T0301600

# Work and Alienation in the Platform Economy

## Amazon and the Power of Organization

Sarrah Kassem

First published in Great Britain in 2023 by

Bristol University Press
University of Bristol
1–9 Old Park Hill
Bristol
BS2 8BB
UK
t: +44 (0)117 374 6645
e: bup-info@bristol.ac.uk

Details of international sales and distribution partners are available at bristoluniversitypress.co.uk



British Library Cataloguing in Publication Data
A catalogue record for this book is available from the British Library

ISBN 978-1-5292-2654-6 hardcover
ISBN 978-1-5292-2656-0 ePub
ISBN 978-1-5292-2657-7 ePdf



Cover design: Liam Roberts Design
Front cover image: 123rf/elenabsl
Bristol University Press use environmentally responsible print partners.
Printed by CPI Group (UK) Ltd, Croydon, CR0 4YY

To those who have supported me and grounded me, my family

To those who have motivated me and inspired me, the workers

And finally to all those whose voices are not heard.

# Contents

# List of Figures and Tables

## Figures



## Tables

# List of Abbreviations

| | |
|---|---|
| AECJ | Amazon Employees for Climate Justice |
| AI | Artificial Intelligence |
| ALU | Amazon Labor Union |
| API | Application Programming Interface |
| ARPA | Advanced Research Projects Agency |
| AWI | Amazon Workers International |
| AWS | Amazon Web Services |
| CGIL | Confederazione Generale Italiana del Lavoro |
| ETUC | European Trade Union Confederation |
| FACE | Former And Current Employees of Amazon |
| FBA | Fulfillment By Amazon |
| FNV | Federation of Dutch Trade Unions |
| HIT | Human Intelligence Task |
| ILO | International Labour Organization |
| IP | OZZ Inicjatywa Pracownicza |
| IPO | Initial Public Offering |
| ISP | Internet Service Provider |
| ITUC | International Trade Union Confederation |
| MTurk | Amazon Mechanical Turk |
| NLRB | National Labor Relations Board |
| NSF | National Science Foundation |
| PPE | Personal Protective Equipment |
| PRA | Power Resources Approach |
| RWDSU | Retail, Wholesale and Department Store Union |
| TCP/IP | Transmission Control Protocol/Internet Protocol |
| TOT | Time Off Task |
| TSS | Transnational Social Strike |
| TWC | Tech Workers Coalition |
| UNI | UNI Global Union |
| UPH | Units Per Hour |
| VC | Venture Capital |
| ver.di | Vereinte Dienstleistungsgewerkschaft |

# Preface

It was both through interest and by chance that I found myself researching Amazon. I am fascinated by the world of workers, who, despite the unequal structures of capitalism, retain their humility, strength and agency. Agency, essentially the ability to act, allows us to imagine possibilities for change and to pursue these, historically and contemporarily. But as we are always bound to a specific moment in time and place, I have been eager to combine my interest with an essential development in our world today: technology, and more specifically the platform economy. These transnational corporations, such as Amazon, Google, Airbnb and Uber, which instrumentalize the Internet to mediate what they may not directly own, intrigue me. While these may not (yet) employ, relatively speaking, the largest amount of global workforces, they continue to grow in power and capital, equivalent to national economies, and contribute to the unequal distribution of wealth globally. I found myself increasingly absorbed into the orbits of Amazon, its exponential growth and what it has come to symbolize. It was Amazon's former CEO, after all, Jeff Bezos, one of the richest humans in our planet's history, who joined the summer 2021 ten-minute Blue Origin flight to the edges of outer space to experience zero gravity. In the press conference he later stated, "I want to thank every Amazon employee, and every Amazon customer, because you guys paid for all this" (Goodkind, 2021; Lopatto, 2021).

The curiosity about what unfolds behind the virtual and physical walls of Amazon fueled my dissertation, on which this book is based. I wanted to dive into the different worlds of those who essentially power it – the workers, both of its e-commerce platform, Amazon.com, and of its digital labor platform, Amazon Mechanical Turk. This book is my thank-you to you, for your trust, time and efforts to let me into your world in an attempt to shed some light on your realities. Having to accept that research itself is bound to the time and space in which we pursue and develop it, I hope that it is in a future step that I integrate not just your class – but also more of your gendered and racialized subjectivities and material realities. This book thus presents part of these realities – but is far from claiming their entireties.

It has always been important to me not to speak *for* the workers. I was eager to access the field through ethnographic participant observations to grasp their dynamics, contexts and experiences in their world of work. Accessing Amazon warehouses has been more traditional and straightforward, as Amazon for one offers public tours. I thank Leo Bieling and Thorsten Schulten, who took on the supervision of my dissertation and encouraged my fieldwork. Thorsten, you helped me establish my initial contact to ver.di, given my focus on the German context. I am grateful to ver.di for allowing me to join meetings and industrial action, during which I first spoke to Amazon workers, and to UNI Global Union – both Nigel Flanagan and Nick Rudikoff – for inviting me to transnational union meetings. Thank you for supporting and defending our positions as researchers and recognizing our role in the struggle. I am indebted to at least a dozen warehouse workers who trusted me in their (in)formal interviews, at times out of a common interest to 'get the word out' – a task intrinsic to research itself, in other times, based on our racialized and gendered subjectivities. For them, it has been a show of solidarity and empowerment to support me as a woman of color. I deeply value these acts of solidarity.

In contrast, the digital shop floor level could not be accessed traditionally, as labor relations are mediated online and workers are geographically and temporally distributed and isolated from one another. Like other researchers in the field, I carried out some tasks on MTurk to gain firsthand insights into the fragmented and individualized labor process. To access the voice of workers, I have learned from the experiences of others, who have highlighted how unpaid surveys of precarious gig workers diverts time away from conducting gigs for piece-wages. Thank you to Greta Jasser for our conversations more generally and to Monique McKenzie more specifically for suggesting I offer remuneration, at least according to the national minimum wage, to those completing my MTurk surveys. This ensured that workers taking my surveys on MTurk are compensated for their labor, reflecting the *Guidelines for Academic Requesters*. I am thankful to Leo's financial support, which allowed me to pay for more than four dozen surveys before and during the pandemic, at the rate of the German minimum wage, which is higher than that of the US and India, where the majority of workers labor. Discussions at conferences, workshops and my teaching courses have helped me at different stages to reflect further on my own research. I am thankful for all the questions, feedback and advice I have received throughout the process from students, researchers and colleagues.

Conducting the research was a struggle, but it was a different kind of struggle to publish it – from Kathleen Sheppard, who read my very first book proposal and encouraged me to start submitting it, to everyone who has been involved in bringing this work to life. Thank you to my editor, Paul Stevens, who saw potential in my work, and to Bristol University Press for taking it on. Thank you to the different teams at the Press that have answered all my questions and have made the production of this book possible. Thank you to the reviewers, who have provided me with constructive, engaging and encouraging feedback.

All of this would not have been possible without the continuous support I have received, not just academically but personally. I am grateful to my mother, Amal, my father, Mohamed, and my brother, Omar, who have given me their unconditional support, which has kept me grounded. I am grateful to friends I have studied, lived and shared conversations with. You have been pillars of support, from those in Cairo to those in Tübingen, who were by my side amidst the struggle. Thank you to Natalie Pawlowski, my constant in this journey, to Míša Zezulková for not letting even a pandemic stop you from being by my side, to Cansu Erdoğan, for always lending me a shoulder, to Mona Kassem, Kerstin Hachenberg and Violeta Bakia, for reminding me how this all began, to Meryem Erren, Sarah Karama and Beatriz Trejo Maltseva for giving me strength over the years, and to those in Cairo – Yara El Razaz, Milda Shawky, Nancy Salem, Alex Machaal, Hoor Alawady, Gehad Abaza and Maheen Hyder – for helping me navigate life over the last decade.

شكراً

[*shukran*, thank you]

To never losing sight of the past, present and future – *sempre*.

1

# Introduction

It is becoming more and more difficult to imagine our daily lives without digital platforms. To order something, we check Amazon and its reviews; to search online, we Google; to go somewhere, we Uber; and we Netflix and chill. We rely on Facebook or its WhatsApp and Instagram for our social relations, while we browse TikTok for content – entertaining at times, political at others. But our contact with these platforms may not always be so obvious. We could just be using a website that is a client of Amazon Web Services (AWS) or stumble across some data that Amazon Mechanical Turk (MTurk) workers contributed to. We could even be one of these very workers. Indeed, it takes a substantial effort to avoid these platforms, as they have come to form an intrinsic part of our social fabric and vocabulary. Relatively speaking, our degree of contact with one or more of these platforms is of course not devoid of privileges, class, racialized and gendered relations, and questions of access that are not uniform across our world. Generally speaking, the presence of platforms in our lives has only been magnified and accelerated by COVID-19, as the Internet plays a growing role in the mediation of our social relations, labor relations and, more generally, our daily lives. In the process, the societal, political and economic powers of platforms have become increasingly apparent in recent years; meanwhile these platforms have accumulated an enormous amount of wealth that has not been shared equally.

It is now clear that these platforms, which were once celebrated in the name of entrepreneurship for the novel ways by which they have instrumentalized the Internet in the pursuit of profit, are shaping and reshaping the world of work and of workers. This is a book about these workers, who power the platform economy, although many of them appear invisible to us behind our screens. This raises an array of questions. What are the different ways in which platforms are structured? How do workers organize and reshape these in the face of their alienating working conditions, which fragment them and atomize them from one another? How do platforms reproduce historical continuities and produce contemporary developments in organizing workers? This book examines these questions by diving into Amazon, and more specifically by looking at two of its platforms: its renowned e-commerce platform and its digital labor platform, MTurk. Amazon is an intriguing corporation to investigate and contextualize because of the ways it navigates and instrumentalizes political–economic and technological conditions. It is also fascinating to study because of the dimensions of its exponential growth and expansions within preexisting and new markets, which it has in some cases monopolized. It has grown and continues to grow its ecosystem far beyond its initial e-commerce platform, becoming in the process a forerunner and trendsetter in terms of its approach to both capital and labor. By investigating the alienating and precarious terrains of two of its workforces and their agency, this book is an effort to contribute to an analysis that moves away from one that regards developments in the platform economy, and Amazon's ecosystem, as predetermined. The way in which the platform economy and the larger economy, more generally, develop is not inevitable; instead, it is dynamic and full of labor struggles.

## The matrix of the platform economy

The 'platform economy' is one of many terms used to conceptualize corporations such as Amazon, Google, Airbnb and Uber within the larger economy. In contrast to the broader terms such as 'digital capitalism' (Schiller, 2000; Fuchs and Mosco, 2016) or 'digital economy' (Huws, 2014), I refer to the 'platform economy'. The former terms center the digital fabric within our current economic system and regard it not as separate from capitalism's larger historical trajectory. Instead, that fabric is bound to, and co-evolves along with, larger socio and political–economic conditions. The 'platform economy' as a term emphasizes more specifically the mediating function of platforms within the larger economy via the infrastructure of the digital: namely, the Internet. Within an asymmetrical relationship, platforms can be understood as connecting two or more groups through the Internet to mediate and facilitate the exchange between those offering products and services, to which work is integral, and those acquiring these at any given moment (Srnicek, 2017; Moore and Joyce, 2020). This book focuses on *capitalist* digital platforms, which have erupted in the dot-com era and following decades. These are fundamentally different from worker-led alternative platform cooperatives, which are re-organized along the collective interests of those workers who power them (Scholz, 2016).

The recent growth of the platform economy and the repercussions of that growth have been accompanied by a vibrant and growing body of literature, some of which examines platforms from the perspective of capital, while some examines them from the perspective of labor. When it comes to the former, Srnicek's *Platform Capitalism* (2017) has been a foundational source in conceptualizing platforms, their functions and roles within the trajectory of capitalism. This helps us categorize different kinds of platforms based on what they mediate, such as advertising platforms or cloud platforms. Bilić, Prug and Žitko (2021) delve deeper into capital's trajectory to analyze through a (neo-)Marxian lens the developments, significance and implications of platforms that have now grown into monopolies. While distinguishing platforms on the basis of their function and tendencies to monopolize provides insights and is relevant to discussions on the growing power of platforms, it mainly constitutes an analysis from the perspective of capital. This book contributes to conceptualizing and examining platforms, but mainly from the perspective of workers. As the platform economy is not homogenous, I look at it from two central dimensions: the *nature of the platform* (location-based vs. web-based) and the *nature of the work* (traditional time-wage vs. gig wage) (Table 1.1). I investigate more specifically the fundamental questions: how do the different *nature of the platform* and *nature of the work* alienate workers, and how do workers respectively express their agency within their political–economic contexts in order to organize in traditional and alternative ways?

When it comes to mediating labor relations, a central distinguishing feature among platforms is the *nature of the platform* itself: for example, workers can be location-based, like a worker in an Amazon warehouse, or web-based, like those who work remotely online via MTurk (Schmidt, 2017; Woodcock and Graham, 2019). The diversity of the platform economy is not only reflected in how class relations are mediated, but researchers have increasingly emphasized

**Table 1.1:** Matrix of the organization of the platform economy

| | | Nature of the platform | |
|---|---|---|---|
| | | **Location-based** | **Web-based** |
| **Nature of the work** | **Traditional time-wage** | Amazon warehouses | |
| | | Amazon Web Services | |
| | | Google | |
| | | Facebook | |
| | **Gig time-wage** | Helpling | Upwork |
| | | TaskRabbit | Toptal |
| | | Deliveroo | Freelancer.com |
| | **Gig piece-wage** | Uber | Amazon Mechanical Turk |
| | | Lyft | Upwork |
| | | Deliveroo | Clickworker |
| | | Airbnb | Prolific |

how a specific part of the platform economy, namely the gig economy, reproduces, normalizes and even celebrates precarious labor (Berg, 2016; De Stefano, 2016; Collier et al, 2017; Graham and Shaw, 2017; Van Doorn, 2017; Graham and Woodcock, 2020). The *nature of the work* is thus also crucial to the organization of the platform. I differentiate between those who receive what can be regarded as a set traditional time-wage, as in Google offices, and those paid by gig, essentially a wage paid per task as an 'independent contractor'. A gig wage can be either time-based as an hourly wage paid for a task, as on TaskRabbit, or of a piecework nature per task, without a minimum hourly wage, as is currently still predominantly the case with Uber.

To investigate my central research question, I therefore contrast two case studies that differ in relation to the nature of the platform *and* the nature of the work. My first case study of Amazon workers can be regarded as organizing workers more traditionally: in location-based warehouses, and according to a traditional time-wage. While investigative journalists have previously exposed working conditions in warehouses, a scholarly interest has only developed more recently. Apicella (2016, 2021) has become known in the field and among unionists as one of the first to systematically investigate Amazon warehouse workers in Germany, carrying out original fieldwork and focusing primarily on the question of class consciousness and strike action. Other scholars have looked at the warehouse, and especially at the role of technology in organizing workers (Struna and Reese, 2020; Delfanti, 2021a, 2021b), and juxtaposing different national settings and labor organization (Cattero and D'Onoforio, 2018; Owczarek and Chełstowska, 2018; Boewe and Schulten, 2019, 2020; Massimo, 2020; Vgontzas, 2020). I build on this research to contextualize Amazon within the broader platform economy to understand its growth in relation to the larger technological, social and political–economic conditions (Alimahomed-Wilson and Reese, 2020; Brevini and Swiatek, 2021). I look at Amazon warehouses in terms of their more traditional organization of work(ers) within the platform economy, underlining how being under the same roof while laboring, and having a guaranteed wage within a time frame, relate to the variety of ways by which workers are organized and organize: both their alienation *and* their agency.

Far from representing the majority of employment relations in the platform economy, a glimpse at the earlier matrix indicates the vast proportion of gig work within it. In other words, the majority of platforms organize workers less according to traditional employment relationships and more according to ones characterized by precarity and outsourcing. This is reflected in the growing body of scholarly work engaging with the gig economy or, as others have called it, the sharing economy or on-demand economy. Scholars have closely examined the political–economic and legal implications of the assigned status of 'self-employed' or 'independent contractor' (I use the latter term in this book), devoid of the historical rights and benefits associated with laboring in the formal economy. In doing so, they underline the role of technology and algorithms in mediating exploitative class relations, and different ways by which workers have (self-)organized (Van Doorn, 2017; Graham and Woodcock, 2020; Ravenelle, 2020; Schor, 2020; Haidar and Keune, 2021; Aloisi and De Stefano, 2022; Boto and Brameshuber, 2022; Christiaens, 2022; Dubal, 2022a, 2022b; Joyce et al, 2022; Kocher, 2022). I take a further step back to underline that both gig and 'non-gig' work in the platform economy are crucial to understanding its growing political, economic and social power. To grasp the continuities and novelties for the world of work(ers) in a theoretically grounded and empirically systematic manner, the matrix of the nature of the work and the platform vis-à-vis two case studies can then augment our understanding not just of the platform economy but also of contemporary trends in the labor market.

My second case study, of MTurk, differs then from the first both because of its gig nature, and also because of its web-based nature – relatively speaking, a novelty in capitalism's development. Unlike location-based platforms, where traditional employment relationships are possible, web-based labor is characterized by gig work – whether paid as a time- or piece-wage. All web-based workers, along with location-based gig workers like Uber drivers, make up the gig economy. These gig workers, despite their different nature of the platform, can be understood as forming part of the larger workforces of digital labor platforms, which I trace and outline more in Chapter 4. While what is considered to be 'high-skilled' labor in developing, designing, project- and product managing is paid by the hour (such as Upwork and Toptal), other web-based digital labor platforms for microtasks, such as MTurk, pay workers by piece-wages.

In comparison with Amazon's warehouses, the interest in MTurk is rooted in a rich body of academic work initiated to a large extent by scholars such as Irani (2013) and her work with Silberman (Irani and Silberman, 2013), which eventually seeped into more journalistic efforts. A recent crucial contribution has been the work of Gray and Suri (2019), who make the invisible digital laborers *visible* by contextualizing these workers, shedding light on their stories and recommending how to make ghost work more sustainable. By historicizing piecework, these authors underline its continuities in platforms today (such as MTurk) and the indispensability of human labor for technological developments. While this book builds on the extensive and grounded research of such scholars, it adds to the conversation by contextualizing piecework within the larger development of the (re)organization of work(ers) in the platform economy and the political–economic conditions alongside which it has evolved.

By differentiating between platforms according to the basis of their nature of the work and nature of the platform, we can identify the repercussions of each dimension for their workers and their agency more systematically and grasp the continuities and novelties of the world of work(ers). Thus, although this book does not delve into a location-based gig platform such as Uber, the two Amazon case studies – which are fundamentally different in their organization – can add in turn to the larger understanding of the platform economy. It can also be telling of contemporary trends in the labor market to which Amazon has become a central player. Based on an analytical framework informed by historical materialism at its foundation, this book contributes to an analysis of agency by, first, systematically investigating alienation on the (digital) shop floor level, an approach inspired by Marx's *Economic and Philosophic Manuscripts of 1844*.

Though the concept of alienation is increasingly found in contemporary labor discussions, it had been a rather philosophized concept in recent years, with few efforts aiming to resurrect its centrality (Jaeggi, 2014; Fuchs, 2019) or to incorporate it in examining technological developments and the platform economy (Wendling, 2011; Fuchs and Mosco, 2016; Christiaens, 2022). While focusing, then, on alienation in one part of the analytical framework can account for working conditions and how platforms individualize the world of work(ers) and can rupture their collective organization, I do not see it as all explanatory. Instead, I also examine the larger (often counteracting) political–economic and technological conditions in relation to the mobilization of labor's power resources to organize and leverage capital for their interests (Wright, 2000; Silver, 2003; Schmalz and Dörre, 2014; Schmalz et al, 2018). Workers do have agency, but the circumstances under which this is translated into action are bound to time and space.

As I integrate alienation and power resources into one analytical framework to examine agency, I understand this book as contributing to those theoretical debates and touching upon different implicit and explicit elements of historical and contemporary ones of labor and social transformation. These include labor process theory that has studied different elements of work(ers') organization – from the deskilling of laborers and division of labor (Braverman, 1974) to processes of consent (Burawoy, 1979) and subjectivity (Jermier et al, 1994). Given the centrality of the agency of labor, I see my work as touching additionally on debates inspired by *(post)operaismo* (workerism) based on "the understanding from below, from the optic of the class struggle of the exploited" (Negri, 2022: 164). These have centered workers' class composition within larger capitalist relations from the initial focus of the 'mass worker' to the 'social factory' (Tronti, 2019; Gray and Clare, 2022). A later emphasis was developed on the autonomy (*autonomia*) of labor in its power to struggle for its class interests, further grasping labor beyond the factory (Cleaver, 1979; Wright, 2008, 2017; Negri, 2022) to include, for instance, unwaged and reproductive labor (Dalla Costa and James, 1975; Federici, 2004). Given the all-encompassing nature of capitalism and the understanding that abstract labor is common to all workers, Open

Marxism has widened the understanding of struggle to include not only struggles of labor but additionally to encompass those necessary for labor's social reproduction (Dinerstein et al, 2019; Dinerstein and Pitts, 2021).

These rich and evolving theoretical strands have been applied by scholars to grasp our contemporary capitalist moment and, of interest here, the platform economy, engaging with how workers are organized in the larger platform economy (Haidar and Keune, 2021) and gig economy (Briken et al, 2017; Gandini, 2019). These have, for instance, investigated platform managerialism (Moore and Joyce, 2020), flexible despotism (Wood, 2020), immaterial and affective labor (Koloğlugil, 2015; Arcy, 2016; Woodcock and Johnson, 2019); digital workerism (Englert et al, 2020; Woodcock, 2021) and power resources (Vandaele, 2018, 2021; Joyce et al, 2022). I understand my book as participating in such debates on labor struggles and the platform economy, given its historical materialist theoretical foundation, which grasps capitalism's trajectory, class relations and labor's agency within the larger context of co-evolving political–economic, technological and social conditions.

In historicizing and contextualizing the platform economy and its workers, I look at how contrasting sites of production and circulation in the platform economy relate to the ways by which the organization of the labor process individually and collectively alienates and fragments workers. I then examine how workers reclaim their collective organization and mobilize their power resources. Focusing primarily on the spheres of production and circulation in the platform economy is by no means meant to ignore the way these have implications far beyond the political–economic sphere and into that of social reproduction (Dinerstein and Pitts, 2021). By examining the workers of Amazon warehouses and MTurk in their political–economic context and on their (digital) shopfloor level, this book argues that the nature of the platform and the nature of the work pose different repercussions for labor organization and reconfigure their different possibilities. Both platforms have hypertaylorized the assembly line by dividing tasks into smaller parts to be carried out as efficiently as possible, and algorithmically manage workers. Gig- and web-laboring, however, additionally rupture the temporal and spatial limits of working beyond what has been traditionally possible. While these may alienate and individualize the workforce, it is crucial to grasp these as sites for their labor struggles across different dimensions of their structural, associational, institutional and societal power.

By analyzing the agency of these platform workers, this book underlines how workforces are confronted with a neoliberal political–economic context characterized by deregulation and precarity that sets obstacles for organizing: Amazon warehouse workers need to navigate their national contexts and Amazon's union-busting culture but still have the advantage of being assembled on a daily basis within a physical space. MTurk workers, who are currently considered independent contractors left without rights and benefits, are additionally confronted with a global race to the bottom, and no physical space to organize. This illustrates, for example, how the platform economy shifts work away from traditional forms to more novel ones through the digital mediation of work and the larger spheres of precarity. However, it also sheds light on how workers adapt to these changing times to navigate alienating working conditions and precarious contexts to build solidarity and organize both traditionally and alternatively by assuming the very infrastructure that organizes them – the Internet. This book humanizes these workers to underline their agency both in the warehouses on whose labor Amazon depends to become the number one destination for all customers, and on MTurk, by virtue of whose labor Amazon can claim an (in)direct role in the future of technology and Artificial Intelligence (AI). While platforms continue to grow and reap profits for capital, they significantly impact the world of work(ers) in present and very likely future terms – of which Amazon has become a forerunner and for which it must be investigated.

## Chapter structure

**Part I: Examining the World of Work and Workers** formulates the theoretical foundation and analytical framework of this book, understanding the development of material production, and thereby social life, as the guiding force of history. Chapter 2, **How to Study Alienation: Marx's Four Relations,** lays out the systematic analysis of the relations of alienation to the labor product, activity, species-being and fellow humans – according to Marx's *Economic and Philosophical Manuscripts of 1844*. This is crucial to Part III, which underlines how platforms intrinsically fragment the workforce and foster atomization and individualization. While I recognize the importance of studying alienation, I understand it as only providing part of the explanation of why workers do (not) organize. Chapter 3 bridges this analysis by underlining the importance of class consciousness and different subjectivities to then focus on **How to Grasp Agency: The Power Resources Approach**. It engages with how workers navigate the (counteracting) political–economic conditions and mobilize their structural, associational, institutional and societal power resources. This too is integral to Part III's analysis, highlighting labor's different efforts in organizing and fostering solidarity given the different nature of the platform and nature of the work.

**Part II: The Birth and Growth of Platforms** traces and analyzes the organic development of the platform economy in relation to the political–economic, social and technological conditions. This part focuses on the perspective of capital, which is crucial to grasp the world of labor, as these both operate in relation to the wider co-evolving context. Chapter 4,

**Historicizing Three Generations of Platforms**, grounds the platform economy within the larger neoliberal context and identifies the first generation as springing up during the dot-com era of the mid-1990s to 2000, the second during web 2.0 in the mid-2000s and the third in the aftermath of the 2008 financial crisis. This analysis interweaves the different ways in which platforms have come to organize workers vis-à-vis their nature of the work and the platform, as these developments have been intrinsically tied to technological and political–economic ones. The platform economy is not separate from, but part of, the larger economy.

Transitioning from the larger historical development of the platform economy, Chapter 5 focuses on **Contextualizing Amazon's Growing Empire** within this larger trajectory. It situates both the Amazon warehouses and MTurk in the platform economy to grasp how these developed vis-à-vis the larger conditions. By underlining the growing empire and ecosystem of Amazon, we can understand Amazon's development not as inevitable. Just as platforms developed in a certain specific way, so they can develop differently, underlining not just the discussed material conditions in Part II but also the role of agency discussed in Part III.

**Part III: Workers on the (Digital) Amazon Shop Floor** interweaves the theoretical–analytical framework and contextual background to engage critically with the two contrasting Amazon case studies, each with a chapter on the alienation and working conditions on their shop floor level, and one that engages with labor's agency within the larger political–economic context. Chapters 6 and 7 are devoted to Amazon warehouses as an example of a location-based and traditional time-wage laboring platform. It focuses on humanizing the backbone of the global corporation of Amazon – the manual labor that circulates commodities sold via the platform in the warehouses. Chapter 6, **Cog in the Machine: Working the Amazon Circulation Line**, examines this manual labor reminiscent of factories in the industrial era – yet brought into the 21st century. The organization of Amazon warehouses appears to reflect Taylorist techniques of scientific management that monitor and control every step of the labor process along the division of tasks to ensure a docile and (also algorithmically) disciplined workforce to keep up with the ever-increasing demand and expansions of the corporation. As this chapter analyzes the shop floor through the relations of alienation, the next investigates how such a platform provides both challenges and possibilities for workers to express their agency. In Chapter 7, **"I Am Not a Robot": (Trans)national Labor Organization at the Warehouses**, I integrate the larger political–economic context and Amazon's union-busting, which can prove to be additional obstacles to the organization of workers. Despite these challenges, we see workers strategically navigating this terrain and organizing physically and digitally through (trans)national unions, grassroots movements and possibly supported by political movements.

Chapters 8 and 9 focus on the contrasting case of a web-based gig work platform, namely the digital outsourcing platform MTurk. **"Artificial Artificial Intelligence": Gigging on Amazon Mechanical Turk** examines the alienation of MTurk workers, who complete monotonous and repetitive microtasks – known as Human Intelligence Tasks – from behind their screens. These range from classifying videos to identifying objects and answering surveys. Workers are paid by piece-wage upon completion and evaluation of these tasks. Confronted with various 'virtual assembly lines' that produce data across geographical and temporal zones, their human labor can be further used for machine learning specifically and AI more generally. This can prove to be central to general contemporary and future technological developments bound to bring their own repercussions with them – including ones we are already witnessing in terms of facial recognition technology that is essentially racist, and algorithms that can hire and fire workers. To grasp the agency of these workers, Chapter 9, **Instrumentalizing Technology: Digital Solidarity with and among MTurk Workers**, focuses on the new challenges and different possibilities this organization of platform poses for dispersed gig workers. These workers appear to fall through the cracks of regulation as a result of the Internet and their precarious status as independent contractors – though there seems to be some potential efforts to change the latter. Interestingly enough, workers instrumentalize existing digital spaces and new ones designed specifically for them to foster solidarity, interact and provide support to one another on how to best navigate MTurk.

While these two Amazon case studies are examined in isolation to one another to grasp their individual complexity, Chapters 10 and 11 take a step back to recontextualize the cases and refer to other platforms that have not been part of the study. Chapter 10, **Alienation across Amazon and the Platform Economy**, highlights how the case of Amazon warehouse workers illustrates, on the one hand, the historical continuation of traditional time-wage laboring in which the workforce is assembled in the same physical space within the contemporary development of the platform economy. It thereby shares similarities with other platforms such as Facebook and Google. The case of MTurk, on the other hand, sheds light on a different historical continuation, namely that of piece-laboring adopted by capital into the new dimension of the digital. Although even time-wage platforms such as Facebook and Google are known to contract labor and depend on ghost work like that of MTurk, the MTurk case is meant to give first insights both into the significance of laboring remotely through the web *and* the significance of piecework, known as gig work, in the platform economy. Given the centrality of agency in this book, Chapter 11, **The Power of Amazon Workers and Platform Workers**, discusses the implications of the different configurations of platform organizations regarding the larger question of agency to formulate some reflections on our current political–economic and social order. This chapter highlights both traditional and more alternative ways of organizing in the platform economy, forming inter- and intra-platform solidarity. This sheds light on the potential of what may be considered a growing labor movement.

As the platform economy is continuously developing, so too are the realities of the work, workers and platforms presented in this book at the time it was written. As we have seen, platforms may acquire one another, may rebrand themselves and may be regulated. The platform economy is constantly in flux – not just as a result of capital developments, but also of labor struggles. This book ultimately emphasizes then that, just as the conditions of the platform economy need to be understood historically and holistically, so too does the agency of workers. The form and appearances by which workers express this agency similarly co-evolve with the material and technological conditions, both of the platforms and of the larger political–economic context.

PART I

# Examining the World of Work and Workers

# 2

# How to Study Alienation: Marx's Four Relations

Worker-centered research allows us to grasp workers as subjects with agency who have the capacity to act individually or collectively and resist their exploitation and oppression. In doing so, they can shape their world, social change and transformation, and thereby history. By humanizing workers and acknowledging their struggle and attempts to bring about change, we can contribute to an understanding of history that is dynamic rather than one that dismisses agency and presents itself as inevitable. To examine the world of work and workers in the platform economy, it is important first to establish an analytical framework grounded in a historical materialist and dialectical approach that contextualizes the political–economic, social and technological conditions in which labor and capital are situated. This chapter focuses therefore on the relations of alienation to shed light on the ways in which capitalism fragments and atomizes workers in their individuality and collectivity and inhibits their organization. Alienation provides part of the explanation of why workers may not organize, but an analytical framework that stops at this point risks falling into the traps of determinism and regarding alienation as all-encompassing. As Ollman states, "it is not enough to treat people as embodiments of social-economic functions" occupying idle, passive and submissive positions with no agency to affect the course of history (1987: 64). In Chapter 3 I bring agency back into the analysis to examine how workers struggle against capital despite their alienation and mobilize their power resources. Just as the relations of alienation come to express themselves differently in relation to the nature of the platform and of the work, so too does the organization of the platform in turn relate to the ways in which workers act and express their agency within their material contexts.

## Historical materialism, dialectics and the labor theory of value

Unlike Hegel, who regards the 'idea' as creating the world, Marx argues that "the ideal is nothing but the material world reflected in the mind of [the hu]man, and translated into forms of thought" (Marx, 1977: 102). I regard historical materialism as forming my theoretical foundation, as I conceptualize the development of material production, and thereby society, as the guiding force of history. Put differently, the material conditions of the mode of production inform how we sustain ourselves, which in turn organizes and determines our social relations (Marx, 1847; Harvey, 2010a). Understanding capitalism historically allows us to grasp it as *one* development within the trajectory of history that organizes society into different classes according to their relation to the means of production. This organization is not devoid of struggles, as workers mobilize time and time again to pursue their class interests. The appearance of their labor struggle against capital is in turn tied to their material context, constantly interacting and co-evolving with one another (Dunn, 2004; Bieler, 2018). As Marx notes, "Men [Humans] make their own history, but they do not make it as they please; they do not make it under self-selected circumstances, but under circumstances existing already, given and transmitted from the past" (1852).

Theory is fluid and constantly evolving, as we apply it to make sense of the developments of our world. One such critical contemporary capitalist development has been that of the platform economy. I am interested in engaging with the ways in which the platform economy (re)organizes labor and the wider social relations, as it has provided capital with a digital dimension and infrastructure for its profit and monopolies by mediating different forms of capital and labor. Kenney and Zysman (2016: 62) accordingly state that

> [i]f the industrial revolution was organized around the factory, today's changes are organized around these digital platforms, loosely defined. Indeed, we are in the midst of a reorganization of our economy in which the platform owners are seemingly developing power that may be even more formidable than was that of the factory owners in the early industrial revolution. ... Whatever we call the transformation, the consequences are dramatic.

The platform economy is a novelty within the trajectory of capitalism, as its digital infrastructure not only mediates labor that is bound to a physical location, as has been historically the case, but now also mediates labor remotely through the web in a variety of ways. It is interesting to analyze how the different organizations of platforms affect social relations, the focus here being on class relations and struggle.

If historical materialism analyzes history through the evolution of modes of production as these inform social relations and so forth, then these elements are in and of themselves dialectically related to each other. The analysis of the material world is bound by a totality of interdependent, interacting co-evolving internal relations and elements of processes of production, technology, humans' relation to nature, the reproduction of daily life, mental conceptions and social relations (Marx, 1977: 493, fn.4). Harvey adds an important seventh element, namely, institutional, governmental and legal arrangements, which can be conceived of as also including industrial relations (2010a, 2010b). Instead of understanding elements such as technology as determining all other elements or as abstract and independent, these are mutually interacting as part of the dynamism. Far from being static, a change in one of these elements is bound to effect change in others – constantly reconfiguring the totality of relations and interacting within a specific moment in time and place, leading to specific developments (Ollman, 2003). Historicizing capitalism allows us to understand it as the expression of the sum of peculiar and particular appearances of these relations, both mutually supportive but also contradictory. They are, in that sense, *dialectically* related. These contradictions do not necessarily result in a single synthesis but can lead to the perpetuation and expansion of contradictions on a larger scale. As these elements are not static, but are in and of themselves interacting, co-evolving, part of a totality and constantly in flux, it is of crucial importance to investigate how these develop and are (re)configured in different moments within the trajectory of capitalism.

Such a holistic and dialectical analysis moves away from one that is structuralist and linear and unmasks instead how any constellation of this totality of relations is subject to change when there is change to its co-evolving elements. The capitalist totality, like all material bases and thus social organizations, is far from being inevitable and is human-made. In reference to Darwin, who engaged with the history of plants and animals, Marx (1977: 493, fn. 4) poses the direct question

> Does not the history of the productive organs of [hu]man in society, of organs that are the material basis of every particular organization of society, deserve equal attention? And would not such a history be easier to compile, since, as Vico says, human history differs from natural history in that we have made the former, but not the latter?

The representation of capitalism, and (re)production thereof, as a natural development is ahistorical, deterministic and damaging. Dialectics allows us instead to question developments and investigate how all things are interconnected and constantly evolving. In turn we can realize the potentialities of agency and possibilities for change. I am particularly interested in investigating exactly these potentialities and possibilities for workers in the platform economy, which has largely rendered its workers invisible behind its technological infrastructure and interfaces. Although platforms mediate and are founded upon a digital infrastructure, the platform economy must not be analyzed from a technologically reductionist or structuralist perspective. It too is grounded in exploitative social relations that do not function outside of the capitalist totality. I historicize the development of the platform economy in Part II, analyzing it in relation to larger political–economic and technological conditions that both reflect and reproduce capitalist trends that organize not just production but also society.

The essence of the capitalist system lies in its organization of its mode of production through the particular social relation of exploitation, in which one is forced to sell one's labor power to sustain oneself. As the platform economy is part of the larger economy, it reflects and reproduces this social relation of exploitation differently depending on the organization of platform, as platforms are positioned in different points of capital's circuit. The latter can be conceptualized as "M – C ... P ... C' – M'" (Marx, 1978: 109). Money capital (M) is used to acquire commodities as labor power and means of production. The means of production along with the exploited labor power in the production process (P) create a commodity of greater value (C'). This results in more money capital (M'). All commodities, despite being of different use-values (utility) and exchange-value (price), are reducible to the same objectified abstract labor through which capital accumulates by extracting surplus value (Marx, 1977; Pitts, 2017; Dinerstein and Pitts, 2021). According to Marx, value can generally be understood as the socially necessary labor time to produce a commodity within the respective society, taking into account both average skill levels and labor intensity. Labor power reproduces, thereby, its own value in addition to an excess amount of value termed surplus value, representing surplus labor time, which capital pockets as profit (Marx, 1977). This forms the labor theory of value.

Both labor in the sphere of production and circulation are necessary for the continued accumulation of capital. While labor in the circuit of production produces surplus value, it is only through labor in the circulation process (C' – M') that surplus value is realized. The commodity is exchanged in the latter circuit rather than produced and is converted back into money form (M') which has now expanded and reaps profit for the capitalist. Labor in circulation is essential in increasing the velocity by which commodities are exchanged and profit is accumulated. While this allows the accumulation of capital to continue as the money form can be reemployed elsewhere in the circuit, its labor needs to be paid through surplus value that has been produced elsewhere as well. In that regard labor in each sphere depends on labor in the other sphere for its survival, just as capital depends on them for its profits. Thus it is not just the sphere of production that is of centrality to capital but so too that of circulation (Pitts, 2017). Different forms of labor are confronted with different forms of exploitation and productivity, yet they are dialectically related and rely on one another within the circuit of capital (Marx, 1981). Understanding different forms of capital and different positions of labor can contribute valuable insights in conceptualizing the various dynamics that operate the economy in general and the platform economy more specifically (Pfeiffer, 2013; Comor, 2014; Robinson, 2014). Far from being homogenous, exploitation takes place in the platform economy in similar and yet different ways according to whether labor is tied to a physical location or takes place exclusively remotely, and this exploitation also changes with the nature of time- and piece labor. Yet regardless of which platform these workers labor for, it is important to approach these not in a digital vacuum but as located in real time and material conditions – all part of the larger circuit of capital. This allows us to shed light on the implications for capital, but also on how capital accumulation (re)organizes class relations. In the process, this exacerbates inequalities, against which labor in turn mobilizes.

## The study of alienation

While my theoretical approach is generally based on a historical materialist and dialectical framework, I find it crucial first to examine the alienation of workers more specifically to delve into the complexity of agency. Alienation is far from being natural and is instead peculiar and unique to capitalism. It is "historic and transitory" (Dunayevskaya, 1975: 56). This allows us to grasp and underline the ways by which work fosters disunity and fragmentation, which may in turn hinder labor organization, before looking at how workers resist and reshape their class relations despite these alienating conditions. This is not meant, however, to dismiss other crucial factors, such as ideology and hegemony (Gramsci, 1971). Although alienation has been previously regarded as outdated, "the *problem* of alienation is still (or perhaps once again) of contemporary interest" (Jaeggi, 2014: xix, emphasis in original).

To analyze alienation systematically, I find it useful to turn to the *Economic and Philosophic Manuscripts of 1844*, in which Marx discusses four interacting relations of alienation to the product of labor, labor activity, species-being and other humans. These provide a way to examine the different dimensions by which alienation comes to engross human life. It is also helpful to tie these where necessary to the concept of commodity fetishism discussed in *Capital, Volume I*. As I agree with scholars who see Marx's ideas as evolving and reject the juxtaposition between what is often assumed to be the young and the mature Marx (see Satterwhite, 2009), the analysis of alienation can be approached based on the previously laid out historical materialist and dialectical analysis.

### *Alienation from the labor activity*

Contrary to Marx's work, I find it more helpful to begin the analysis with the labor activity and not product, as the former constitutes the basis for all exploitation. I then conclude with the relation to fellow humans (Ollman, 1971). As workers labor, they perform a certain task that is an expression not of their own decision but of capital. Marx states accordingly that it is not for

> the satisfaction of a need; it is merely a *means* to satisfy needs external to it. ... [T]he external character of labor for the worker appears in the fact that it is not his [their] own, but someone else's, that it does not belong to him [them], that in it he [they] belongs [belong], not to himself [themselves], but to another. (1844: n.p., emphasis in original)

Rather than being a result of self-activity, workers can only survive under capitalism by selling their labor power to someone who has power over them. It is thus alienated from them, as capital appropriates commodities through its domination of labor and exploitation. This constitutes the basis for all reproduction of capital. While Marx focuses on labor activity in the sphere of production, that focus should be extended to the sphere of circulation, given the generally exploitative nature of the labor activity regardless of labor's different roles in the circulation of capital (Pitts, 2017).

The estrangement of humans from their own labor is intrinsic to capitalism and directly tied to the division of labor, which allows for the specific exploitative organization and domination of workers (Marx, 1977). It effectively fragments the labor activity by assigning workers specific tasks, thereby obscuring the purpose of the specific activity and ensuring that the labor process in its entirety is unknown to any single worker. This relation of estrangement becomes exacerbated by the fact that this labor activity does not belong to workers. It can be further accentuated through developments in the labor process, Taylorist organizations of work, (scientific) management and the instrumentalization of technology (Braverman, 1974). While alienation is fundamental to capitalism, it is continuously reconfigured in relation to wider political–economic, social and technological conditions. It needs to be contextualized and investigated, therefore, to establish the specific ways by which the platform economy estranges workers through various organizations of capital–labor relations. This raises important questions as to how alienation differs according to whether workers labor in a physical location or when their work is digitally and remotely mediated; when labor is centralized or decentralized; when it is remunerated by an hourly or a piece-wage; and how the nature of the labor activity relates differently to the (digital) division of labor.

### *Alienation from the product of labor*

The relationship to the product of labor is closely tied to the worker's position in capital's circuit of accumulation, making it inseparable from the previous relation. As workers do not control their labor activity, they have no influence over the produced commodity, which now conceals in its exchange-value the objectification of labor and exploitation. The product of their labor confronts them "as *something alien*, as a *power independent* of the producer ... an alien object exercising power over him [them]" (Marx, 1844: n.p., emphasis in original).

Just as alienation from the labor activity cannot be analyzed without reference to the division of labor, it is also integral to understanding this relation of alienation. Labor's product is both an embodiment of the division of labor as well as private property. The commodification of labor activity by capital allows for the privatization not only of labor but also of its products. The concealment of social relations through an alternative appearance constitutes a fetishism – another particularity of the capitalist moment. In the case of the commodity, relations "do not appear as direct social relations between persons in their work, but rather as material [*dinglich*] relations between persons and social relations between things" (Marx, 1977: 166, emphasis in original). Through the mystified appearance of the commodity, workers find themselves feeling detached from their products. They only confront these in terms of their quantitative appearance, rather than their qualitative essence. It is in the product of labor that the labor activity is fetishized, obscured and concealed, the same labor activity that produces and circulates commodities, without which capitalism cannot sustain itself. As Dunayevskaya states, "*[t]his* is the essence of *all* that is perverse in capitalism" (1975: 59, emphasis in original). If the labor activity is strongly related to the wider conditions, such as those of the platform economy, so too must the same analysis be extended to the estrangement from labor's product in the platform economy in relation to their varying (digital) appearances and possibly gig nature.

### *Alienation from species-being*

I conceptualize the alienation from '[hu]man species-being' as the third relation, dialectically related to the others, as it comes to encompass additional dimensions of existence. One becomes alienated from one's species, estranged from nature and any organic relations to it. Labor activities appear as a "*means* of [one's] *individual existence*", making "individual life in its abstract form the purpose of the life of the species" (Marx, 1844: n.p., emphasis in original). Capitalism objectifies our species-being through labor, reducing our life activity to merely sustaining our existence through it. Creativity is constrained and choked, alienating humans from their potentialities. The life of the worker becomes dominated by exploitative activities through the extension of the working day, including unpaid time, and working space. Capitalism absorbs thereby further temporal and spatial aspects, as well as activities, within its domain.

The appearance of this relation of alienation can vary according to different developments within the capitalist trajectory: technological conditions, for instance, can push the labor activity processes outside of what has been traditionally known. It is important to shed light on what happens when the limits to the working day and workspace are no longer bound by physical limits as a result of connectivity to the Internet. Similarly, this relation of alienation from species-being can be impacted by political–economic conditions where workers are constantly facing precarity and a global reserve army of labor, essentially the unemployed. As the dimensions of both time and place are broadened, workers have less time to spend on activities beyond their laboring, while capital benefits by the further exploitation and accumulation of surplus value. As such, the life of the worker comes to evolve around work and the activities associated with their subsistence and essentially their social reproduction (Federici, 2004; Bhattacharya, 2017; Dinerstein et al, 2019; Dinerstein and Pitts, 2021). Dunayevskaya (1975) underlines the idea that true self-realization and freedom cannot be achieved therefore under capitalism, as it is not with the emancipation of labor but with its abolishment that these can ultimately be obtained.

### *Alienation from fellow humans*

All the relations of alienation project themselves onto the relations of humans to one another, in which humans confront each other the way they confront themselves. In other words, "[w]hat applies to a [hu]man's relation to his [their] work, to the product of his [their] labor and to himself [themselves], also holds of a [hu]man's relation to the other [hu]man, and to the other [hu]man's labor and object of labor" (Marx, 1844: n.p.). As capitalism reduces us to our class position, we project this onto the perception of other humans, perceiving them first and foremost as workers. While fetishistic work cultures, as in the platform economy, give an illusion of community and solidarity among workers, they are in essence individualistic. The previous relations of alienation ensure that workers are separated from one another and confront each other as an external other. Each worker is reduced to their productivity and thus in so far as the worker exists in relation to another and confronts another, they constitute an element of competition. Alienation as such translates into the fragmentation of workers that is strategically essential for the continued accumulation of capital, the reproduction of class relations and expansion of social control. Humans can be alienated from fellow humans in different ways depending on whether they labor in a single physical place or are distributed across the globe behind their screens in their own time zones and whether their labor takes a more traditional wage-form or an individual gig and atomistic one. These factors may directly impact the extent by which workers encounter and identify with one another and organize, having significant consequences for labor and its potential struggle.

When regarded holistically, these relations of alienation can be understood as dialectically related to the totality of capitalist relations, including social, political–economic and technological conditions. Their appearances and expressions may differ in relation to the wider context in capitalist temporality and spatiality. Focusing the analysis on these relations of alienation is designed to contribute to our understanding of the complexity of agency, and by no means ignores, as has been claimed, the importance of crucial dimensions and relations under capitalism such as ideology, hegemony and social reproduction – just to name a few. The examination of alienation can shed light on how the organization of the labor process and labor activity estranges workers and projects itself onto the dimensions of their social world, inhibiting the development of solidarity, class consciousness and labor organization. As the platform economy is in and of itself not homogenous in how it organizes workers, an analysis of it can contribute to the various appearances of alienation within the larger discussion of the complexity of agency in the 21st century.

3

# How to Grasp Agency: The Power Resources Approach

If we were solely to study the relations of alienation of workers, we would risk reproducing a dehumanized understanding of capitalism and its trajectory – at most accounting for only its internal interacting contradictory relations. It comes as no surprise that Adam Smith and Frederick Taylor dismiss the agency of workers, the former describing those laboring simple tasks as "stupid and ignorant as it is possible for a human creature to become" (Smith, 1776: n.p.), the latter arguing that it "would be possible to train an intelligent-gorilla so as to become a more efficient pig-iron handler than any [hu]man can be" (Taylor, 1911: n.p.). Such disempowered depictions of workers deny them all consciousness and agency, immobilize them and strip them of their emancipatory potential. In contrast, Gramsci underlines that

> not only does the worker think, but the fact that he gets [they get] no immediate satisfaction from his [their] work and realizes [realize] that they are trying to reduce him [them] to a trained gorilla, can lead him [them] into a train of thought that is far from conformist. (1971: 310)

While I do see it as crucial to analyze the different relations of alienation, we cannot dismiss how workers resist these to express their agency, which can in turn take on different appearances depending on their context. Before diving into how we can conceptualize the agency of workers, it is important to at least underline the important role of class consciousness and acknowledge workers as subjects within the bounds of a historical materialist analysis. The discussion on subjectivity, which later grew into labor process theory, is a broad one. It has come to range from initial analysis by Braverman (1974) to later post-Marxist and Foucauldian perspectives that expanded the debate to further interrogate the manufacture of consent and theoretical conceptualizations and empirical strategies for resistance (Burawoy, 1979; Knights and Willmott, 1990; Jermier et al, 1994).

The subjectivity that I focus on is one based on class. I understand it as stemming from one's position and function in the capitalist system. This is bound to the historical function and political and economic role of that class, which forms solidarity to collectively struggle for its interests in opposition to capital (Lukács, 1920; Booth, 1978; Ollman, 1987; Kelly, 1998). In underlining class, I do not deny different gendered and racialized subjectivities, as the formation and reformation of class is itself bound by the context in which it develops and the realities of these very workers (Rose, 1997). These intertwine within a fabric on which solidarity can be built, bound to their material contexts and experiences. Patriarchy, colonialism and imperialism have been and continue to be central to capitalism's existence and trajectory (Bohrer, 2019). Understanding these processes as bound to the material conditions and contexts in which one is situated, "[i]t is not the consciousness of men [humans] that determines their existence, but their social existence that determines their consciousness" (Marx, 1859: n.p.). In the most ideal case for capital, workers are caught in the webs of their alienation and confront each other as competitive individuals. In the most ideal case for workers, they form solidarity and associations based on their class interests, to which their various subjectivities and class consciousness interrelate, to mobilize effectively and collectively in opposition to material conditions and capital. It is neither a dichotomy nor must it constitute a linear, given or inevitable process (Sayers, 2011).

Acknowledging the importance of class consciousness to the agency of workers that is constantly in flux and within a process of "transformability" (Negri, 2022: 18), I grasp it as growing out of the interplay of various relative and general conditions. The relative material conditions and relations of production that organize and thereby alienate workers entail contradictions. In other words, the organization of workers and division of labor that individualizes and atomizes them leads by its very nature to their social organization, by which workers seek to overcome these. As such, the division of labor depends on the sum of cooperative labor processes to produce or circulate a commodity, which forms the 'collective worker'. The power derived from these conditions can prove integral to the mobilization of labor. Essentially, the process that brings workers within the same place *can* bring about their cooperation, as possibly "this mass [of workers] becomes united, and constitutes itself as a class for itself" (Marx, 1847, 1977). This can be further complemented by workers' access to knowledge as a resource. This may relate both to knowledge of capital and its profits, decision-making and future plans, as well as knowledge of labor from its history and rights to associations and institutions for seeking out help and support (Braverman, 1974; Ollman, 1987; Collinson, 1994). The status of a worker within a country, and the systemic inequalities associated with it, are additionally entangled within their experiences, knowledges and material realities, which can both leave them vulnerable and also provide further ground for solidarity and their class interests. While I do not delve into the complexities of this process, given the diverse ways in which the platform economy organizes workers, it is interesting to shed light on how the platform economy relates to these relative conditions, and I focus on the socialization of the labor process.

As workers are bound by the larger context in which they are situated, there are also capitalist conditions that workers generally face, regardless of where they are positioned in the economy and the platform economy more specifically. Such political–economic and societal conditions are marked by capitalism's continued development and survival, changes in the intensity of exploitation in times of crises and trends toward concentration and monopolization. These are accompanied in turn by growing precarity and unemployment, possible loss of previously attained welfare benefits and finally "the evident failure of traditional economic and political strategies" (Ollman, 1987: 80). The combination of these general and relative factors in the context of growing contradictions, inequalities and injustice, as for example in our current neoliberal moment, may appear more visibly as incompatible to workers and their interests. As these conditions are bound to the context in which they develop, I understand class consciousness as historical processes formed and reformed differently with regards to the relative and general conditions and larger context in which workers are situated. These project themselves in turn more generally on "labor and labor movements [which] are continually made and remade" (Silver, 2003: 19).

Though an empirical investigation of class consciousness and its formation is intriguing and illuminating, this requires a closer and more systematic interrogation of class composition, to which the former is integral (Negri, 2022: 33). Class consciousness refers to the "technical composition" as "*class as an economic category*" within specific relations of production in time and space and "political composition" as "*class as a political subject*" (Mohandesi, 2013; Gray and Clare, 2022: 6, emphasis in original). I am interested, however, in examining more systematically how workers translate their agency into praxis, and do not examine for this analysis more closely the development of class consciousness, class composition or their different subjectivities. Just as these cannot be understood as predetermined, these cannot be grasped as necessarily pre-determining resistance, as the material realities of workers can pose additional obstacles. I use class consciousness, therefore, as a bridge to connect my larger analytical framework of agency and also to speak to crucial existing research on class consciousness with regard to Amazon warehouse workers (Apicella, 2016, 2021). Integrating, then, class consciousness into my analytical framework in order not to attribute explanatory force to alienation alone, I am interested in examining how workers, despite the relations of alienation and their material contexts, navigate these – at least for now – within the parameters of our capitalist moment. Such a discussion of labor's agency can shed light on the potential for the formation of a general labor movement or for one of the platform economy more specifically.

I turn, therefore, to the Power Resources Approach (PRA), which developed out of the discussion of the revitalization of labor and the labor movement, aiming to grasp the relation between these and recent sociopolitical developments, economic crisis and changing global conditions. In doing so, scholars underline how workers can organize and act in their own strategic interest (Silver, 2003; Turner, 2005). PRA can be understood as developing over several decades, having originated in the late 1960s and 1970s "with the re-discovery of class as an analytical category and as a mobilising and organising principle among left scholars and social activists" (Schmalz et al, 2018: 114). Sparking a discussion on the agency of workers across the world, the PRA is in its core based on the engagement of Beverly Silver (2003) and Erik Olin Wright (2000) with two specific powers: the structural and the associational power of workers. Scholars have expanded on these powers in relation to the material and global contexts of their case studies, to include, for instance, institutional and societal powers (Schmalz and Dörre, 2014).

I am interested in examining in detail the various forms of interacting structural, associational, institutional and societal power resources (hereafter referred to directly as powers) that workers mobilize. In doing so I account for their larger political–economic contexts and industrial relations. Similar to the relations of alienation, I find it helpful to think of these powers as dialectically related, as they are tied to one another and co-evolve with each other. Acknowledging how labor revitalization studies and PRA provide central theoretical and analytical tools for the discussion of labor's agency, it is important to highlight that these primarily focus on unions. I find it fruitful, therefore, to account for the changing terrain that workers navigate by expanding these power resources to focus not just on traditional associations of workers. Just as the varying nature of the work and of the platform alienate workers in different ways and present obstacles to their agency, so I investigate the possibilities that manifest themselves out of these in both traditional and alternative forms.

## Structural power of workers

This power can be regarded as the most foundational for labor's struggle, as it is derived from its general class position – the essence of the capitalist system. Silver builds on Wright to identify two forms of structural power: *marketplace bargaining* and *workplace bargaining power* (hereafter marketplace and workplace power). The former stands in relation to the labor market (Wright, 2000) in which the power of workers is derived from "(1) the possession of scarce skills that are in demand by employers, (2) low levels of general unemployment, and (3) the ability of workers to pull out of the labor market entirely and survive on nonwage sources of income" (Silver, 2003: 13). The different interplay of these factors can strengthen or weaken this power, bound by the specific position of workers within the circuit of capital, the nature of their work and the larger political–economic context. Workplace power refers in contrast to the power derived "from the strategic location of a particular group of workers within a key industrial sector" (Wright, 2000: 962). It is a source of power to workers regardless of existing collective representation, as it is based on the potential and ability to interrupt and disrupt the circuit of capital and profit.

I find it helpful to divide workplace power into two forms: *individual everyday forms of resistance* and *collective forms of mobilization and organization.* The appearance of agency can range from protests and strikes to more subtle repetitive activities. These can be local or (trans)national, un(organized), (de)centralized, non(violent), appearing invisible or as directly challenging power. These are not fixed, exclusive or exhaustive categories, and should be conceptualized neither as a linear process culminating in social transformation nor as a dichotomy in which one form is regarded as 'real' resistance and the other as not (Scott, 1985; Rose, 1997; Schmalz and Dörre, 2014). Workers find themselves in different material situations increasingly characterized by precarity, bound to the growing "deregulation of labour market institutions and labour protection" to make these more flexible and competitive (Bispinck and Schulten, 2011: 1). Other factors, such as unemployment and fear of retaliation, may severely change the possibility and appearance of resistance. It is important to account for how differing political–economic and technological conditions in the platform economy may open up certain spaces for the expression of this structural power and close others.

Focusing solely on collective and organized expressions risks reducing workers' resistance to being non-existent and invisible unless it has been historically recorded, for example in the form of strikes. James Scott, who examines what he terms the "weapons of the weak" of peasants in Malaysia, argues that, unlike political revolts, these "[e]veryday forms of resistance make no headlines" (1985: 213). Scholars have predominantly studied such subversive and informal practices which may appear initially as 'apolitical', accommodating or invisible, in the Global South (Scott, 1985; Shehata, 2010; Bayat, 2013; Butler et al, 2016). These actions may not be emancipatory or "overtly counterhegemonic" (Rose, 1997: 153). These may in many ways (re)produce the system, as workers may sustain production while subverting its rules. Everyday forms of resistance may or may not take place repetitively, and may be dispersed (Lilja and Vinthagen, 2018). These can range from symbolic "resistance through distance"(Collinson, 1994) – referring to a dismissal and rejection of corporate culture and management on the shop floor – to individual actions to disrupt capital by working at a slower pace, taking more bathroom breaks, sabotage or theft (Scott, 1985). While such individual forms of power shed light on how workers can mobilize on an individual basis in contexts in which it is difficult to challenge the exploitative conditions directly, it can be important both to acknowledge these and not to dismiss them, while not overestimating or romanticizing them either. How we make sense of such individual everyday forms of resistance can vary depending on the kind of research, its aim and focus; in my specific case it is on examining how workers mobilize their workplace power to disrupt capital.

I turn my attention, therefore, to what I refer to as collective and organized mobilizations of this structural power. These are more identifiable, visible and closely tied to class consciousness and solidarity and involve more direct sabotages of the laboring process through industrial action, strikes and occupations. Such mobilizations of workplace power are closely tied to the position of the workers involved, as those facing high productivity pressures in production lines or in export may have a relatively large power compared with other workers. Such assembly lines and the division of labor can be seen as empowering forms of resistance for workers. The socialization of the labor process, the collective labor and the potentialities arising out of their instrumentalization by workers can play a crucial in mobilizing their disruptive power. This can in turn result in stoppages in key nodes that are costly for capital (Schmalz and Dörre, 2014; Schmalz et al, 2018). Given our current political–economic context, where capital is in many forms transnational, it is important to understand the structural power of the platform economy not just locally and nationally but also transnationally. Workers in transnational corporations may have increased workplace power because of the global supply chain of value that can be disrupted. Capital may attempt to counter and undermine it through a series of strategies, from threatening jobs through global reserve armies, relocation, decentralization of production and circulation and the 'hypermobility of capital' to changes in the organization of production, increased pressures in productivity and profit maximization (Silver, 2003; Schmalz and Dörre, 2014). Just as labor organizes in relation to its conditions, so capital too responds to these labor struggles by (re)organizing workers. These are in and of themselves dialectically related and co-evolve.

It is important to incorporate into this analysis, then, how capital and the political–economic conditions undermine different forms of workers' power to underline the complex terrain that workers navigate. These can range from specific conditions related to the dimensions of the reserve army of labor, the possibility of capital to relocate, or specific way by which capital has come to organize the labor process (Silver, 2003). These play a crucial role in explaining why workers may not organize, regardless of their subjectivities and their consciousness of their alienation. By analyzing two contrasting platforms we can juxtapose the different roles of the nature of the platform and of the work in reconfiguring the structural power of workers throughout their (virtual) assembly lines. In doing so, this allows us to examine the potentially changing appearance of marketplace and workplace powers of platform workers when an anonymized, dispersed and isolated workforce no longer convenes in a centralized manner under a single roof but does so behind a screen in a (digital) labor market characterized by precarity and a global reserve army of labor.

## Associational power of workers

The associational power of workers is closely tied to their structural power and their ability through collective solidarity to increase their wages and improve their position in relation to capital. Wright explains that it is derived from "the various forms of power that result from the formation of collective organizations of workers", such as unions and parties (2000: 962; Silver, 2003). While Wright also discusses works councils in relation to the associational power, I refer to these in the next power resource of institutional power considering the gains they can achieve within their institutional setup. Though union membership and power then declined within the context of neoliberalism for the last decades of the 20th century, unions initially developed in a context different from that of today. Unions have historically provided workers with associations through which they can mobilize cohesively and effectively. Often measured in terms of their membership numbers, industrial actions and strikes, these are closely tied to the available resources and their inner cohesion (Tilly, 1978; Fantasia, 1988; Dribbusch, 2015).

Unions do not, however, operate or organize in isolation from their material contexts, but are also bound to specific national industrial relations. Richard Hyman explains that these refer to "the regulation of work and employment through some combination of market forces, state intervention and collective bargaining", characterized by different obstacles, production processes, work organization and competition (2005: 10). It is, therefore, important to investigate to what extent workers with different natures of work can organize in the form of unions based on their precarious positions within the labor market and industrial relations context, and how this is affected once they are separated by the decentralized nature of the Internet. Within this discussion, I regard it as critical not to reduce all associations to traditional unions, and also consider and examine alternative formations and grassroots efforts that have developed in relation to current political–economic and technological conditions.

The transnational dimensions of capital and labor also project themselves onto the associational power given the close relation to the workplace power in disrupting global supply chains. Transnational organization is in many cases premised on the existence of national unions or other associations that become part of a more global network which can then mobilize. These are embedded in their distinctive political–economic and national industrial relations context, and thus their activity may be constrained by these. Unifying these into a labor movement may be difficult, as international solidarity is not formed, developed and expressed in a vacuum but is directly linked to such underlying challenges, which need to be confronted. Capital deliberately exploits the industrial relations of national contexts to rupture workers' unity and solidarity (Kelly, 1998; Gumbrell-McCormick and Hyman, 2013; Dribbusch, 2015). Capital can also undermine these through various efforts from delegitmizing unions and labor organization to union-busting actions (Silver, 2003). The platform economy assumes a transnational character in the way it organizes both capital and labor, and this in turn is interesting to consider in the investigation of the diverse expressions of associational power, the critical role played by technology and the different terrains workers maneuver.

## Institutional power of workers

If associational power is based on the structural power of workers, institutional power is intertwined with, and the result of, labor struggles and negotiation processes. It refers to a very specific context and industrial relations situation in which attempts of cooperation and concessions between labor and capital are possible. If associational power is conceptualized initially in PRA as necessitating the existence of unions, then this institutional power, if understood literally, can only be investigated in contexts in which workers and unions have already acquired certain rights, ranging from collective bargaining to co-determination. Institutional power has a twofold character: it strengthens the position of workers through specific rights but can also limit the spaces in which they can maneuver and negotiate within a specific constellation of power struggles, institutions and possibilities for co-determination (Schmalz and Dörre, 2014). Bound to the specific industrial relations system, this power too is essentially reformist in character.

Institutional power is closely tied to the activities of unions as representatives of workers, as well as works councils and collective bargaining agreements to further improve their working conditions and possible leverage then over capital. Unions are thought of as balancing their grassroots efforts within an institutional setting to promote their interests. Depending on this setting and the larger context in which unions operate – which can restrict their actions and goals and spaces to maneuver – it is crucial for them to pertain some form of autonomy. Struggles are thereby separated from their political content and transferred into the economic sphere to be regulated by institutions within this specific industrial relations context. Resulting concessions and cooperation are bound to a specific context resulting in some short-lived and fragile outcomes as well as far-reaching, robust ones, such as the freedom of association. In fact, a stronger associational power that can result in a stronger institutional power can essentially be of interest to capital, if these concessions result in higher productivity and profit for instance (Wright, 2000). Considering then that I understand works councils as part of and inseperable to the institutional fabric and context itself, I analyze these in relation to the institutional power and not associational power (different to Wright, 2000; Schmalz et al, 2018).

Generally speaking, institutional power too is not immune from being undermined by political–economic conditions. These have ranged from union recognition within national contexts (or lack thereof), neoliberal attacks on the institutional power, as witnessed most prominently by Thatcher and Reagan, to employer associations and governments withdrawing from relevant dialogues altogether. Accordingly, different strategies and conditions can weaken labor and strengthen capital, where the former attempts to push back (Schmalz and Dörre, 2014; Schmalz et al, 2018). It is, therefore, interesting to investigate to what extent such an institutional power can be identified on the current labor market and, specifically of interest here, in the platform economy – where gig workers are still predominantly misclassified as 'independent contractors' external to workforces altogether, though we may be witnessing a potential relative shift as some examples demonstrate.

## Societal power of workers

In addition to structural, associational power and institutional power, I find it crucial to include societal power, referring to the ability of different social groups and organizations to cooperate and support unions. This power extends the political agenda of unions beyond the workplace within broader society. It can be broken down into coalitional power and discursive power. While the former relates to the support unions receive from additional societal actors such as NGOs or social movements, the latter refers to the extent by which struggles are framed as legitimate in the broader society and potentially tie these to larger moral understandings within that society. The stronger the discursive power, the higher the probability of unions applying public pressure for their struggles and interests. This discursive power is then intertwined with coalitional power (Schmalz and Dörre, 2014).

Considering how power resources interact and co-evolve with one another where a change in one is bound to bring a change in the other, stronger societal power can in turn translate into stronger associational, institutional and structural powers and vice versa. I find it essential also to generalize the societal power to the position of workers, and not necessarily limit it to unions. The weakened position of unions in certain countries or sectors must not negate the overall societal power of workers in which their struggles are regarded as legitimate. This is especially interesting for the platform economy, in which, depending on the organization of the platform, certain workers may be more visible than others to society at large, while others are distributed globally and may seem almost invisible. Similarly, as with the previous forms of power, it is important to understand how political–economic conditions and capital's countervailing strategies may undermine this power and its framing as a unifying social struggle. The power resources of workers are dialectically related, and co-evolve within the larger context in which they are situated. It is thus important to also identify how these interact and how a change in one power resource can affect another.

Because of the novelty and the diversity of the platform economy, I aim to examine how the different interacting dimensions of platform organization both impede and also possibly facilitate workers' organization. To grasp this complexity of agency, I understand my analytical framework as, first, requiring an investigation of the concrete organization of capital–labor relations for their (re)production of alienation. Recognizing that alienation is not all-encompassing and recognizing the critical role of class consciousness, my framework then examines expressions of agency in relation to various power resources and how these interact in relation to the organization of the platform within their wider contexts. Given the platform economy's patterns of growth it is even more important to highlight the potentialities for workers' agency, which in a way strengthens their societal power. In reference to cloud-computing and big data, to which I add the platform economy, Vincent Mosco states these not only

> deepen the chains of accumulation that power digital capitalism[,] [b]ut they also produce chains of resistance, from China to Silicon Valley. The success of resistance will depend on how well workers … are able to unite and develop strategies both locally and globally. (Mosco, 2016: 531)

The platform economy must be analyzed not just for how it has developed out of technological and political–economic conditions to mediate all possible formations of capital, which is the focus of Part II, but also for how it (re)organizes temporally and spatially dispersed workers and how workers resist in return, which is the focus of Part III.

PART II

# The Birth and Growth of Platforms

4

# Historicizing Three Generations of Platforms

The historical development of technology has never been neutral or inevitable. As all other developments, it too is bound to its context. It is helpful therefore to grasp the platform economy as evolving in relation to the political–economic, social and technological conditions. Before delving into the world of workers, I historicize and contextualize three different generations of platforms. I begin with tracing the first generation of platforms during the dot-com era in the 1990s, evolving from the creation and wider dissemination of the Internet. Following the dot-com bubble burst in 2000, technological conditions resulted in a user-friendlier Internet while political–economic conditions pushed a second generation platforms to search for a new source of financial capital. As changes in the wider conditions also bring about changes in the platform economy, I finally delve into third generation platforms that erupted after the 2006–8 economic crisis. This chapter ultimately demonstrates that each kind of platform, with its own way of organizing workers, has organically developed in relation to the wider conditions within capitalist temporality.

## A brief history of the Internet: its creation and dissemination

As an ever-growing decentralized network of tubes, circuits and packets of data that connect computerized devices globally, the Internet provides the digital infrastructure necessary for the creation, development and expansion of platforms. A series of conditions coincided at a very specific historical time and place. The US government responded to the political conditions of the time by pouring massive amounts of funding into its research and initial development. This had been taking place in a context where, technologically speaking, the US had both an extensive telecommunications network and firms that specialized in and produced the technical equipment necessary for the infrastructure of the network, such as routers. The requisite economic conditions were also present, given the wide availability of venture capital (VC) essential for the dot-com era in the 1990s. These combined conditions would prove crucial for the Internet's later proliferation and commercialization beyond its initial military purpose and restrictions. While it is important to underline the role of the US in the development of the Internet and platforms, we must also keep in mind that the history of the Internet is not limited to the US and is interconnected with various research developments elsewhere (Abbate, 2000; Kenney, 2003a).

Responding to the political climate of the Cold War, the roots of the Internet can be traced back to its development as a military experiment in response to the Soviet launch of Sputnik in 1957 and fear of a nuclear attack. The US Department of Defense set up the Advanced Research Projects Agency (ARPA, later renamed DARPA, Defense Advanced Research Projects Agency) to intensively research technology and funded researchers across US universities by also providing technological resources such as mainframes. Among ARPA's research foci was the need to create a complex decentralized network to facilitate communication between various computers. Messages would be broken down and sent through separate packets that were combined at their eventual destination. Accordingly, the message would keep moving even in the event of a nuclear attack by searching for a still functioning route (Chayko, 2018). Four servers were connected for the first time in 1969, creating a computer network between the University of California in Los Angeles, the Stanford Research Institute, the University of California in Santa Barbara and the University of Utah. It was three years later that ARPANET was complete and ready for a public demonstration at the International Computer Communication Conference (Keefer and Baiget, 2001; Naughton, 2016). The context of the ongoing Cold War provided the conditions in which the US, with its strong military interests and dominant economy, could pour resources and capital into the technological development of ARPANET and what would become the Internet.

Given this historical context, the creation and growth of the Internet were dependent on its expansion beyond the restricted military project only accessible to those funded by ARPA, and on additional technological developments that allow for more computers to interconnect. While the former was in part achieved through the separate creation of MILNET for the exclusive use of the military, the latter was facilitated by the creation and adoption of Transmission Control Protocol/Internet Protocol (TCP/IP). As its name indicates, the Internet is not a unitary network but a *network of networks* (Cerf, 2004; Schafer and Serres, 2017). TCP/IP broke messages down and sent the fragments separately, to be rearranged at the destination, enabling different kinds of machines and networks to interconnect beyond

ARPANET, such as CSNET and later NSFNET, funded by the National Science Foundation (NSF). These expanded the user pool to also include institution-based computer scientists, who could pay an annual subscription fee to connect to it for non-commercial purposes. It was only in the 1990s that the Internet proliferated beyond this academic and scientific community. This resulted in part from the decommissioning of ARPANET, which marked the end of military involvement in the Internet. Additionally NSFNET was later defunded, which now opened the gates to VC-funded Internet Service Providers (ISPs) to commercialize the Internet to operate its backbone via dial-up connection (Kenney, 2003a; Naughton, 2016; Chayko, 2018).

The dissemination of the Internet was accelerated by the integral technological development of the World Wide Web by Tim Berners-Lee at the European Organization for Nuclear Research (CERN) based in Switzerland. With its idea laid out in 1989 and initial technologies written the following year, it was made accessible outside of CERN by 1991.[1] The web made the Internet more navigable for the everyday user, as it linked documents through hypertext, thereby connecting sites that users could access. While it operates on the Internet's infrastructure, the web is not the same as the Internet. Given the Internet's open architecture, the use of the web did not pose any restrictions. Subsequent user-friendly graphical navigators, such as Mosaic in 1993, Netscape in 1994 and Internet Explorer in 1995, popularized the use of the Internet and allowed anyone to surf without needing any specialized knowledge (Leiner et al, 1997; Chayko 2018). The commercialization of the Internet was consequently contingent on such technical simplifications and developments, the already growing network of personal computers in the US and ISPs. Additionally commercial products that incorporated TCP/IP technology and local area networks connecting PCs through routers, modems and later optical fiber telecommunications were instrumental for the Internet's dissemination. The overlapping political, economic and technological conditions demonstrate that the trajectory of the Internet was an organic one. The way these conditions came together leading to the creation of the Internet was in and of itself not predetermined, as "there is nothing preordained about technological development" (Naughton, 2016: 12). Technological development is, as other developments and processes, always bound to the context in which it unfolds and must not take one specific and concrete path. It too develops dialectically.

## The dot-com era and first-generation platforms

With the groundwork laid for the dissemination and commercialization of the Internet, capital was now presented with new opportunities by instrumentalizing precisely this novel infrastructure to mediate the exchange of commodities *digitally* for the first time. First-generation platforms were formed within this context with the vision to be 'first movers', seeking to establish themselves within their new market in order to dominate it, and to reap benefits and later profits. Their growth was fueled by financial capital in the form of VC and trading on NASDAQ, essentially creating a frenzy (Naughton, 2016). The potential of the Internet was seen as limitless: an untapped market that created a wealth of opportunities for the expansion of capital for both creators and venture capitalists alike. It is within this context that the 1990s would come to be known as the dot-com era – an era that demonstrated once again that, just as technological developments respond to political–economic conditions, so the latter equally respond to the former.

The dot-com era and its bubble developed within the neoliberal context that facilitated the growth of finance capital and all speculative activities through instruments such as derivatives or hedge risks. Neoliberalism has been characterized as attracting wealth away from workers and their welfare toward the orbits of capital, for which finance capital has been integral. This entails favoring interest rates and tax reductions, for example through the 1981 Economic Recovery Tax Act (Sloan, 1999; Harvey, 2005; Haiven, 2011). Platforms were able to grow so rapidly within the neoliberal context as they directly depended on financial capital from venture capitalists. VC, which focused on investments in high technology traceable to the post-World War II era, had grown dramatically at the end of the 1970s and early 1980s. It had already financed technological firms such as Cisco, Oracle and Sun Microsystems, which produced items necessary for the Internet's infrastructure, and was now turning to investing in dot-com firms and platforms. VC increased heavily during this period from around US$5 billion in 1995 to over US$30 billion in 1999, peaking at almost US$70 billion by 2000. Given that many platforms lacked start-up capital, they turned to venture capitalists for initial funding, as evidently 60 percent of VC funding in 1999 went to information technology (Gompers and Lerner, 2001; Kenney, 2003b; Srnicek, 2017). When viewed geographically, it comes as no surprise that the largest concentration of platforms and more generally tech corporations coincides with the largest concentration of VC in California, more specifically the San Francisco Bay area and Silicon Valley (Kenney, 2003a). Within this neoliberal context, the interlocking of such technological capital along with such financial capital provided novel opportunities through the now commercialized Internet – one of which was the platform economy.

Developing organically within a specific context in time and space, the digital infrastructure of the Internet was initially claimed by first-generation platforms. Platforms such as Amazon, eBay, Google and Yahoo! (hereafter Yahoo) organized labor according to traditional time-wage contractual agreements within a physical space by coupling these with the newly available digital infrastructure. Founded in 1994 by Jeff Bezos, Amazon.

com (hereafter Amazon) instrumentalized the Internet to mediate exchanges by taking the marketplace into the digital sphere and creating an online commercial retail platform also known as e-commerce. Amazon was primarily an online bookstore, backed by location-based warehouses, that allowed users to "[s]earch one million titles [and] [e]njoy consistently low prices" (Spector, 2002: 70). Given the centrality of Amazon for this book, I look at its specific development in the next chapter. In contrast to Amazon, which mediates between producers or sellers and consumers, eBay mediates first and foremost between Internet users. Initially called AuctionWeb, and renamed in 1997 as eBay, it was established as a bidding platform in 1995 for all sorts of commodities, where users could sell products online and ship these to buyers. In a way it brought garage sales and thrift shopping online (Sundararajan, 2016).[2] EBay and Amazon both transported the marketplace into a digital sphere, which was not isolated from the non-digital and immaterial, as these platforms existed through labor in physical locations to circulate commodities. Both Amazon and eBay would survive the dot-com era and come to dominate within their spheres. In fact, Amazon would later even expand into new fields and new generations of platforms.

The dot-com era did not just witness the birth of e-commerce but also brought about the creation of web directories and search engines that further helped users navigate the web. Founded in 1995, Yahoo constituted the first web portal, with additional features such as email, apps for music (Yahoo Music) and videos (Yahoo TV) and various sections, ranging from weather to news. Yahoo came to dominate the Internet: it was the most valuable company worldwide by 2000 and shaped the dot-com era in many ways. It would, however, never truly recover after the bubble burst in 2000, despite attempts to later acquire Google and Facebook (Tynan, 2018b). Among the companies that would come to displace it in the later years would be precisely Google with its better-ranking algorithms and data commodification starting in 2000. Google, renamed from the earlier BackRub, was incorporated in 1998 by Larry Page and Sergey Brin with a VC investment of US$100,000 from Sun Microsystems' co-founder Andy Bechtolsheim (Verge, 2018). It was meant "to organize the world's information and make it universally accessible and useful", as would become evident over the following decades.[3] Workers, from the corporate offices of these platforms to those in warehouses, were location-based and labored according to time-wages that did not differ in nature from other jobs at the time. In essence, first-generation platforms, which initiated the platform economy, did not reorganize the workforce.

While VC fueled the creation of platforms, Initial Public Offerings (IPOs) played a crucial role in the expansion of the dot-com bubble, further fetishizing the value of platforms. IPOs were vital to liquidate investments and receive returns. In 1995 Netscape went public with US$28 per share, valuing this one-year-old company at a shocking US$2.9 billion. Netscape was trading based on what was expected to be its value in the future, rather than its past profits and earnings (Naughton, 2016). Caught in this frenzy, more and more dot-coms, including platforms, followed Netscape in a political–economic context now characterized by excessive speculation in technology stocks. The NASDAQ stock exchange was central to the growth of platforms, as it increasingly specialized in exchanging stocks for these young companies at a time in which these were often valued more highly than dominant companies with larger workforces. Within this frenzy, the political–economic conditions created a vicious circle of an ever-increasing and -inflating dot-com bubble, as more and more companies were established with higher and higher valuations on the stock market. Unleashing a VC investing frenzy with hopes of exiting right before the crash, this "virtual gold rush" was regarded by venture capitalists as "a special once-in-a-lifetime opportunity, just like the railway booms of the nineteenth century, and the car, airplane, and radio booms of the 1920s" (Goodnight and Green, 2010: 123). Platforms relied on such financial capital from VC and IPOs to become 'first movers' and 'get big fast' in this highly competitive market to claim a certain market, dominate this market and grow into monopolies, some of which persist until this day.

The dot-com bubble continued to expand, reaching its height in early 2000. Overvaluations were accompanied by mergers such as the largest (at that time) merger, valued at US$182 billion, announced between the leading dot-com, America Online (AOL) and the world's largest media giant, Time Warner (Goodnight and Green, 2010). In early March 2000 the Chair of the Federal Reserve, Alan Greenspan, insisted that

> the capital spending boom is still going strong [which] indicates that businesses continue to find a wide array of potential high-rate-of-return, productivity-enhancing investments. And I see nothing to suggest that these opportunities will peter out any time soon. (Federal Reserve Board, 2000)

Despite these perceptions, the bubble finally burst just a few days later. As always with bubbles, it was only a matter of time before speculations, completely detached from real material conditions, ran ahead of actual economic developments and profits. Finance capital appears in the form of money breeding more money in future terms, meaning claims on future value. It appears to be detached from social relations and the exploitation of labor that takes place for the realization of value (Marx, 1977, 1981). As stocks boomed in the dot-com era, there was often an extreme difference between fictional stock market value and real value of accumulated profits. The total valuation of more than 370 Internet firms that had gone public by 9 March 2000 "was $1.5 trillion, though they had only $40 billion in sales" (Kenney, 2003b: 42; Goodnight and Greene, 2010). Given that the once-projected growth could not be achieved, investors began to question the possibility of actually making profit.

The selling off of stocks and shares was triggered by a series of overlapping moments such as the height of dot-com stock prices, an increase in interest rates by Federal Reserve at the turn of the century and the expiry of an extraordinary amount of lock-up agreements that no longer restrained short sales. A total of nearly US$300 billion worth of shares had been unlocked by the summer of 2000 and thus it comes as no surprise that the market value of such dot-coms crashed by the end of the year (Ofek and Richardson, 2003). As more and more dot-coms burned through financial capital, they were delisted and disappeared from the market. Once known as dot-coms, they were now being termed 'dot-bombs' (Goodnight and Green, 2010: 130). Profitless and stagnant e-commerce dot-coms were the first to disappear, such as the then famous Pets.com, followed by other network equipment and telecommunications companies. The stock market collapse of 2003 was (at the time) second only to the Great Depression of the 1930s, though it would later be eclipsed (Kenney, 2003b). Along with the delisting of more and more dot-coms, the financial market was further rocked by the largest bankruptcy of the bubble of WorldCom – the telecommunications giant which was found guilty of corporate fraud, improperly recording US$ billions of profits and recording expenditures as capital investments (Tran, 2002). The end of the dot-com bubble did not, however, mean the end of the platform economy or the disappearance of all first-generation platforms. Nor did it discourage platforms from their initial vision of the possibilities and potential of the Internet and of capitalizing from these. While Amazon, eBay, Google and Yahoo survived the burst and attempted to evolve, new platforms were also created, characterized by novelties in their organization of workers within a political–economic context that would lead to the next bubble – the housing bubble.

## Web 2.0 and second-generation platforms

Just as the dot-com era and first-generation platforms were intrinsically tied to the commercialization of the Internet, so Web 2.0 and second-generation platforms were dependent on the infrastructure that resulted from the dot-com era and the growing dissemination of the Internet. This new period of Web 2.0, a term popularized by Dougherty and O'Reilly, was framed as a transformative period of a more user-friendly and dynamic Internet (Musser et al, 2007). In its discursive spirit of innovation and peer-to-peer interactions across various media, Web 2.0 revolved around concepts of 'public collectivism', 'democratized digital spaces' or 'mass collaboration', as embodied in Wikipedia. Such communal terms were inflated with positive meanings, and presented users as having "unprecedented power for participation, conversation, collaboration, and, ultimately, impact" (Musser et al, 2007: 11). Within this context platforms were established that have become among the most used today, such as YouTube, acquired by Google in 2006 both of which are under Alphabet since 2015, and Facebook which is part of Meta since 2021. Accordingly, the integral economic motivation for capitalist platforms to be first movers was now to a large extent framed and discursively veiled behind social interaction and collaboration on the Internet and the desire to participate in the (re)defining of their digital possibilities. The democratic discourse of Web 2.0 should be regarded critically, as it not only connotes positive qualities but can also give the impression of a new form of Internet. Web 2.0 was no radical transformation, but rather an organic development within the trajectory of technology and, in many ways, of capitalism.

The increased number of users and the decentralized nature of the Internet were largely dependent on developments in terms of both software and hardware through the dissemination of bandwidth and cheaper technologies, as well as infrastructure and hardware tied to the Internet. A growing user base translates to more user activity, ranging from content creation and commenting to searching, sharing or writing reviews, crucial to platforms as a result of network effects. These refer to the phenomenon in which more users translate into more activity and online content, which produce more data that can be commodified, making the platform more valuable. At the same time, large masses of collected data allowed and continues to allow platforms to constantly update and evolve (Srnicek, 2017). Unlike first-generation platforms, those of the second generation were characterized by digital social interactions and labor appropriated by both old and new platforms.

The development of the latter was intrinsically tied to technological developments of the dot-com era and political–economic conditions following the bursting of the bubble. Economically speaking, the bursting of the bubble resulted in a recession that also translated into a drop of VC activity in the US, with investments declining in early 2001 by 42 percent and further decreasing to a total of 85 percent by 2003 (OECD, 2009). With the drying up of such financial capital given the hesitation of VC to fund new platforms, platforms needed to find alternative sources. As the Internet user base had reached over 1 billion by 2005 (Statista, 2021b), second-generation platforms sought to capitalize precisely from this continuously growing user activity, identifying different sources of profit. The first of these was the commodification of data by advertising platforms such as Google and the then newly created Facebook, and the second was the creation of cloud platforms that would rent out cloud space such as AWS. These location-based platforms were additionally accompanied for the first time by the creation of a new nature of platform, namely the web-based platform. One such platform was MTurk, which digitally outsourced labor and paid per task, thereby presenting a novelty both in the nature of the platform and in the gig nature of work.

One of the most central developments during this period has been profit generation through the commodification of data for targeted online advertising, for which Google and Facebook have become iconic. Both first- and now second-generation platforms thrived through the massive amounts of created, tracked, collected and analyzed data through users' digital activity, essentially translating into the monetization of large-scale user surveillance (Fuchs, 2012; Srnicek, 2017; Zuboff, 2019). Google generated unprecedented profits through its Google AdWords in 2000, later renamed Google Ads, which transformed Google into an advertising platform. By virtue of being a search engine, one of the most accessed websites along with YouTube (acquired in 2006), it has access to a wealth of data essential to its business model, which matches advertisers with users. Web 2.0 then also saw the springing up of social networking platforms, such as YouTube, Facebook and Twitter in line with its discourse on 'mass collaboration', which obscures the commodification of user participation. Mark Zuckerberg's Facebook, now Meta, which came to eclipse MySpace, provided users with a digital space to set up a profile to connect and interact with others. Although Facebook relied on VC in the millions in its early years, it introduced Facebook Ads in 2007 to commodify its growing user data (Meta, 2007; Mangalindan, 2011). This translated into a wide debate around the production of free data by users, as well as around the commodification of user surveillance on platforms (Fuchs, 2012; Zuboff, 2019). In 2021, 97.6 percent of Meta's revenue came from Facebook advertising, amounting to almost US$115 billion, while around 81.6 percent of Google's revenue came from advertising, amounting to US$209.49 billion.[4] The commercialization of the Internet now meant that capitalism could combine large-scale digital surveillance with its pursuit of profit.

The wide expansion of the Internet, bandwidth and users meant that growing platforms needed more computing power, online storage and servers, leading to the natural development of cloud computing and with it a new kind of platform: cloud platforms. The term 'cloud' describes the virtual storage space used for data tied to physical servers accessible from all devices connected to the Internet. Cloud platforms own the software and hardware connected to the cloud and rent these out to other platforms or companies, thereby cutting for these third parties the costs associated with producing their own software and hardware. These platforms, which de facto provide the platform economy's infrastructure, are extremely lucrative (Kenney and Zysman, 2016). The leading example has been Amazon, which instead of outsourcing its data centers and infrastructure created AWS in 2005, which I further contextualize in the next chapter. AWS, alongside Microsoft and IBM, would come to dominate among cloud platforms. As

Srnicek (2017) states, if Google and Facebook were the first to commodify data and become advertising platforms, then Amazon is regarded as the first to commodify what appears as the means of production in the platform economy, since companies need cloud space to operate in our current day and age. While these two kinds of second-generation platforms found new sources of profit, they were nonetheless organized similarly to the previous generation. Workers labored in physical locations and their contractual agreements, characterized by a monthly wage, were not too different from those in other sectors of the economy.

A novelty was to come with the development of digital labor platforms that in this period differed both in nature of the work and the platform. This kind of platform would grow even more after the economic crisis with third-generation platforms, expanding from web-based digital labor platforms to also include location-based ones. The specific configuration of social, technological and political–economic conditions within that moment allowed capital now to seize the digital infrastructure to mediate the exchange of outsourced labor, also referred to as 'crowdsourcing platforms'. Though coined by Jeff Howe in 2006, the term 'crowdsourcing' refers back to the early 18th-century British government, which awarded a prize at the time to whoever identified the best way to measure the longitude position of ships. Today, crowdsourcing encapsulates the outsourcing of labor to a larger 'crowd' to compete for tasks through web-based platforms (Howe, 2006). The Internet's ever-growing user base meant that an ever-growing pool of laborers across the Global North and Global South could now be tapped into and paid online. Cloud platforms allowed digital labor platforms more generally to save on hardware and software costs by offering these for rent (Barnes et al, 2015; Valenduc and Vendramin, 2016).

Among such platforms were MTurk, which I discuss in more detail in the next chapter, later joined by TaskRabbit, Freelancer and CrowdFlower (renamed to Figure Eight Inc. and later Appen). These create and manage a marketplace that mediates between requesters who post tasks, ranging from organizations and corporations to researchers, and a pool of flexible workers seeking remote paid work. These digital labor platforms of this nature represent, therefore, a fundamental moment for capitalism by allowing for the "spatial unfixing of work" (Graham et al, 2017: 136). Compensated by a piece-wage, workers complete different gigs within assigned timeframes, varying from smaller microtasks like image tagging to macrotasks such as software development or a graphic design project. The larger the task, and the greater the skills and qualifications required, the higher the compensation (Irani, 2015; Lehdonvirta, 2018). The remote mediation of labor meant that capital could competitively undercut wages while separating and displacing workers geographically and temporally from both the capital that employs them and from the other platform workers.

Outsourcing via digital labor platforms would only magnify after 2008 with third-generation platforms, which were now both web-based and location-based, creating drastic consequences for labor regulation and protection, the growth of precarious work and the organization of labor. These may be regarded as providing new opportunities for those constrained within their labor markets and seeking flexibility and autonomy. The decentralized nature of the Internet allows capital to access a 24/7 (global) labor market that is unregulated, with no set of industrial relations reigning over the digital sphere and within the physical locations of these workers. The gig nature of these platforms which pay workers based on independent tasks, however, presents a first step towards the precarization of platform workers which would become intrinsic to its very fabric via the gig economy. In other words, the platform economy has since been developing along a trajectory in which it increasingly organizes labor precariously and away from what has come to be understood as traditional employment relations. Behind the flexibility is the status of an independent contractors that strips workers of their benefits and increases economic insecurity, all within a system that does not guarantee payments (Berg, 2016; De Stefano, 2016; Kässi and Lehdonvirta, 2018; Howcroft and Bergvall-Kåreborn, 2019). The dot-com era and the period that followed it created, then, the conditions for the organic development of first- and second-generation platforms that could now be both traditionally organized and newly organized around web-based gig work. These second-generation platforms proved fundamental and foundational to the trajectory of the platform economy, tapping into new markets framed around social interaction, the mediation of labor relations and (digital) infrastructure.

## The growth of the gig economy and third-generation platforms

Unlike with the bursting of the dot-com bubble in 2000, technology was not the source of the financial crisis of 2008 and the subsequent recession, but it was certainly affected by it and paved the way for third-generation platforms. This crisis, as with all capitalist crises, did not emerge within a vacuum but resulted from specific capitalist developments. The dot-com bubble had already demonstrated how neoliberalism facilitates the growth of the financial sector and all accompanying speculative activities and institutions. Financial deregulation essentially fuels the growth of bubbles based on speculation and overvalued shares that expand through financial lending and borrowing, pushing prices up – in the 2008 crisis of real estate. Record low interest rates following the dot-com bubble and increased borrowing and lending through instruments linked to (sub-prime) mortgages, such as mortgage-based securities and insurance against defaults, led to an increase in house prices. These peaked by the summer of 2006 in the US (Andrews and Calmes, 2008). Increased prices translated into more lending and borrowing, further inflating the bubble until it eventually burst and led to a chain of financial collapses, bankruptcies and bailouts. These ranged from the 2008 bankruptcy of Lehman Brothers, a New York investment bank that had been deeply involved in mortgage-based securities, to that of the largest insurer, the American International Group, which insured mortgage-backed securities and would later be refinanced by the Federal Reserve. As this crisis and the credit crunch hit the New York Stock Exchange and other international stock markets and spread to the rest of the world, this sparked a deep recession, impacting the financial climate for years to come (Duménil and Lévy, 2011; Evans, 2015; Tooze, 2018). Given that the growth of the platform economy has proven to be directly dependent on financial capital, the former would not be immune to the crisis of the latter.

This crisis, as is the case with all crises, had different repercussions for capital and labor in general, and for our interest here the platform economy. This expressed itself in the nature of third-generation platforms. Though VC had been substantially increasing up to early 2008, it, along with IPO activity, dramatically decreased with the crisis and following recession. Modeled on growth-before-profit, new platforms experienced once again a gap in funding (Keuschnigg, 2004; Block and Sandner, 2009). As when the dot-com bubble burst, the financial climate was initially characterized by lowered interest rates, easing and accommodative monetary policies. Eventually, however, the climate fostered more funding once again, resulting in VC tripling since 2009 (reaching billions by 2015), along with increased funding by investment banks, mutual funds and hedge funds. With this financial backing, a new kind of platform could grow, as the crisis also resulted in a surge of unemployment and search for new and alternative sources of income. For these workers, the new generation of platforms would offer such an option (Sundararajan, 2016; Srnicek, 2017). This crisis and its repercussions, coupled with an ever-disseminating digital infrastructure from previous platform generations, planted the seeds for what became known as the on-demand, gig or sharing economy.

If we understand neoliberalism as bringing "all human action into the domain of the market" (Harvey, 2005: 3), then third-generation platforms embodied "neo-liberalism on steroids" (Morozov, 2013). Gig labor may have found its way into second-generation platforms, but third-generation platforms are *specifically* characterized by their gig nature. While initial estimations of the global annual revenues of the so-called sharing economy were to reach US$335 billion by 2025 (PwC, 2015), we can assume that the COVID-19 pandemic is bound to have accelerated and magnified these. In contrast to Web 2.0, which was positively associated with collaboration and community, platforms of the sharing economy were presented as sustainable, utilizing existing 'untapped' resources and making these accessible and efficient (Botsman and Roo Rogers, 2011; Frenken and Schor, 2017; Murillo et al, 2017). These third-generation platforms essentially commodified and monetized additional services that granted through the Internet 'temporary access' such as transport with Uber or Lyft, accommodation with Airbnb or delivery services with Deliveroo. Accordingly, the central desire of platform capital to become first movers in these markets in order later to dominate these, was this time cloaked in the discourse of 'sharing'. This umbrella term of the 'sharing economy' presents capitalist exchange as a paradox "framed as both part of the capitalist economy and as an alternative" (Richardson, 2015: 121). How one refers to this stage of the platform economy is fundamental in highlighting different aspects and viewpoints of third-generation platforms, blurring the world of work and how labor is organized and understood. I use the term 'gig economy', as it highlights its specific nature of work.

Generally speaking, the period after the financial crisis was one in which surviving first- and second-generation platforms came to dominate and develop into monopolies, as we currently see with Amazon, Google or now Meta (Bilić et al, 2021). Taken the political–economic context, it also meant the growth of web-based digital labor platforms such as UpWork or Crowdflower, now Appen. Third-generation platforms mediate the exchange of first and foremost labor power to complete tasks or services through gig work offering workers a piece-wage, but in some cases, depending on the platform, they can also be paid by a gig time-wage. The latter meant that workers with a specific set hourly wage were paid per task depending on the necessary work time needed to complete it.

Accordingly, this period did not just witness the growth of web-based platforms, but the gig nature was also absorbed by new location-based platforms, ranging from transportation and accommodation to grocery and food delivery platforms. This period generally saw then a growth of digital labor platforms both of web-based nature and now also location-based ones, which operated on the same logic of the gig nature of work. While these platforms also employ other workers, such as their customer service staff, I refer here to the precarious workers whose labor power is mediated via the platform. The two location-based pioneers of this generation are 2008 Airbnb, initially Airbedandbreakfast.com, and 2009 Uber, initially UberCab, both of which were established in San Francisco and quickly grew to operate internationally. Airbnb mediates between those who are willing to rent out (parts of) their home on short-term basis to those seeking accommodation. In contrast, Uber provides transport options for drivers with cars, and now even other vehicles, and those looking for a ride – though it too would later expand its ecosystem into food delivery with its Uber Eats.[5] Airbnb and Uber generally reflected the neoliberal understanding at the time, where owners could now monetize their home or vehicle when not in use. The fascinating fact is that "Uber, the world's largest taxi company, owns no vehicles. … And Airbnb, the world's largest accommodation provider, owns no real estate" (Goodwin, 2015).

These platforms depended first on the Internet's ever-growing user base, which could now access platforms from anywhere by mobile devices. As of 2021, the number of Internet users had more than tripled to 4.9 billion users from the 1.5 billion in 2008 (Statista, 2021b). Second, they could cut down significantly on costs because of the very model on which they were built. The 'hyperoutsourcing' model shifts costs onto the workers, who bear the variable capital through their labor power and much of the constant capital through the means of production, such as an Uber driver's car, maintenance costs, gasoline and any training. The fast growth of third-generation platforms was further facilitated by cloud platforms such as AWS, which allowed them to cut down on time and costs necessary to build their own infrastructure. All that was left for these platforms to do was to mediate between 'demands' and 'underutilized assets' via the platform infrastructure. While Airbnb depends on AWS, Uber uses Google for mapping, while collecting data to plot the best routes (Srnicek, 2017). Though tightening VC meant initially a slower start, these platforms adopted the earlier model to 'get big fast' guided by the concept of 'winner takes all'. Both Airbnb and Uber skyrocketed from small start-ups to international corporations of double-digit billion-dollar value within the course of less than half a decade, essentially contributing to the unequal distribution of wealth despite a discourse of 'sharing' (Martin, 2016; Murillo et al, 2017). These platforms may be feeding a new bubble of their own as they hide their true costs and low or even non-existent profits. This was reflected for instance in Uber's initial projection to be worth US$120 billion and later US$70 billion, as its overvalued shares at US$45 closed 7.6 percent lower than its IPO pricing (Rajaraman, 2017; Clark, 2019). Reminiscent of the dot-com era in different ways, it seems that the long-term consequences of platforms on the general economy remain to be seen.

While this frenzy has meant a lucrative time for capital, both location- and web-based laboring presented a different reality for workers. The growth of third-generation gig platforms has meant increased precarization, as previously mentioned, a trend initiated by second-generation platforms and de facto accelerated by third-generation platforms that framed the deregulation of labor markets as a positive development. This generation of platforms was built accordingly on a neoliberal model that cut costs and resources as much as possible by outsourcing as much as possible. Geographically and temporally dispersed workers could compete both remotely through the Internet and directly on-location for the same work without the benefits usually derived from regular employment. Labor regulation could now be dodged by web-based and location-based platforms alike, further contributing to a race to the bottom that threatened fair wages and labor rights, while stripping platforms of all sorts of legal liability. Such developments and co-evolving discourses are in many ways telling of how precarity "is normalized, reproduced, and even romanticized by those firms and platforms ... [which] seek to naturalize and reify flexible and precarious circumstances as ethically appropriate for contract and other workers" (Cockayne, 2016: 75). At the same time, workers face additional surveillance through the system of user ratings and reviews which is encouraged by platforms. These can have fundamental consequences and result in their termination as independent contractors. As I discuss in the later chapters of this book, there could be a potential shift in such labor relations as seen in Europe, given the efforts to reclassify gig workers, though it remains to be seen to what degree these are implemented and monitored (European Commission, 2021a). As will become clear throughout this book, "technological developments cannot be understood without reference to broader material dynamics centred on the restructuring of labour markets and the labour process" (Dinerstein and Pitts, 2021: 48).

Historicizing and contextualizing the platform economy demonstrates, then, that its creation and expansion have been organic and bound to larger political–economic and technological developments. These ranged from instrumentalizing the Internet to attracting financial capital for its growth within a neoliberal context characterized by crises. Each generation and organization of platforms was premised on previous developments. For one, first-generation platforms essentially organized the Internet as a space and focused on creating digital marketplaces through location-based time-waged platforms. Second-generation platforms saw the evolution of previous platforms and novel ways of profit generation through data commodification, as well as the creation of clouds. It also pushed laboring into the realm of digital outsourcing. Accordingly, this period saw the creation of new location-based platforms and growth of web-based platforms that introduced gig work into the orbit of the platform economy. After the 2008 crisis, third-generation platforms further disseminated the gig economy in society in both location- and web-based platforms, possible because of the hyperoutsourcing model, which intrinsically meant continued precarization. At their essence, the different generations of platforms share their desire to tap into a new market and be first movers, and as time would show many of these would establish themselves indeed as monopolies within their respective markets (Bilić et al, 2021). Discursively, their vision was framed around the Internet's untapped potential and framed in relation to new possibilities that could (re)define our daily lives, social relations and labor relations. By analyzing the development of the platform economy, we can account therefore for the ways by which it is (re)configured and continues to do so in terms of capital and labor in relation to different moments in time (Table 4.1).

**Table 4.1:** The development of the platform economy

| | **Dialectical conditions** | | **Platform function** | **Forms of platform organization** | **Platform examples** |
|---|---|---|---|---|---|
| | *Technological* | *Political-economic* | | | |
| **Generation I: 1990s** | • Commercialization & dissemination of the Internet | • Neoliberalism<br>• Rise of VC, IPO<br>• Dot-com bubble | • Commodity circulation<br>• Index and search | • Location-based<br>• Traditional time-wage | • Amazon<br>• eBay<br>• Google<br>• Yahoo |
| **Generation II: Mid-2000s** | • Further dissemination of the Internet<br>• Interactive, Multimedia Web 2.0<br>• Possibilities for data surveillance and commodification | • Post dot-com bubble burst<br>• Decrease in VC<br>• Digitalization of labor markets<br>• Precarization of workers | • Advertising<br>• Cloud<br>• Digital Labor | • Location- and web-based<br>• Time- and piece-wage | • Facebook<br>• MTurk<br>• AWS |
| **Generation III: Post-2008** | • Further dissemination of the Internet<br>• Possibilities for hyperoutsourcing | • Post-financial crisis<br>• Initial decrease in VC and lowered IPO<br>• Hyperoutsourcing | • Accommodation<br>• Transport<br>• Additional services | • Gig economy: location- and web-based gig work | • Airbnb<br>• Uber<br>• Deliveroo |

# 5

# Contextualizing Amazon's Growing Empire

Amazon spreads its roots across the platform economy, becoming foundational to it and making it increasingly difficult not to encounter Amazon in one way or another while using the Internet. Essentially, it constitutes an example "of a corporation thriving under the current organization of capitalism which, in absence of regulatory frameworks, favours market concentration and dominance" (Brevini, 2021: 65). I trace in this chapter Amazon's development within the larger platform economy from its establishment in the 1990s to the monopoly it has grown into today, as it has organically created platforms across all three generations. I focus especially on its e-commerce and digital labor platform, as these constitute the focus of my investigation of the world of workers. Amazon is increasingly regarded as a trendsetter for other platforms and industries in the global political economy looking to *Amazonify* the way they organize themselves and their workforces (Alimahomed-Wilson, 2020; Alimahomed-Wilson and Reese, 2020). The repercussions and implications of this may very well extend beyond the platform economy.

## Amazon as a first-generation platform

The creation of Amazon in 1994 was a response to the conditions of the dot-com era – a time in which Bezos, for decades the personification of its capital, was celebrated as a "pioneer of the new economy" and Amazon as "the poster child of the Internet" (Spector, 2002: xv). With Internet use growing by a staggering 2,300 percent annually with the wide availability of Mosaic for computers, Bezos recognized the opportunity to instrumentalize this new infrastructure of the Internet for the creation of platforms (Stone, 2013; Leisegang, 2014). After surveying a list of 20 possible products, ranging from computer software to music, Bezos opted for creating a digital marketplace for books, although his was not the first of its kind. While bricks-and-mortar stores such as Barnes & Nobles dominated the book industry, an online bookstore would be convenient for both the platform and for users. Books are familiar to users, and their sale could now be mediated on a 24/7 accessible digital marketplace. Users could place orders via a credit card-secured method and have books delivered to them as soon as possible. For the platform, an online bookstore saves on costs of employees and store locations, eliminates physical limits to the range of books and simplifies the purchase through online content such as reviews, excerpts and synopses (Spector, 2002; Kenney 2003a). Given the Internet's growing significance and economic potential for platforms in the dot-com frenzy, there was a sense of urgency for Amazon to 'Get Big Fast' and be in that regard, a first mover.

Amazon was established in Seattle as a result of interrelated conditions: its access to a technical talent pool with the University of Washington and companies like Microsoft and its proximity to Ingram Book Group's largest book distribution center in the country only a six-hour drive away. Additionally, being a state with a small population was important, as only state residents are charged a sales tax. Bezos, along with Shel Kaphan and Paul Davis, created the platform in his garage. After it was officially incorporated in Washington State in 1994 as Cadabra and initially misheard by the attorney as 'Cadaver', it was renamed Amazon.com. In addition to the link to the Internet in its name, it referred to the Amazon river – a river that was "10 times larger than the next biggest river … [and] so much bigger than its next nearest competitor" (Spector, 2002: 36). The name strategically placed Amazon at the top of the alphabetically listed online websites, while keeping it broad enough to expand beyond its 1995 tagline of 'Earth's biggest bookstore'. Crucial to the establishment of Amazon was the financial capital of Bezos and his family which was able to fuel its initial growth despite operating at a loss. Within the first month it had already delivered books to 45 countries and 50 US states, only to boom after Netscape listed it on its 'What's new' page (Spector, 2002). This laid the foundation for Amazon to tap into a globalized market, essential for it to grow into the considerable platform it is today.

Amazon's growth did not merely depend on the financial and political–economic conditions, but was strongly related to regarding customer satisfaction as its very DNA, claiming to be "Earth's most customer-centric company".[1] The customer is regarded as Amazon's gravitational pole to the extent that one warehouse worker in Germany states that "Amazon treats me better as a customer than [it does] as a worker". With customer service available 24 hours a day and a simplified shopping experience, customers could track orders and have a smooth virtual experience to ensure their continued return. This was even more so smoothened with its later trademarked one-click shopping. Reviews left by customers not only attracted new customers but also resulted in immense data that could be utilized by Amazon to further personalize the experience. This was aided by certain acquisitions such as that of Alexa Internet Co. Named after the Egyptian library, Alexa tracked site visits to make tailored suggestions with a database of 12 terabytes (Spector, 2002). With the exception of possible contact with customer service, this e-commerce platform essentially facilitated an online shopping experience for customers devoid of any human contact or interactions with workers.

With favorable conditions in place, Amazon, like other first-generation platforms, benefited from the stock market hysteria during the dot-com era. Despite a fast, efficient system and inventory, Amazon was operating at a staggering loss as high as US$303,000 in 1995, reaching US$5.78 million in 1996 (Wilhelm, 2017). In desperate need of new capital, Amazon turned to venture capital (VC). While the idea of an online bookstore did not excite many, Bezos had been featured on the front page of the 16 May 1996 edition of the *Wall Street Journal*. Amazon ultimately went with Kleiner Perkins Caufield & Byers, which Bezos considered a "gravitational center of a huge piece of the Internet world" (Spector, 2002: 103). The dot-com bubble was characterized not just by VC injections but also by financial capital from the stock market. Despite facing initial lawsuits from the likes of Barnes & Nobles, Amazon went public on 15 May 1997 with an Initial Public Offering (IPO) opening price of US$18 a share. The growth of Amazon's fictitious value translated into greater wealth for Bezos, explaining how he would later become among the richest humans. As of then, he had a wealth of US$177.8 million, holding 42 percent of Amazon with an additional 10 percent held by his family, therefore constituting a majority voting power. While shares had gone up to US$52 by 1997, they rose to a staggering US$300 the following year around the 'Internet Christmas', during which Amazon became the second most visited website, with over 9 million visitors. Though Amazon was regarded among the most overvalued stock, it demonstrated the potential of capitalizing off the Internet (Spector, 2002; Stone, 2013).

If Amazon's mantra was initially to 'Get Big Fast', it was now to 'Get Bigger Faster' with financial capital ready to inject into the expansion of its workforce, warehouses and products. These steps were essential for it to dominate as a first-generation platform and later monopolize. As the customer base grew, so too did its workforce, which was organized within its location-based warehouses according to traditional time-wages. These years present the initial steps in systematizing a division of labor within its circulation line to pack and ship, and molding a certain work culture and hierarchies by also fishing for managers from, for instance, Walmart. Amazon's expansion was not limited to the US but also seeped into Europe and Asia through acquisitions of British Bookpages and German Telebuch in 1998 and later expansions in France and Japan by 2000. So the 1990s did not just see the creation of the platform but effectively its *transnationalization*, crucial for its later developments. The spatial expansion of Amazon was accompanied by the diversification of sold commodities, as Internet analyst Mary Meeker stated in 1999: "[m]aybe a decade from now we'll be looking at books and concluding that it was a Trojan horse that built the rest of the company" (Spector, 2002: 93; Kruse, 2004). Amazon's redesign of its logo into an upward facing arrow in the shape of a smile linking A to Z reflected its transformation far beyond an online bookstore into an 'everything store' – selling commodities ranging from books and toys to home supplies and kitchen appliances. As Bezos had stated in 1997, "[o]ur strategy is to become an electronic commerce destination. When somebody thinks about buying something online, even if it is something we do not carry, we want them to come to us" (Spector, 2002: 191). Amazon's creation and growth, fueled and developed within the dot-com context, was also not immune to the bursting of the bubble. Its overvalued shares dropped rapidly and it only reported its first ever profit in the fourth quarter (Q4) of 2001 (Hansell, 2002). Amazon, however, managed not only to survive but in fact to thrive in the years that followed.

## Amazon's second-generation platforms

If Amazon initially developed as a location-based platform with a more traditional workforce, it evolved organically along with capitalist and technological conditions by expanding, creating and rolling out second-generation platforms. These include MTurk, which mediates outsourced labor, and Amazon Web Services (AWS), which mediates cloud computing. MTurk differs from the e-commerce platform in the nature of both the work and the platform. On the one hand, technological conditions facilitated its web-based laboring; a novelty for platforms at the time. Its piece-wage laboring, on the other hand, has been historically part and parcel of the development of capitalism (Gray and Suri, 2019). MTurk, an invisible digital assembly line, joins many platforms that bring together new and old dimensions to the organization of capital–labor relations, "appear[ing] to be a permanent fixture of a 'new world of work' that is flexible, digital, and globally networked" (Harmon and Silberman, 2019: 913).

Interestingly enough, Amazon created its second-generation platforms primarily for its own internal use before commercializing these. As the e-commerce continued to expand after the dot-com bubble burst, its growing database of books required additional labor for additional tasks. These included identifying duplicates, outdated book cover images, typos and embedded keywords to match customers' searches better with as many books as possible. Engineers understood it to be an 'insurmountable' task to create Artificial Intelligence (AI) algorithms for these tasks, emphasizing that they required human intelligence. Amazon initially turned to employing temporary contracted workers from India and the US. As it expanded and diversified its product range, it increasingly required a larger workforce. Venky Harinarayan, an Amazon manager at the time, patented his idea of breaking down tasks into smaller ones to be distributed across a larger network of workers – a form of "hybrid machine/human computing arrangement" (Schwartz, 2019). It was more efficient to outsource these tasks to temporary workers via Amazon's own platform than to contract agencies. This would give Amazon direct access to a global army of workers for microtasks that could be paid in small piece-wages. Shortly afterwards, Amazon recognized its potential beyond its internal use and publicly launched MTurk in 2005 as a "crowdsourcing marketplace".[2]

Amazon, as other platforms would do, thereby instrumentalized the technological conditions that made it possible for work no longer to be geographically fixed (Graham et al, 2017). Information and communications technology developments had previously enabled capital to cut costs by coordinating a globally dispersed labor force through relocations such as customer service and data and information processing. India is one of the countries with the highest number of MTurk workers. Along with its history of outsourcing, based on its English-speaking colonial history and degree of scientific education, it has channeled funds into the development of broadband Internet infrastructures, which had in turn meant away from public utilities. Outsourcing presents capital with an opportunity to cut costs, weaken the labor movement and unions, and circumvent labor rights and regulations (Gray and Suri, 2019). By the mid-2000s, Amazon could take outsourcing into the digital sphere via its platform, where workers only needed an Internet connection and a device. MTurk was thus amongst the platforms that planted the seeds for digital labor platforms, the de facto digital outsourcing of online gig work that was to grow with third-generation platforms (Kuek et al, 2015; Webster, 2016; Casilli, 2017). The digital mediation of labor is deemed to have accelerated through COVID-19 as a result of the increased shift to working from home and online education in light of surges of cases and national lockdowns (Kassem, 2022).

While MTurk's web-based nature was a product of its time, it is important to keep in mind that piecework is not a novel development of the 21st century but reaches far back to the times of automating the first assembly lines. Gray and Suri (2019) argue more specifically that the employment of labor pools for a temporary duration of time through piecework, often regarded as 'unskilled labor' and ghost work, has been indispensable to technological advancements. This refers to workers who have been in the shadows of automation and technology such as the crucial human computer pools in Langley, VA, that performed the necessary calculations for the Apollo 13 launching. Rather than understanding automation as replacing labor, it is understood historically for its role in displacing labor, as "the long march toward automation has historically created new needs and different types of human labor to fill those needs" (Gray and Suri, 2019: xvii). Essentially this reflects the general understanding that "[t]echnology has not replaced work, but created new forms of work and augmented others, often with negative consequences for those who perform it" (Dinerstein and Pitts, 2021: 29). While organized labor and unions channeled attention to securing rights for time-wage labor in mines and factories, piece-wage labor fell through the cracks and became part and parcel of the larger economy. Today's ghost work offers capital a large pool of expendable labor with the status of independent contractors, stripping workers of rights and benefits and freeing capital of responsibilities offered to time-wage laborers. Within our current capitalist moment, such forms of labor, which conduct (micro)tasks, have become increasingly integral to both small and larger capital formations concerned with the production and analysis of big data and algorithms necessary for the development of AI (Gray and Suri, 2019). As such, the platform economy combined this historical form of work with its technological infrastructure and normalized it through the gig economy.

Unlike other web-based digital labor platforms where workers labor for larger projects, MTurk mediates through its Application Programming Interface the exchange of labor power for microtasks. These can range from data gathering and crosschecking information for clinics and restaurants, transcribing/digitizing data to answering market and academic surveys or identifying objects across different media. Much of this is for the purpose of contributing data for machine-learning algorithms for AI by workers who are meant to be completely invisible. The name of the platform is a reference to Wolfgang von Kempelen's chess-playing automaton, the 'Mechanical Turk', presented in the late 18th century at the court of the Empress Maria Theresa of Austria (Figure 5.1). The automaton toured Europe and the Americas for nearly a century and defeated the likes of Benjamin Franklin and Napoleon Bonaparte. The Turk, embodying Orientalist conceptions of a docile 'Other' of the time, appeared as an automaton playing chess independently of any humans, presenting a case of "simulated machinic intelligence". In reality, a smaller chess master was concealed within the case to play on behalf of the automaton (Aytes, 2013; Irani, 2013; Aloisi and De Stefano, 2022).

Amazon's MTurk transports the Mechanical Turk into the 21st century, stating that

> humans still significantly outperform the most powerful computers at completing such simple tasks as identifying objects in photographs – something children can do even before they learn to speak. … [MTurk] provides a service for service requesters (hereafter "Requesters") to integrate Artificial Artificial Intelligence directly into their applications by making requests of humans.[3]

By adopting Mechanical Turk in its name, Amazon frames the vast, diverse, global workforce on MTurk as *artificial artificial intelligence*. Where a chess

**Figure 5.1:** Kempelen's Mechanical Turk – originally in Karl Gottlieb von Windisch, *Briefe über den Schachspieler des Hrn. von Kempelen, nebst drei Kupferstichen, die diese berühmte Maschine vorstellen*, 1783

Source: Accessed on public domain of Wikimedia Commons, 24 July 2022, https://commons.wikimedia.org/wiki/File:Turk-with-person.jpg#file.

master was secretly controlling the chess game, now a vast global workforce runs the automaton from behind their screens. MTurk describes its microtasks as "break[ing] down a manual, time-consuming project into smaller, more manageable tasks to be completed by distributed workers over the Internet".[4] If Amazon mediates the sale and purchase of commodities, then MTurk is in its essence a digital marketplace for one commodity: labor power. In the words of Bezos, "You've heard of software-as-a-service. Now this is human-as-a-service" (Irani, 2013: 720).

As Amazon developed MTurk for its internal use, it also required additional infrastructure to operate its platforms and logistics. Accordingly, it developed its cloud-computing AWS and similarly rolled it out to the public in 2006. Today, it operates on six continents and has become "the world's most comprehensive and broadly adopted cloud platform".[5] AWS constitutes Amazon's crucial source of profit which can absorb the losses of its e-commerce platform. In addition to clients such as General Electric, partnering with

NASA and receiving a contract from the CIA, AWS has also facilitated the creation of third-generation platforms such as Airbnb and Lyft by reducing and outsourcing their data storage to its digital and material infrastructures (Gregg, 2019; Williams, 2020; Bilić et al, 2021).[6] Those working for AWS labor in their location-based offices and are offered a time-wage, quite similar to those working for Google. Within the empire of Amazon, these white-collar workers can be considered at the top of its pyramid, especially when compared with the manual warehouse workers or MTurk workers who seem invisible. While AWS operates part of the very infrastructure of the platform economy, Amazon's growing workforces across its different platforms demonstrate how it has come to encompass various sectors of the platform economy. This became even more crucial in the context of COVID-19 as relations were pushed online and corporations that experienced a surge in activity, such as Netflix and Zoom, were already operating and supported via AWS.

The development of Amazon's platforms appears to have evolved from its most central and very first platform. It was crucial therefore for the e-commerce platform to continue to expand and grow its customer base. This was in part possible through the launch of its Amazon prime membership in 2007, which ensured free two-day delivery and additional benefits such as access to Amazon's video streaming service. This would be later complemented by the 2019 introduction of one-day delivery.[7] Amazon has additionally expanded its market reach by mediating third-party sales of products on its platform through Fulfillment By Amazon (FBA) or Fulfillment By Merchant (FBM). While the former refers to Amazon handling the circulation process and shipping in the warehouses, in the latter sellers take on these responsibilities. Regardless of the chosen method, which accordingly differ in cost, third-party sellers have become increasingly integral to Amazon sales, while Amazon's growing market reach has become crucial for sellers. Since 2017 these have constituted at least half of Amazon's sales – a number that continues to rise (Statista, 2021a). Amazon has additionally developed its own exclusive technological products which were central to its growth, such as its 2007 e-book reader Kindle, which now has a 90 percent of e-book market share, its 2014 Fire TV and its 2015 Amazon Echo, which virtually assists through the program Alexa (Day and Gu, 2019; UNI and ITUC, 2019). The context of first- and second-generation platforms was thus central to paving the way for Amazon's establishment and growing influence across the platform economy, cementing and translating its vision of being a first mover across markets.

## The growth of Amazon and its third-generation platform

The previous periods were foundational to Amazon, however its exponential growth can be attributed to the last few years. While it has come to monopolize many markets, such as in the US, it expands in others, such as the Middle East and North Africa, where it has done so by acquiring the Emirati e-commerce souq.com (Lunden, 2017). It comes as no surprise that US politicians like Elizabeth Warren and Bernie Sanders, as well as the then General Secretary of the International Trade Union Confederation (ITUC) Sharan Burrow, are among those critiquing and stressing the importance of breaking up Amazon, its concentration of power and monopoly (Perticone, 2019; UNI and ITUC, 2019). Amazon's growing power has only been magnified by the context of COVID-19, during which it has seen its share prices, profits and workers more or less double in the course of a few months. Its growth, power and reach over the global political economy have been dubbed '*Amazon capitalism*' by researchers (Alimahomed-Wilson et al, 2020).

Amazon's growth goes hand in hand with its increasing control over its logistics and supply chain, as we have seen with its introduction of Amazon Flex in 2015 – essentially a third-generation location-based gig platform, though one (for now) exclusively tied to its first-generation platform. Just like Uber and food couriers, workers are hired by gig as independent contractors. As the name suggests, it offers those willing to do the job with – what the gig economy most widely celebrates – *flexibility*. Initially tested in the US, it now operates in various countries, including some in Europe, such as the UK and, until around mid-2022, Germany. All one needs is to be at least 21 in the US or 18 in Europe, to have a valid driver's license and a smartphone by which to access the app and have access to a mid- to large-sized vehicle to carry out the deliveries. Amazon Flex estimates the hourly rate, depending on locations and tips, to be US$18–25 in the US. As with other gig platforms, individuals must still consider other expenses such as paying for gas. Signing up for hourly time blocks, Amazon Flex allows workers to "have the freedom to really be yourself" and be "actively engaged in delivering smiles to happy customers" or, as it sums up in the tagline, "Do it your way. Set your own hours, listen to your own tunes, and get paid."[8] As other gig platforms demonstrate, flexibility can be valued by workers as providing work in an economy characterized by looming crises. Amazon Flex reflects, for one thing, how Amazon adapts and evolves along technological conditions to further expand. It also sheds light on the future implications of such increased control within its supply chain and logistics network, which depend less and less on external services and sectors – some of which have been known to be unionized and organized.

Co-evolving along with the wider political–economic, societal and technological conditions, Amazon has come to grow its ecosystem over the last years – even within healthcare, at least in the US (Thorbecke, 2022). In a seemingly fascinating way, Amazon may have initially been created to be an online bookstore – taking bricks-and-mortar into the digital sphere.

However, in recent years we have in fact seen, in addition to its exponential expansion in the digital, a move in the opposite direction, into the world of the bricks-and-mortar stores. These include the first Amazon Books bricks-and-mortar shops, though it was decided in 2022 that these were to close to focus more on its Whole Foods, acquired in 2017. They also include (since 2018) its cashierless grocery stores, Amazon Go, and its new Amazon Style clothing store (Schaverien, 2018; O'Brien, 2022). At the same time, Amazon's acquisitions and developments can be regarded as having established trends in the automation of labor: take, for instance, its Kiva System, acquired in 2012 and later renamed Amazon Robotics. These circular robots can be incorporated into warehouses by sliding under shelves and moving them around, thereby automating certain steps within the circulation line (Pepitone, 2012; Day and Gu, 2019). Finally, it is important also to highlight Amazon's expansion of its distribution network, spanning all its warehouses, which it calls Fulfillment Centers (FCs), referring to customer fulfillment, and its further sorting centers, delivery stations and even airport hubs. These underline its growing control of the supply chain, as it now even holds its own cargo airline to deliver its packages. Thus, while Amazon already locates its warehouses close to airports and highways to facilitate the fast delivery of orders (Boewe and Schulten, 2019), it is increasingly assuming last-mile delivery and what Alimahomed-Wilson refers to as the "Amazonification of logistics" (2020). A contemporary development along the lines of increased logistics chain control has been, for instance, its Amazon Delivery Service Partner program, in which one can participate in Amazon's deliveries through one's own business.[9] Given the unprecedented rate at which Amazon has opened new warehouses and centers, boosted by the surge in online shopping during the COVID-19 pandemic, it is increasingly difficult to pin down the growing number of the hundreds of warehouses both in numerical and geographical terms.[10]

Amazon's expansion has implied different things for capital and labor: as its warehouses network grows, so too does its workforce. While in 2009 its workforce amounted to 24,300, by the end of 2019 the workforce had grown to an astonishing global workforce of almost 800,000 (Statista, 2021a). While this number includes full- and part-time workers, it can be assumed to be much higher, as it excludes temporary workers and contractors. Amazon relies heavily on these workers during its most profitable quarter, Q4, which includes Black Friday and the Christmas season. In 2019, for instance, seasonal workers amounted to 200,000 in just the US (Bloomberg, 2019). These numbers expanded to a whole new dimension in light of COVID-19. Though it had an extensive supply chain and logistics network, Amazon had to hire hundreds of thousands of workers at different stages of the pandemic to keep up with orders (Kassem, 2022). By the end of 2020 it had officially almost doubled its direct workforce in the span of less than a year, amounting to almost 1.3 million in 2020 and 1.6 million in 2021. These numbers also exclude the workers in peak seasons during Prime Day, Black Friday and Christmas sales (Statista, 2021a; Statisa, 2022). As platforms struggle to maintain growth levels experienced during COVID-19, resulting in waves of layoffs by the end of 2022, it remains to be seen how these and their workforces will develop in the coming years.

Amazon's growing market share is reflected in the frenzy around its financial capital. Upon announcing its 2019 Q4 earnings, tied to its peak season, Amazon stocks had soared to over US$2,000 per share, adding close to US$13 billion to the wealth of Bezos (Debter, 2020). While stocks rise and fall, the share value rose exponentially in relation to Amazon's expansion in 2020, doubling between March and September 2020 from US$1,600–1,800 to almost US$3,500 (Kassem, 2022).[11] These numbers, refer, however, to Amazon prior to its stock split of a 20:1 ratio that was announced and came into effect in 2022 (Curry, 2022). Without legal and political regulation and enforcement, Amazon, like other platforms, has been able so far to evade taxes despite its growing wealth. Amazon ultimately demonstrates that "[t]here's no clearer example of corporate abuse than an Amazon warehouse worker paying more income tax than Jeff Bezos, the [then] world's richest [hu]man" (UNI and ITUC, 2019: 13). If Bezos was already the richest human before the pandemic, his wealth grew even further in 2020 (though Elon Musk would overtake him). It is yet to be seen how the historic G7 agreed deal in 2021 to tax multinational corporations a minimum of 15 percent where they make sales, regardless of HQ location, will impact Amazon in the future, as these must report a minimum profit margin of 10 percent to be taxed (Jolly, 2021).

Contextualizing and historicizing Amazon allows us to trace its development and grasp how it has grown into the monopoly power it is today, and how it consolidates itself given the context of COVID-19. Indeed, Delfanti (2021b) argues that Amazon has grown by maneuvering crises: from the dot-com bubble, the aftermath of the 2008 recession and now COVID-19. As it extends its influence across the supply chain and the platform economy through first-, second- and third-generation platforms, it is important to recognize how, as Christy Hoffman, the General Secretary of UNI, states, "Amazon has acquired unparalleled influence and it presents an unparalleled threat" (UNI and ITUC, 2019: 3). With this threat has come one to the larger labor movement, as many platforms and sectors beyond the platform economy regard Amazon as the model for efficiency and wealth. Given the dimensions of its growing power, a defeat and by the same token a victory for the workers is bound to be felt by those elsewhere and vice versa. Having analyzed the developments from the perspective of capital, I now turn my attention to the workers of the first of two case studies: its backbone, the manual workforce of its warehouses.

PART III

# Workers on the (Digital) Amazon Shop Floor

# 6

# Cog in the Machine: Working the Amazon Circulation Line

"I am not a robot."

Warehouse worker

Warehouse workers of Amazon's e-commerce platform occupy a complex role: they are manual workers reminiscent of those inside factory walls in the industrial era, now transported into the technological conditions of the 21st century. Whereas factories produce, Amazon circulates. The organization of these warehouses reflects Taylorist techniques of scientific management. These monitor and control every step of the labor process to ensure a docile and (algorithmically) disciplined workforce to keep up with massive expansions and ever-increasing demand. In the process, this location-based traditional time-wage platform systematically alienates workers across the dimensions of their laboring and being. As one worker puts it, they do not just become "part of the machine, [they] are the machine". To dive into the walls of the warehouse, where the division of labor and organization of work(ers) is similar across the globe, I abstract the larger material context. I return to this in the next chapter to shed light on some relative differences in the working conditions that play a role in the agency of labor.

## Alienation from the labor activity

As all estrangement and labor exploitation is rooted in the process of laboring, the alienation of Amazon's workers is founded on the systematic division of labor. Given that these workers occupy a place in circulation, the corporation realizes value that it does not necessarily produce. It is, therefore, in its interest to shorten the turnover time of products as much as possible (Marx, 1978). Amazon has a highly productive and efficient circulation line that can organize workers in ways more traditionally known in factories, while applying various social and technological mechanisms of surveillance.

A hierarchy of supervisors, ranging from leads, who directly supervise manual workers, to various managers, who supervise leads and others, ensures that workers labor productively as interchangeable cogs in the Amazon machine. The ability to labor according to the demands of Amazon is *the* criteria to get hired. Amazon stresses that it is "committed to a diverse and inclusive workplace. Amazon is an equal opportunity employer and does not discriminate on the basis of race, national origin, gender, gender identity, sexual orientation, protected veteran status, disability, age, or other legally protected status."[1] Yet, since these warehouses do not operate in a vacuum, they are not immune to the wider trends of the labor market in which they operate. In other words, if manual labor is generally racialized or gendered in a particular local and national context, then this will be reflected in the composition of the labor force in Amazon's warehouses. Depending on the geographical location of a warehouse across the globe, but also within a specific country, the manual workers, seasonal and/or permanent, may be predominantly people of color (Reese, 2020; Vgontzas, 2020; Kassem, 2023). The same logic applies to supervisory and management roles, which may require a university degree and, depending on location, can be predominantly filled by white men or in some cases even (former) military personnel (Transnational Social Strike Platform, 2019; Reese, 2020; Delfanti, 2021b).

Rather than focusing on the vertical hierarchy of the division of labor that includes such supervisory functions, I am mainly concerned with four steps within the horizontal circulation line of manual laborers. I engage, therefore, with the supervisors and managers to the extent that they oversee the labor process of the manual workforce. Amazon does not hire a worker for each of these four steps within the circulation, but generalizes the labor activity and calls its workers *associates*. These, unlike those laboring in management, do not need prior work experience or special skills (Massimo, 2020). They can accordingly be easily hired but also replaced. Amazon advertises these jobs as follows: "You'll be part of the Amazon warehouse team that gets orders ready for customers relying on Amazon's services" within "fast-paced, active roles".[2] The general description of its warehouse labor appears as masking the division of labor, as workers know how to labor all subtasks along the circulation line. This proves efficient for Amazon, which can shift workers interchangeably depending on the volume of orders.

The circulation line can be simplified and imagined as beginning in the *Inbound* and ending in the *Outbound*. The former can be subdivided into receive/prep and stow, the latter in pick and pack (Figure 6.1). Let us imagine a customer, Hana, who has ordered a set of six light bulbs from Amazon directly. These light bulbs have initially traveled to the warehouse to arrive in the Inbound. The Inbound prepares, indexes, registers and stows the commodities. Upon unloading the trucks, the first crucial group of workers that encounters the light bulbs is the one in *Receive* and *Prep*. Once workers

**Figure 6.1:** Circulation line of Amazon warehouses

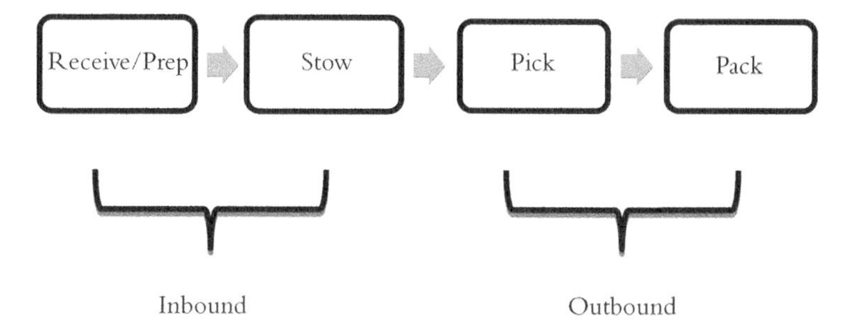


are assigned a task, it is to be performed repeatedly and continuously, though they can be shifted around. The Receive/Prep and the packing workers are physically restricted to their assigned numeric and daily interchanging desks. The Receive/Prep worker unpacks the larger boxes of light bulb sets, registers/indexes each on the system and scans these to double-check that they fit their description. Unlike light bulbs, if products such as hats were shipped in bulk, they would have to additionally be individually repacked and labeled with a scan code. Returning to our light bulbs, once on the Amazon system, they are placed in carts and/or yellow tote boxes that move on to be *stowed* on the shelves. Whereas in the previous step the set was digitally registered on the system, stowers do it physically. Since Amazon warehouses have an optimized disorganized storage system, products can be stowed wherever there is available space within the rows of shelves to which the worker is assigned. The light bulb sets are not all stowed beside each other so as not to cause any confusion when picking these, given the differences in kinds and sizes. Once a space is identified, the stower's task is to use a hand scanner to register the light bulb set to the virtual system by now linking it to the specific physical space where it is placed so that it can be found once ordered (Delfanti, 2021a). As soon as this is done, the light bulbs are available and deliverable to Hana. While in Receive/Prep it is important to unpack and register products as fast as possible, stowers need to stow as many products in as little space as fast as possible.

Workers assigned in the *Outbound* need to get Hana's light bulb set to her in the shortest time possible. The picker under the guidance of a hand scanner, which displays the index code of the set, locates it and places it into a yellow tote bin. Pickers can walk up to 20 km a day to keep up with customer orders in these warehouses, which stretch over an area the size of several soccer fields. Once workers log on with their ID via their hand scanners, their relationship to their managers becomes mediated and regulated through their scanner (Cattero and D'Onoforio, 2018). The labor activity of the picker is the opposite of the stower's, with the exception that they are not restricted to certain shelves. Once the light bulbs are picked, these move on to the packers. While prep and pack workers are assigned a physical place in the circulation line, stowers and pickers appear to be part of a mobile circulation line, as they are distributed across the warehouses (Boewe and Schulten, 2019).

Just as pickers are subdivided in ones picking numerous single or multiple products ordered by customers, so too are packers. In our case, Hana only ordered one product, which is single packed. If she had ordered something else along with the light bulbs, a worker would sort these items together for a packer to pack together as 'multi', should these products all be available in the same warehouse. The packer then scans the set, so that the computer can display the right box size for it to be packed in. After adding some filler material so the light bulbs do not get damaged during transport and delivery, a machine spits out the corresponding amount of tape to seal off that specific size of box before it continues on the conveyer belt. Human decision-making in this process is restricted to the amount of filler material placed in the box. Put in too much and the box falls off the conveyer belt, because it is too heavy, which could mean the wrong product has been packed and Hana would not receive her order. The key is to put in as little filler material as possible while ensuring the product is not damaged. Once the package is on the conveyer belt, a machine spits out a label with Hana's address, before a worker loads her package onto the delivery truck.

At every step of the circulation line, it is apparent that workers are not in control of their labor activity, but have it dictated to them. In a process of "machinic dispossession" workers are alienated from their labor activity, with no special knowledge over the labor process or inventory as has been essential in the past. As long as workers have technological access to the system, they can labor but also be replaced (Delfanti, 2021b). The whole process of laboring is impersonal, from the tasks to the workplace. Just as the shelves and benches have their designated space marked by yellow tape and often labeled with a sign, so workers laboring the circulation line are assigned at any given moment a specific task that physically restricts them to a space, with the mere exception of the pickers. Within this fast-moving circulation line in which all steps depend on the previous ones, each worker, regardless of their background, is reduced to their ability to meet the same productivity rate dictated in that moment for their specific task. The Taylorist organization that "break[s] the unity of the labor process" is essential to its management and ensures efficiency, while removing any sense of control from the hands of the workforce (Braverman, 1974: 114). This systematic division of labor, which divorces, atomizes and fragments each step from every other step, has been a development within the trajectory of capitalism and only appears to have intensified. The worker turns into the gears of the machine, in which their individuality becomes irrelevant. Only their function is of importance. In the echoes of Marx's words, "[i]n the factory we have a lifeless mechanism which is independent of the workers, who are incorporated into it as its living appendages" (1977: 548).

To extract as much labor as possible considering national legal limits to the working day, Amazon replaces traditional factory clocks with individual *Units Per Hour* (UPH) rates for each part of its circulation line. This refers to how many commodities should be received, prepped, stowed, picked or packed per hour and accordingly depends on the department. These are presented as objective and calculated. Workers are informed of their specific rate at the beginning of each working day with pressure to then achieve it and "make rate" (Alimahomed-Wilson et al, 2020; Apicella, 2021; Delfanti, 2021b; Delfanti et al, 2021). Along the lines of scientific management, these start-meetings do specify not only "what is to be done, but how it is to be done and the exact time allowed for doing it" (Taylor, 1911). Those in the *Outbound* are especially confronted with a higher rate that must be achieved before cut-off times when delivery trucks leave the warehouses to make their way to the customers. Accordingly one stower states, "[Amazon] controls us. We have no decisions that we can make ourselves. ... [Amazon tells you] this is what you should do and this is how to do it."

These UPH rates do not just differ according to task but can also differ from one national or even local context to the other, which is highlighted in the next chapter. During my fieldwork and union meetings, I was informed at the time that, while a German warehouse worker could be confronted with a UPH pick rate of 100–150, a Polish one in contrast is given one of 240. Some workers in the US have reported a rate as high as 400, which means that such a US worker is meant to pick an item every nine seconds (Sainato, 2019). Such expectations explain why the issue of health and safety is central to warehouse workers, who have high rates of sickness to the point that Amazon introduced a 'health bonus' to be awarded to a team with a certain attendance rate (Kessler, 2017). Although Amazon offers a traditional hourly wage, workers find themselves evaluated according to their productivity rates, which may determine whether or not they have their contract renewed. Amazon's traditional time-wage arrangement disguises in a way how such labor is at its heart organized not by time but in fact by piecework. Instead of workers controlling their labor activity, workers are expected to constantly function and perform as machinery – never be sick, never be exhausted, never needing a break. As work becomes dictated by numbers, workers come eventually to regard themselves as "just a number in the whole system".

As a location-based platform, Amazon can additionally enforce its regime through disciplining supervisors using both social and digital surveillance. Warehouses are essentially factories that have "turned the laborers into an industrial army under a hierarchy of officers and sergeants" – the officers and sergeants being here the leads and managers (Dunayevskaya, 1975: 57).

Their human eye is used as 'social surveillance' to ensure that the working day is not disrupted, as leads and managers break up and limit times in which workers are not productive. Examples of the latter are attempts of conversing with fellow workers, building support to one another or simply taking 'too many' bathroom breaks. Workers are disciplined for their (lack of) productivity through feedback talks, possibly receiving disciplinary points for work infractions. Those not achieving their UPH rate may be labeled 'underperformers'. While the social dimensions of surveillance are possible because of the nature of the platform, the labor activity is ultimately under a technological panopticon (Cattero and D'Onoforio, 2018; Delfanti et al, 2021). This is predominantly managed not by the human but by the machine, through *algorithmic management*. This refers to "software algorithms that assume managerial functions and surrounding institutional devices ... [something which] allows companies to oversee myriads of workers in an optimized manner at a large scale" (Lee et al, 2015: 1603). Labor activity is turned into data and quantified while placing workers under constant surveillance.

If workers codify the inventory of Amazon's disorganized and chaotic storage system in the warehouses, which depends on technology to be navigated (Delfanti, 2021b), they are in turn managed by technology. It records their activity log accessible to managers, who can then infer times of both activity and inactivity. The extremes of this are exemplified by documents obtained by *The Verge* showing that "Amazon's system tracks the rates of each individual associate's productivity and automatically generates any warnings or terminations regarding quality or productivity without input from supervisors" – though Amazon argues this could be overridden (Lecher, 2019). While Amazon is not unique in implementing algorithmic management, it exemplifies *digital Taylorism* (Barthel, 2019). The alienation of workers is magnified by the machine, as workers are meant to labor as machines while simultaneously being managed by them. Each and every step (and mistake) is registered on the system, either through the computers at which workers are stationed or through hand scanners. These leave behind a log that displays the 'time off task' (TOT) – though in the summer of 2021 it was announced that the latter is to change and only show an average time over longer periods (Hamilton, 2021). Pushing this system to the extremes, Amazon in 2018 patented wristbands, which capture workers' hand movements through ultrasonic tracking to monitor performance and correct movements by vibrating (Solon, 2018). Algorithmic management assumes thereby the role of the organizer and implementer of the division of labor. This is reflective of the wider capitalist trends on the labor market, as "[t]he robots are here, they're working in management, and they're grinding workers into the ground" (Dzieza, 2020).

This digital Taylorization of the circulation line and larger division of labor demonstrates capital's complete power over labor activity, further dividing and isolating intellectual and mental labor from physical and manual labor. They present two separate hierarchical work spheres in which the former manages and designs the labor process to be carried out by the latter. The manual workers are to perform physical tasks: as one picker reports, they were instructed during training to "leave [their] brain outside the gates" of the warehouse. While management is concerned with developing what appears to be Taylor's "science of work", Amazon depends on manual and physical labor activity to turn over commodities – at least until it can eliminate and replace human workers. Dead labor, meaning robots, always function; one worker states, they "do not get sick and do not go on strike". Seeking to automate and optimize its circulation line, Amazon is increasingly introducing these into warehouses. One such example is the little robots previously mentioned that shift shelves to workers at a pick station, thereby eliminating subtasks altogether. Yet, for now, Amazon still predominantly requires manual labor, which it continues to treat like robots – prepping, stowing, picking and packing as fast as possible. Estranged from their own labor activity, as one worker put it, they "must always work ... for the corporation, [and] think for the corporation, not for [themselves]". What ultimately goes on in the warehouses of Amazon cannot be understood as peculiar within our current moment but can be regarded as among the most efficient examples of the implementation of such a Taylorist division of labor in contemporary capitalist temporality.

## Alienation from the product of labor

The estrangement of the worker from their labor activity projects itself onto the product of labor. While warehouse workers interact with commodities in their material form, these appear as divorced from the social relations of exploitation and the gendered and racialized division of labor through which these have likely been produced. Both their use-value, meaning their useful property and function, and their exchange-value, meaning their price, are insignificant to the workers who are circulating these in the warehouses (Dunayevskaya, 1975; Marx, 1977). Whether it is a Fulfillment by Amazon (FBA) product or an Amazon product, these are all processed and treated equally by Amazon workers.

While general performance pressures limit the contact workers have to any one commodity, this contact itself may differ depending on where they are assigned within the circulation line. It is in the Inbound that the commodity, such as Hana's light bulbs, becomes reduced to a series of numbers, which the Outbound workers are then confronted with. Upon the delivery and unloading of trucks, it is the worker in prep who physically sees the commodity by checking it. Opening box after box of the same product, only to move on to a different product, it does not matter to the worker what it is, as long as it can be registered on the system and matches the description. As such these workers receive the labor products of geographically dispersed workers and do not, therefore, contribute to their production but ensure the realization of their value by circulating them. In the warehouse, workers digitally create in a way the products for the platform by registering them on the system. The stower further contributes to this process by taking this product with a registered number and tying it to a physical location in the warehouse so that it can be later picked and packed for the customer. Owing to the chaotic yet efficient stowing system, it does not even matter where the product is stowed as long as it is stowed, with the exception of hazardous commodities.

The workers in Outbound are confronted with higher UPHs to collect and dispatch the commodities to the customer, leaving them with too little time even to acknowledge what the commodity or its exchange-value is. It is crucial for capital in the sphere of circulation to shorten the turnover time as much as possible, which translates in the warehouses in these high UPH rates. These stand in an inverse relation to the worker's contact per labor product. The product is merely a code on the hand scanner that is registered to a shelf that must be picked and placed in the trolley. To take the example from earlier, it is irrelevant to the worker whether Hana ordered a set of light bulbs or a hat. If a US picker needs to limit their interaction with the commodity to no more than 10 seconds to achieve the dictated rate, the worker cannot spend additional time reflecting on the nature of commodity and the social relations at its essence, wondering where or by whom it was produced. When the packer receives the product, the contact is merely limited to scanning and placing it in the assigned box. What matters is the size of the commodity, as this relates to the UPH metric system that dictates the worker's performance and determines how much can be picked or packed. Larger items are picked more slowly and are more difficult to pack. In the same manner, it makes a difference whether the worker is assigned 'multi' commodity picks/ packs. As customers are confronted with an endless choice of products, workers confront the accumulated labor within these on equal terms both in their use- and their exchange-value.

Workers ultimately encounter these fetishized commodities in their physical form, yet these become reduced to a number to be fulfilled within their UPH log. The nature of the product itself becomes utterly irrelevant to the worker, who attempts to keep up with their UPH and functions as gears in the machine whose bounds of productivity are continuously pushed. This only further estranges workers because of the paradoxical relationship they have to labor products, given that they are paid a time-wage but are evaluated to a large extent based on their piecework. While the nature of the platform and of the work defines the specific appearance of this relation of alienation, it is important to keep in mind that this relation too is not peculiar and particular to the Amazon warehouses but also appears across temporally and geographically dispersed workers of our world today.

## Alienation from species-being

The alienation of workers is not limited to the workplace but comes to absorb their species-being. Under capitalist conditions "[w]ork has become a means to stay alive rather than life being an opportunity to do work", as Amazon exemplifies (Ollman, 1971: 153). As a result of the first two relations of alienation, for Amazon manual workers each working day is similar to the previous one, draining them of creative abilities. Each day is a race to achieve the UPH; every day is labored in fear of being disciplined and punished. Drained by performance pressures and recovering from the day's manual labor, life activity is reduced to sustaining oneself and revolves around the continued labor activity. In its attempts to focus on the physical and mental wellbeing of workers to "help them recharge and reenergize", Amazon announced in a May 2021 press release its "WorkWell program". One of its "dystopian" initiatives that have come under fire is the "Zenbooth", a kiosk described as a small "coffin-sized booth in the middle of an Amazon warehouse where workers can use a computer to view 'mental health and mindful practices'" (Gault, 2021). While one could argue that introducing such a program could potentially be understood as Amazon recognizing the pressure workers are under, its de facto implementation with such an initiative loads the stress onto the worker. The worker can now meditate in a tiny pod, rather than requiring capital to engage with its UPH and the performance pressure at the root of its labor regime.

Different mechanisms, some of which are common in the platform economy, further alienate workers from their species-being. For one, Amazon states it "want[s] to empower associates" to "make sure that we are better tomorrow than we are today" by preparing suggestions – known as *kaizens*, which is Japanese for "change for the better".[3] In its essence, this allows Amazon to capitalize on the creativity of its workers to optimize and increase productivity. In return, workers report receiving no more than perhaps a T-shirt, a piece of cake or a verbal thank-you – at least, this was the case in Germany. Second, Amazon extends the working day by the way it marks its beginning and end. Workers must already appear at the 'start-meeting' with their necessary gear (such as hand scanners), and from there their long walks from the gates through security to the get the equipment and be present for the meetings are not factored in the same way. Any time that workers need to leave their workstations or areas to get to the cafeterias or go outside constitutes part of their breaks. Amazon may also offer financially compensated overtime, especially in peak seasons – such as Easter, Prime Day, Black Friday and the Christmas season, though this too extends the working day, possibly taking time away from fulfillment beyond work.

While the working day is limited by the nature of the work and the platform, as workers are bound by a time schedule for their manual labor and a location, work may consume workers beyond the workspace and working time. Amazon claims to value "work–life balance", stating, "we know work is an important and necessary part of your life. But we also know that what matters most is your time away, on your own, with family, and with friends."[4] Yet some workers report that they find it difficult to leave behind performance pressures, with deeply rooted fears of being fired for not meeting the dictated metrics and not being able to scan in to work the following morning. This is exacerbated by the material conditions of workers, especially if they are on precarious contracts with no guarantee of receiving a fixed contract, which I look at in more detail later. Additionally, workers may perceive their time for recreational and social activities outside of work as fragmented, given the bi-monthly rotating shift-work and non-consecutive days off. Workers recall barely having time to see their family, let alone pursue creative interests, as they are physically and psychologically exhausted. Given the additional reproductive labor that they may have to perform outside of work to take care of the family and home, this relation of alienation could be exacerbated for women as well as people of color, who historically perform(ed) reproductive labor. If humans are drained from work and must take care of their family, children and household after work, they are left with little time to rest, let alone to explore their creative being, which may be what fulfills them. These dimensions appear quite characteristic of our larger contemporary capitalist context, where Amazon is in no way unique, but rather reproduces these through its organization of work and workers.

## Alienation from fellow humans

This final relation, which relates dialectically to the others, is instrumental for capital to individualize and fragment the workforce, possibly rupturing labor organization. Amazon constructs a work culture based on a sense of community. In discussing "[w]hat it means to work at Amazon", it states:

> There's a reason Amazon has been ranked among the best workplaces in the world. It's a commitment to our employees, our customers, our communities, the environment, and the world. Everyday we strive to be Earth's Best (and Safest) Employer. What does that mean for you, someone considering not just a job, but a career at Amazon? We hope it is everything you're expecting – and more.[5]

Such a presentation of the work culture can mask the ways by which productivity takes center stage in the warehouses. After joining the team and becoming an *Amazonian* (if one is directly hired by Amazon and not contracted), warehouse workers are confronted with the slogan "Work hard. Have fun. Make history" to inspire and motivate them. The Amazon work culture is one that centralizes productivity and hard labor, but frames this in a positive light. It is meant to remind the worker to constantly become 'top-performers' as their labor is of great importance – for the customer and for history, a history that the worker gets to be part of (Boewe and Schulten, 2019; Massimo, 2020; Delfanti 2021b).

The sense of community is rooted in it being "welcoming and inclusive" where fellow workers form part of a "work family", as Amazon writes "even when you can't get away for a while, we make coming to work the best it can be for you – and your work family".[6] Work culture is further fetishized by free T-shirts on days like Prime Day, special social events around holidays such as Christmas and daily safety tips such as to use the handrail and stay hydrated. Priding itself on its 'team spirit' and support of diversity, this work culture and environment mask the exploitation of workers. Some workers strongly identify with the employer and are proud to be part of Amazon, which seeks to please its customers. These workers may regard the surveillance as legitimate and think that sufficient possibilities for co-determination and social mobility as already existing in the corporation (Apicella, 2016, 2021). The fact that Amazon has a work culture is telling of its platform organization. It is an embodiment and product of Amazon's nature of work and of its platform, as it assembles time-wage workers within the same space, where a work culture can be integral to bind workers together as a workforce. This stands in stark contrast to gig workers, who may be denied employee status altogether.

This culture obscures nonetheless how Amazon systematically alienates workers and pits them against each other by "deliberately promot[ing] fragmentation and the erosion of solidarity among the workforce" (Boewe and Schulten, 2019: 18). The different elements of workers' gendered and racialized subjectivity and material conditions are equally masked by the overarching work culture, which presents workers as a single community united by their manual labor. As the next chapter explains by accounting for the differing contexts, not all workers are confronted with same material conditions across warehouses, let alone within the same warehouse. The degree of precarity can also strongly differ, according to whether one is a temp, contracted, seasonal worker or on a permanent contract. The work culture masks the individualistic nature of labor characterized by "competition, not collaboration".[7] Individual productivity is the premise on which one is disciplined and punished or rewarded, though Amazon may also pit shifts and departments against each other. Here too Amazon is not very different from other platforms, such as Google, that pride themselves on their team spirit and work community, which equally conceal competition and metric systems meant to act as a driving force among workers.

The individualistic nature of warehouse work that is characterized by the Taylorist division of labor, along with the high surveillance and performance pressure, ensures that interaction between workers is limited. Those both at prep and at pack stations communicate not with humans but with computers when laboring their tasks. The stower's interaction with the system is also not through a human but through the hand scanner. The picker finds the product not through a human but thanks to the same hand scanner that tracks all activity. The workers that may run into each other are stowers active in their rows and pickers that may come to the same shelves. Leads and managers break these up should they be found interacting, especially for longer periods (Cattero and D'Onoforio, 2018). The worker interacts with technology more than with humans while laboring and is disciplined by it, dividing, rather than unifying, work and workers.

As workers may come to be consumed by these four relations of alienation, they may be uninterested in organizing, with little time to reflect on their class position, let alone organize or take action (Table 6.1). While Amazon reproduces many trends on the labor market from Taylorization common in production lines to the work culture similar to many platforms, it pushes these to new dimensions. By instrumentalizing technological conditions, it accelerates and dictates the pace of labor through its enforced UPH regime of productivity rates. In hopes of balancing their work life, workers may find it more valuable to spend time outside of work with their families, friends and

**Table 6.1:** Four relations of alienation of warehouse workers

| | **Appearance for worker** |
|---|---|
| Alienation from the labor activity | Hypertaylorization of circulation line<br>Division of manual labor: Inbound and Outbound<br>Productivity measured by UPH and algorithmically managed<br>Social and technological surveillance |
| Alienation from the product of labor | Circulation of commodities, appearing fetishistically through quantitative character that obscures social relations |
| Alienation from species-being | Difficulties in leaving performance pressures behind<br>Absorption of creativity through *kaizens*<br>Working day extended through uncalculated times to start/end and breaks (like long walks)<br>Additional dimension of reproductive labor |
| Alienation from fellow humans | Fetishistic communal work culture masking competition<br>"Work hard. Have fun. Make history." |

for their general wellbeing, rather than organizing. Finally, workers may come to identify with the very corporation and its work culture. Depending on the larger contexts of warehouses, workers may not have cultivated solidarity among each other, may have a negative and distrustful impression of unions or not be aware of earlier labor struggles that acquired many of their rights. It is crucial, therefore, to now turn our attention to contextualizing these workers and examining their agency in relation to their power resources.

7

# "I Am Not a Robot": (Trans)national Labor Organization at the Warehouses

Analyzing how Amazon warehouse workers are alienated explains in part labor's (dis)organization but risks presenting a deterministic portrayal of a compliant and submissive manual workforce that Smith and Taylor portrayed. While some warehouse workers may identify with Amazon, others may be politicized, recognizing their class position and interests, to translate these ultimately, but not necessarily, into industrial action (Apicella, 2016, 2021). Both general capitalist conditions and relative conditions to the worker and labor process continuously form and reform their class consciousness, subjectivities and solidarity. Amazon warehouse workers are distributed across the globe and have their own labor histories and different relative conditions which may spark a formation or further development of class consciousness.

One of the crucial factors regardless of geographical location lies within the labor process itself and its hypertaylorized division of labor. The circulation of Amazon's commodities only continues through the collective labor of the Inbound and Outbound workers. The nature of the platform plays a crucial role here in first facilitating the process of socialization, as workers experience the division of labor and circulation line in its physical form. Given that Amazon hires them as associates to be shifted around the circulation line, workers are aware of all the subtasks within the division of labor. Second, as the analysis of structural power in the next section indicates, the location-based nature of the warehouses facilitates the cooperation of workers derived from their assembly within the same space. It becomes their most foundational source of power. This process of socialization can, therefore, be one central condition for the development of workers' class consciousness and solidarity.

This is intrinsically linked to workers identifying with one another in opposition to Amazon. As Amazon measures its labor force and manages them as gears in the machine, some workers insist that they are *not* machines; they are not defined by their Units Per Hour (UPH). In the words of one warehouse worker, "I am a human. I am not a number. I am not a robot." Such workers are conscious of their exploitation and robotization and may resist these very conditions that alienate them. In doing so, they insist that they are not paid by piece and thus should not be evaluated on its basis. The perception of the labor process, including surveillance, as illegitimate, feeling stressed or fearful of getting sick and of the consequences of being sick can be decisive for workers to mobilize (Apicella, 2016; Apicella and Hildebrandt, 2019). These can be further coupled with personal experiences of specific workplace accidents, the retraction of certain rights or the threat of it. Given the dimensions of Amazon's growth and the wealth of Jeff Bezos, which is dependent on their collective labor, another worker further explains:

> Jeff Bezos is not the face of [A]mazon. We the employees are the face of [A]mazon. We the employees are also the customers, we break our backs for. We the employees are what makes [A]mazon successful. If it wasn't for us, he wouldn't be a billionaire, and he sure wouldn't be praised for any of his so called success. We are his success, and without us. He has nothing.[1]

Of course, their class subjectivity can be coupled with those in relation to their sex, gender and race and own experiences. While it is difficult to generalize, as these co-evolve along with the wider context, it can be said that overlapping subjectivities can foster collective solidarity and push these to organize, as demonstrated later with the case of East African workers in the Minnesota warehouse. Such relative conditions central to the formation of class consciousness can be coupled with general capitalist ones in relation to the daunting reserve army of labor and precarious employment in the labor market, which play a crucial role in their mobilization.

To provide a more holistic analysis of the question of agency, it is essential now to engage with the wider political–economic context, which can strongly inhibit and constrain the dimensions of labor organization. Class-conscious workers who want to organize may ultimately not do so, given the material obstacles (Ollman, 1972). It is, therefore, not a dichotomy of either fully unorganized alienated workers or fully conscious organizing workers. It is important to further grasp labor organization at Amazon within the reformist parameters of our capitalist system rather than being revolutionary per se. Amazon is after all the employer and source of income for workers. Accordingly, when workers organize, they do so to improve their working conditions, rather than to eliminate Amazon altogether. While the structural, associational, institutional and societal power resources provide workers with the potential and opportunities to organize, it is not a smooth process.

**Table 7.1:** Power resources of warehouse workers vis-à-vis Amazon

| | **Workers** | **Amazon counterstrategy** |
|---|---|---|
| **Structural power** | Low marketplace power<br>• Manual labor<br>• Hierarchy of workers<br>• Reserve army of labor<br>High workplace power<br>• Limited individual power<br>• Strong collective disruptive power<br>• Majority of labor is manual labor<br>• Different spatial and temporal dimensions | • Reroute orders, decentralized network of warehouses<br>• Reserve army of labor<br>• Precarious labor on short-term contracts |
| **Associational power** | • Traditional and grassroots national unions<br>• Transnational union (alliances): UNI, AWI<br>• Transnational Social Strike (TSS)<br>• Digital organization | • Anti-union strategy through intimidation, termination<br>• Union-busting also through anti-union firms/consultants<br>• Relocation of warehouses |
| **Institutional power** | • Works council achievements<br>• Possible collective bargaining agreements | • As few concessions as necessary |
| **Societal power** | Growing discursive power through media<br>Growing coalitional power with wider society | • Positive image construction<br>• PR campaigns, public tours<br>• Amazon ambassadors |

Amazon continually attempts to disrupt, undermine and diminish these, as it "consistently tries to exploit to the maximum the leeway granted to it by national legislation" (Boewe and Schulten, 2019: 28). The (dis)organization of labor is ultimately a result of several factors and cannot be explained by any single one of them. Their ability to act, organize and mobilize is intrinsically materially and contextually bound, as workers navigate their terrains and demonstrate the national, transnational and digital potentials and possibilities (Table 7.1).

## The structural power of workers

Workers' structural power is foundational to labor's struggle and ability to disrupt the circuit of capital to push for their class interests. When it comes to Amazon's warehouse workers, their marketplace power appears relatively weak. The manual nature of circulating products in warehouses is not regarded as 'high-skilled' or scarce on the labor market. According to Amazon's homepage, Amazon does not require previous experience and merely underlines the minimum age limit of 18. The application is fairly simple, fast and practical: hourly roles may not even require a CV, merely the completion of an online application and assessment, choosing a shift time and finally watching a virtual preview of what to expect in the job. The rest consists of attending in-person office hours for possible new hires.[2] Warehouse associates receive on-the-job training that can take a few hours (Massimo, 2020; Delfanti, 2021b), which reflects once again the straightforward hiring process at Amazon that may prove advantageous to workers but can also highlight how easily replaceable they are.

As part of its image as an 'equal opportunity employer' Amazon presents itself as embracing diversity, and as not differentiating in its hiring process between different workers' backgrounds as long as they are willing to perform the required manual labor.[3] Amazon by and large strategically opens warehouses in areas with higher unemployment rates (there are exceptions, such as in Poland), further guaranteeing the availability of labor power (Boewe and Schulten, 2019). Workers compete with those unemployed in the reserve army of labor who have no alternative employer nearby, and also those willing to accept part-time jobs and contracted seasonal work. Given how easy the hiring and training is for these Amazon jobs and that Amazon offers above national minimum wage and additional benefits, these may seem appealing to workers. It will be interesting to observe how these levels change in the future when national minimum wages are raised, as in Germany starting October 2022, as well as across the EU, given the recent proposal and possible directive aimed to increase minimum wages relative to the national contexts (Syrovatka, 2022).

The general dependence on Amazon's wages can be magnified then in national contexts where working conditions or minimum wages are less protected and more precarious, considering that such a job offers a guaranteed wage which increases respectively after 12 and then 24 months. These jobs also come with healthcare, vacation days, the possibility of paid time off and the promise (at least) of a flexible work schedule.[4] Amazon states on its blog that it has been "certified as a '2022 Top Employer' in Italy, Spain, France and Poland", which "distinguishes employers who create optimal conditions for the development of their employees".[5] Workers may navigate therefore toward these jobs and are then highly dependent on their wages and benefits, given the way society and labor markets are organized. Amazon can rely on this revolving door of masses of workers through which the labor process can continue without interruption. This severely weakens the leverage these workers have in relation to Amazon.

Both temporal and spatial dimensions further weaken the marketplace power. Amazon hires hundreds of thousands of temporary workers during its peak season, marked by increased demand in the period of Black Friday and Christmas. This is crucial for Amazon, as its highest turnover comes in Q4.

Workers additionally find themselves more vulnerable on the labor market in times of crises, such as the economic crisis of 2006–08 or, more recently, in the first months of COVID-19. For one, this can be connected to job loss in certain sectors such as hospitality, but is also related to for instance Amazon initially raising the hourly wage by an additional hazard pay of US$2, €2 or £2 associated with laboring during a pandemic (UNI, 2020; Kassem, 2022). These points are indicative of how Amazon can continue to hire new workforces to keep up with what has appeared as an exponentially expanding network of warehouses.

Scholars have observed how these labor forces are becoming increasingly racialized and gendered (Reese, 2020; Alimahomed-Wilson and Reese, 2021; Delfanti, 2021b). This can be understood both in relation to the geographical locations of these warehouses outside of and close to urban centers, and also a possible race to the bottom of those willing to accept the working conditions at Amazon. The decision to work at Amazon is closely tied to the options of jobs available for workers in and near these communities, reflecting in turn the larger vulnerabilities of (previously) unemployed workers, as well as of racialized and gendered labor in finding a job. To grasp the growing dimensions of at least those with permanent Amazon jobs in the EU and the UK as it continues to expand, Amazon states they amount to two thirds of those in the entire European steel industry or as exceeding those working globally for top car manufacturers BMW and Renault Group.[6] Such examples of Amazon becoming what appears to be a top employer in numerical terms in Europe further weaken workers' marketplace power, given the nature of the labor activity and Amazon's ability to continue to find workforces to fill these positions (Kassem, 2023).

Depending on their geographical context, workers may feel the pressure of a larger race to the bottom both as a result of the nature of the platform and the nature of the work. In the case of Germany, Amazon can pit workers against each other because of the eastward enlargement of the EU. It has hired to varying extents Czech and Polish workers for the German market, only launching Amazon.pl in Poland in 2021.[7] In the case of Poland, the first warehouses opened in 2014, close to the German border yet in areas with lower unemployment rates. These have had to attract workers from further away, especially during the peak season (Owczarek and Chełstowska, 2018). Warehouses across the border for the German market allow Amazon implicitly if not explicitly to threaten job relocation, but also extend the labor time and push the UPH even higher. In the process, Amazon pays contracted workers across the German border a fraction of what the German worker earns. While gross hourly wages tend to show small increases over the years, we can take a look at job advertisements for warehouse associates on their homepages in March 2022 to grasp wage levels – though, as previously stated, it will be important to observe how these may change given ongoing and possible developments in minimum wages across the EU. While Amazon advertises a gross hourly wage for a German worker of €12.6 (which differs depending on which German warehouse we are looking at), the worker in Poland receives for the same job 22.5zł, which converted then to around €4.5. Capital's instrumentalization of the eastward enlargement of the EU to its own advantage is not unique to Amazon but is observable in other sectors such as outsourced steps within the supply chain of the automobile industry (Krzywdzinski, 2014).

The various spatial dimensions of warehouses and their low entry requirements relate in turn to the composition of the workforce and reflect racialized labor markets and may be different in terms of their gendered compositions. Additionally, nationalities in Germany range from North Africans, East Africans and West Africans to those from Eastern Europe, Balkans and Germany. To list another example, in the UK, at least before Brexit, the majority of workers were Polish or Romanian. The different subjectivities of workers may bind certain workers together but can also fragment them because of the language barrier and their different material conditions and contractual agreements (Kassem, 2023). The nature of the platform as location-based can be therefore instrumentalized to weaken the overall marketplace power of Amazon warehouse workers, while the nature of the work in terms of different national and contractual time-wages creates a hierarchy among them.

In contrast to the marketplace power which is weakened by the platform's organization, the latter can in fact be the source of the workplace power. Though the competitive nature of work may divide workers, their common collective interests to improve their working conditions can unite them. Factories have historically been central in concentrating within the same walls large crowds of workers who do not know each other. The location-based nature concentrates Amazon workers within a single warehouse, which can play a crucial role in their socialization. As each customer order depends on their collective labor, the hypertaylorized division of labor facilitates the possibility for workers to resist across this circulation line. Warehouses are like factories in which workers "were united and disciplined by the very instrument of production which coerced them" (Dunayevskaya, 1975: 47). Amazon's organization of platform may alienate workers, but precisely the nature of its platform provides conditions for them to instrumentalize their workplace power.

Before delving into collective forms of disruptive power, it is helpful to shed light on the possibilities for individual everyday forms of resistance. While workers have historically been able to slow down their productivity through individual acts of resistance, these appear to be constrained in the warehouses because of technological and political–economic conditions. As Amazon's hypertaylorized division of labor is managed by algorithms and the social eye of their supervisors, it is easy to observe and track workers' activities, the time taken for tasks and times of inactivity (Delfanti et al, 2021). It is more difficult for workers to resist by attempting to reduce their productivity because of this pervading surveillance and the fact that the time-wage disguises how workers are evaluated based on UPH performance. In fact, some workers mentioned that they tend to skip health and safety instructions as given by Amazon so they can fulfill their rates. Similarly, workers may skip the 'six-sided check' to examine all six sides of a commodity to ensure it is not damaged, as this process takes additional time away from achieving the UPH rate. Workers may relieve themselves by taking longer to get their equipment and additional social breaks to communicate with co-workers or go to the bathroom. In doing so however, they run the risk of being questioned by supervisors, labeled as a 'low performer' and asked to attend a feedback talk (Transnational Social Strike Platform, 2019). The technological conditions that organize and surveil the labor activity, along with the social dimensions assumed by supervisors in a location-based platform, strongly inhibit smaller forms of resistance that affect productivity when workers are governed by metrics.

Individual resistance is additionally restricted by material and political–economic conditions, closely related to their weak marketplace power. Workers often find their contract to be initially fixed, and only feel relief after receiving a permanent contract. The conditions of the latter differ according to the specific industrial relations in which workers labor. The German warehouse worker, for instance, can only be given fixed contracts for a sum of two years and must subsequently receive either a permanent contract or not have it renewed, a decision for which Amazon does not need to provide an explanation (Boewe and Schulten, 2019). The more precarious the contract, given the weak marketplace power, the less likely it is that even a class-conscious worker will risk resisting individually through everyday forms of resistance, let alone more direct collective ones. The same logic applies to those on a work visa or residence permit in a foreign country, where their status within it is bound to their employer, in this case Amazon. Some workers may symbolically resist by distancing themselves from the work culture and ridiculing various facets: from the "Work hard. Have fun. Make history" mantra and Amazon's safety tips to its culture of greeting by fist bumping. Workers may also decide not to attend holiday events or the summer festival, where the latter has taken place on a Sunday, a day off for German warehouse workers. Similarly, workers may refuse to hand in *kaizens*, as these are not financially compensated, or to answer the voluntary end-of-day survey question that pops up, for instance on their hand scanner. While these forms of symbolic distancing could be considered as rejecting the work culture, these should not be romanticized in terms of their disruptive effect on the circuit of capital.

The essence of the structural power is rooted in the collective strength of workers. The location-based nature of warehouses may facilitate the formation of different solidarities and allows for physical disruptions of work through industrial action such as strikes. Workers, depending on their national and material context and work contracts, may, however, have different obstacles to deal with. Whether a contract is fixed or permanent acts as a central motivation to pursue industrial action and strike (Apicella and Hildebrandt, 2019; Krähling, 2019). It is more difficult for workers to strike if their right to do so is not protected and may result implicitly or explicitly in the termination of their employment. While those in Germany are more likely to receive a permanent contract and be directly hired by Amazon, the situation is less homogenous and more precarious across borders. Amazon states that warehouses typically employ between 1,000 and 2,000 workers on permanent contracts, yet those in the UK report many on fixed and zero-hours contracts. In the case of Poland, contracts can be as short as one month to three months mediated through temp agencies.[8] Contexts strongly vary in their industrial relations, legal parameters and material conditions, which further project themselves on the composition and fragmentation of the workforces.

These compositions can be integral to how workers organize and communicate and have repercussions for the mobilization of their power resources. While the disruptive power in the UK is further complicated by two thirds of the workforce not speaking English as their native language (at least pre-Brexit), in Poland workers face restrictive labor laws that necessitate a ballot vote in which half of workers place a vote to support strike action in the first place (Owczarek and Chełstowska, 2018; Boewe and Schulten, 2019). In fact, one worker in Germany, who works at one of the newer warehouses known to have an especially racialized manual workforce, stated to me that there are around 90 nationalities within their warehouse, where the realities of these workers, their languages and their knowledge regarding their rights can strongly differ. The implications of these different national contexts become clearer when discussing the associational power where unions and workers attempt to coordinate their workplace power.

Given however these political–economic dynamics where in Germany the industrial relations and material conditions allow at least more room for labor organization, the first strike in Amazon's history took place in Bad Hersfeld, Germany, on 9 April 2013, as overall 1,100 workers formed a picket line in front of its gates. Bad Hersfeld, the first warehouse to open in Germany in 1999, along with warehouses in Rheinberg, Werne and Leipzig, is among the warehouses with the strongest disruptive power, with around a half of shift-workers likely to lay down their tools and walk out. Disruptive power today can additionally range from temporary blockades and unannounced walkouts during busy shifts to 'in-out' strikes where the corporation is meant to bear additional costs by preparing for the strike, rerouting orders or employing additional workers (Cattero and D'Onoforio,

2018; Boewe and Schulten, 2019). As Amazon continues to grow its empire, industrial action has expanded beyond Germany, with workers across Europe and the US, but also the Global South such as India, increasingly claiming their agency to collectively protest, strike and walk out. Through their labor struggles, these workers resist the conditions by which they are alienated. Poland's first spontaneous protest, in 2015 in Poznań, was sparked by workers who were supposed to labor longer to undermine the strike in Bad Hersfeld (Owczarek and Chełstowska, 2018; OZZ Inicjatywa Pracownicza, 2019; Boewe and Schulten, 2020). While this underlines the importance and the potential for transnational industrial action and labor organization, the case of the national strike in Italy in March 2021 highlights, on the other hand, the power of mobilizing on the national level even beyond the warehouses and across Amazon's distribution chain (Delfanti, 2021b).

The different labor compositions within a local, yet alone national context, are bound however to project themselves on the transnational one – both in terms of the fabric of solidarity, but also the difficulties, a point I return to shortly. The struggle to improve working conditions and health and safety measures was further magnified in light of COVID-19, a time in which Amazon experienced a surge in orders (Kassem, 2022). Amazon claims to have invested US$11.5 billion in 2020 on health and safety measures, ranging from temperature checks, testing and additional cleaning to Personal Protective Equipment (PPE) and social distancing (Amazon Staff, 2020). Yet health and safety concerns associated with COVID-19 triggered a series of industrial action across warehouses and continents to disrupt the circuit of capital. Workers "on the front lines of this crisis" initially reported a lack of PPE, an inability to maintain social distancing given the pace of work and a lack of transparency when it came to outbreaks (Heikkilä, 2020b). These instances of labor organization and mobilization were therefore initially concentrated around the beginning of the pandemic, but continued at different instances – especially during the peak season. Workers thus demonstrate how they mobilized their workplace power even during times of weakened marketplace power amidst a pandemic (Kassem, 2022, 2023).

These instances also demonstrate that despite the rather heterogeneous compositions of the manual workforces, these can come together and form solidarity through their similar material interests for better working conditions – may these be health and safety conditions or higher wages. In the context of rising inflation, these political-economic conditions appear to further motivate and spark continued labor unrest at various warehouses. Amazon unilaterally decided to raise wages by a mere 3 percent at the German warehouse of Winsen in September 2022, despite inflation at the time being around 10 percent. Considering that Amazon raised wages elsewhere by up to 7.4 percent, workers at Winsen from dozens of different nationalities, organized and mobilized in an unprecedented manner to strike during different shifts for better working conditions (ver.di, 2022; Kassem, 2023).

Meanwhile in the US, home to Amazon's largest workforce and potentially largest disruptive power, workers too mobilized during these times. The first industrial action at Amazon warehouses unfolded, however, in Europe and not the US, as a result of the latter's anti-union landscape and Amazon's union-busting activities. It was only in 2019 that the first strike took place in the US, in Minnesota, initially sparked by Amazon refusing to give the majority Muslim East African workforce additional breaks and space to pray during the upcoming Ramadan. While this industrial action was small in size, it was strongly supported by the worker-led Awood Center, a community center that aims to strengthen and support East African workers. The name is derived from the Somali word *awood*, which translates as "power". As Abdirahman Muse, its executive director, emphasizes, "[p]eople thought we were crazy and that we would never achieve anything. But we created a space that's culturally relevant to organize migrant workers and we had organisers who spoke their language" (UNI and ITUC, 2019: 5).[9] Such an action cannot be underestimated as it set a precedent in what had remained a strike-free terrain for Amazon workers for around a quarter of a century and would be followed by other protests such as on Prime Day. The case further demonstrates the strengthened potential when additional dimensions of race and/or gender complement class solidarity.

Given the mentioned health and safety concerns of workers during COVID-19, workers across the US mobilized their workplace power through walkouts – one of which gained a lot of attention after organizer Christian Smalls at the warehouse in Staten Island was fired for supposedly violating his quarantine. He was described in a leaked report as "not smart, or articulate", and smeared as the face of the labor movement (Blest, 2020; Paul, 2020; Kassem, 2022). When viewed holistically, labor mobilizations of workplace power are increasingly gaining momentum across Amazon warehouses globally. These underline their collective potential, guided by similar health and safety concerns and against intense and alienating working conditions with the aim of improving these. These are bound to further intensify in light of the political—economic conditions that are characterized by rising inflation, which as of fall 2022 has not been accompanied by a proportionate rise in wage levels. The contemporary material conditions thus play a crucial role in motivating and sparking labor struggles of workers in an unprecedented manner.

While spatial and temporal dimensions of marketplace power weaken workers' leverage, workers can magnify their disruptive power by instrumentalizing these. The moment in which workers disrupt circulation can be vital, as they have strategically coordinated action on Prime Day and during Amazon's peak season during Q4. This has taken place both prior to and during COVID-19: from coordinated national industrial action on

Black Friday in 2018, when Spanish, German, Italian and British took global strike action and protest, to Black Friday in 2020 and 2021, when there was industrial action in over 20 countries (Biron, 2021). This temporal dimension has been especially crucial in the context of the pandemic, as Q4 overlaps, at least in the northern hemisphere, with winter and therefore a surge in coronavirus cases. In 2020 this was followed by more national measures such as lockdowns that pushed many into online shopping. Given Amazon's growing market share and global supply chain, such coordination of action on Black Friday is also instrumental in spatial terms, potentially causing a ripple effect across warehouses. The Italian national strike exemplifies in contrast the importance of coordinating action spatially across the supply chain, especially given Amazon's growing concern of controlling last-mile deliveries and relying less on the better-organized workers of the postal sector (Różycki and Kerr, 2019). While the nature of the platform presents obstacles to (trans)national labor organization because of the differing industrial relations and material conditions, the location-based nature of the platform can be a source of strength as their collective labor gives workers various points at which they can disrupt the accumulation of capital (Kassem, 2022).

Amazon attempts to counter these efforts by instrumentalizing the political–economic and technological favorable conditions, coming to hold the "'dubious record for longest labor dispute' in the history of the Federal Republic of Germany" (Boewe and Schulten, 2019: 9). Amazon has previously used 'strike-break' rewards of, for example, €200 there to divide and polarize workers by incentivizing them to labor during strikes such as on Black Friday. It may also move workers prone to striking from strategic positions ahead of a strike (such as loading and unloading trucks) and provide them with the most laborious tasks, such as picking (Boewe and Schulten, 2019). As previously mentioned, Amazon additionally exploits the larger context of precarity and unemployment, low marketplace power and national legal boundaries to (in)directly threaten workers with the termination of their contracts. Just as workers worry about not having their contracts renewed, so they fear similar repercussions if they talk about organizing, let alone pursuing, industrial action.

The fixed, precarious and seasonal contracts may not only rupture the formation of solidarity and willingness to mobilize, but can also further fragment workers by creating a hierarchy according to their different rights and wages. Thus workers may be either unwilling to jeopardize their contract by sympathizing and organizing or be completely uninterested if their employment does not last long enough for them to benefit from potential gains. This can be exacerbated for migrant workers on a visa or with a temporary residence permit, who do not want to risk jeopardizing their status or their employment relations both to secure their living in their new home, but also as they may be sending money to their family in their countries

(Kassem, 2023). Fluctuations and turnover further complicate the formation of solidarity within the warehouse or newly opened warehouses, which requires continuous efforts and resources (LaVecchia and Mitchell, 2016; OZZ Inicjatywa Pracownicza, 2019). While the peak season provides workers with a high potential for disruptive power, this may be weakened by Amazon's revolving door of seasonal workers on short-term contracts, which is not conducive to labor organization.

Amazon can further instrumentalize the (trans)national nature of the platform to further undermine solidarity and industrial action, appearing one step ahead by adapting delivery times and shifting orders to other warehouses with largely similar inventories. As Barthel identifies, the decentralized network of warehouses means there are no clear choke points within its logistics network and supply chain. No one warehouse occupies a strategically more important position that could bring their totality to a halt (Barthel, 2019; Vgontzas, 2020). Amazon cannot just shift orders to warehouses within a country, but in the case of Europe it benefits greatly from the EU enlargement and hence can shift these across borders to absorb strike impacts. As previously mentioned, when workers strike in Germany, Amazon can quickly shift the orders to Polish warehouses and in effect use Polish workers as strikebreakers. This only further underlines the necessity for workers to organize transnationally, considering the measures Amazon resorts to in order to ensure customers receive their orders in time (Krähling, 2019).

Accordingly, Amazon warehouse workers, who have a weak marketplace power, must navigate both Amazon's counterstrategies and the general political–economic conditions. The location-based nature of the platform provides both opportunities and obstacles for workers' agency, though limits to the time-wage in the form of temporary contracts ensure workers are kept in precarious and vulnerable positions. As Amazon continues to monopolize the e-commerce market and expand across transport and logistics, it becomes increasingly important for solidarity to be cultivated among its heterogeneous manual workforces. It is integral for their labor organization that the workplace power be mobilized locally and (trans)nationally across its supply chain and even different platforms. As discussed in Chapter 11, given that Amazon Web Services (AWS) is its profit-making platform which can absorb losses from Amazon.com, it would be a further opportunity for different Amazon workers to strategize and coordinate collective action to increase their leverage.

## The associational power of workers

The nature of the platform and of the work at Amazon's warehouses, reminiscent of factories, allow for a more classical understanding of labor organization through unions that may help workers in recognizing their class interests and mobilizing. Far from the days in which unions were radical and revolutionary, unions today can be perceived as ineffective or restrained by the political–economic systems in which they operate. "[H]elp[ing] workers sell their labor as advantageously as they can" (Azzelini and Kraft, 2018: 5), unions have become a component of the institutional fabric within capitalism. While it is necessary to critically evaluate unions in our current neoliberal age, it is important to emphasize that they *can* offer workers supporting structures, resources or compensations for missed wages when striking. Workers in turn may decide whether to support a union depending on past experiences or the union's accomplishments in representing workers' interest (Apicella and Hildebrandt, 2019). When workers come from a national context in which such rights are not protected, they may additionally find themselves feeling more vulnerable, unprotected and possibly unaware of their rights within the new national context.

Though union membership rates, strategies and national industrial relations may differ, the landscape of the associational power on a national level shows potential. While Amazon organizes the division of labor similarly across warehouses, the nature of its platform strongly impacts opportunities for workers to organize themselves to further mobilize their workplace power. Germany, where the right to join a union is constitutionally protected, is often regarded as an exemplary case because of the activity of ver.di (*Vereinte Dienstleistungsgewerkschaft*) and resources dedicated to organizing Amazon warehouses.[10] It was over a decade after the first warehouse opened in Germany that ver.di began its organizing effort in pursuing a collective bargaining agreement. This was in turn crucial in sparking the first industrial action in 2013 in Amazon's history, because of Amazon's unwillingness to bargain. Ver.di has since channeled resources in rank-and-file and shop steward structures to further raise awareness among workers of their rights. While ver.di aims to increase its membership, the previously mentioned composition of the laborforce can prove critical and require additional efforts. Depending on the local context – migrant workers may be more reluctant to join the union given the associated risks and financial cost of one percent of their gross monthly wage (Kassem, 2023) – yet warehouses also demonstrate that these workers can (especially once they receive a permanent contract) unionize and become part of the organizing workforce.

Engaging with ver.di's labor struggle would, however, mean a recognition of the union on Amazon's part (Cattero and D'Onoforio, 2018; Boewe and Schulten, 2019; Vgontzas, 2020; Apicella, 2021). While Amazon currently aligns its wages with that of the logistics industry, interestingly enough, it deems itself a retailer and not a logistics company as in other countries, such as the US. This is one of many examples that reflect how Amazon exploits the system to its advantage. While ver.di has not yet been able to win the long sought-after collective bargaining agreement, workers have made some gains discussed in the section on institutional power (Boewe and Schulten, 2019; Apicella, 2021). Victories in any national context are considered instrumental to those elsewhere, sending ripple effects for workers across their power resources, setting possible precedents and strengthening solidarity among Amazon warehouse workers.

While in Germany Amazon workers unionize freely and have relatively higher union membership rates than in other EU countries, the situation is certainly more complex in other European countries. The UK, for instance, has a more labor-restrictive legal system, allowing for more union-busting. The GMB Union, which is not allowed on Amazon's premises, has struggled to become a recognized union, as this necessitates support by a majority of workers – though it can still turn to the highest labor authority under specific conditions to claim statutory recognition (Boewe and Schulten, 2019).[11] Within this struggle, the GMB has found other ways to support workers, ranging from the creation of an online game, through which online users experience the productivity pressures during peak season, to surveying workers about their health and safety concerns and working closely with reporters to expose how 600 ambulances were called over a three-year period (Butler, 2018; GMB Union, 2018a).

While the UK is interesting as it is in a close race with Germany for the largest market outside the US, the Polish case is integral to the German market, as workers there can be used as strikebreakers and are organized by two competing unions. The coordination of workplace and associational power of German and Polish workers can prove integral to the larger labor struggle given their interdependence; however, workers in each country are confronted with their own industrial relations landscape. Within Poland's labor-restrictive landscape, which requires a ballot vote to strike, both the anarcho-syndicalist rank-and-file OZZ Inicjatywa Pracownicza (IP) and the more social partnership model-based Solidarność compete to organize its precarious warehouse workers. Cooperating could strengthen their associational power, which showed potential after their joint call for wage increases in 2019, when the Amazon-recognized Solidarność refused to negotiate without the presence of IP (Owczarek and Chełstowska, 2018; Boewe and Schulten, 2019; OZZ Inicjatywa Pracownicza, 2019). Such cross-national differences underline the difficulties workers navigate in organizing uniform transnational industrial actions.

As these labor struggles continued and intensified during COVID-19, the associational power was crucial in many cases in coordinating the mobilization of workplace power on Prime Day, Black Friday and the peak season more generally. The French and US cases particularly underline the evolving nature of labor struggles where the context surrounding COVID-19 can be regarded as further strengthening the associational power. For one, the French Union syndicale Solidaires (SUD) played a crucial role during the first lockdown by taking Amazon to court after protests were followed by labor inspections over health and safety concerns. The first ruling limited sales to essential items or risk a fine of €1 million per day until conditions were improved in warehouses, later magnified by a €100,000 fine for every non-essential item. Amazon initially shut down its warehouses to avoid these financial costs, only to reopen once it had reached an agreement with the union (Alderman, 2020; Kassem 2020, 2022). In this case the union was able to push for regulation of Amazon, even if it was short-term.

In contrast, across the Atlantic workers in the US have been pushing for their organization: from Amazonians United, "an independent and democratic organization of workers" to unprecedented, organized union drives.[12] Warehouse workers in Bessemer, AL, presented the first example of this kind of organized drive to legally oblige Amazon to recognize the Retail, Wholesale and Department Store Union (RWDSU), an expression of their traditional associational power. In quite a historical moment Amazon workers at the Staten Island, NY, warehouse JFK8 have presented the first successful majority to join the newly established grassroots union, the Amazon Labor Union (ALU). ALU was in fact created by Smalls, the previously mentioned warehouse worker that was dismissed after organizing a walkout in 2020 (Kassem, 2022, 2023). According to the 1935 National Labor Relations Act, workers must prove through a vote to the labor authority that the majority of the workforce supports unionization. While winning such a vote allows the union to conclude collective bargaining agreements that apply to the entire workforce, without this initial majority vote workers find themselves without such a legal collective organization (Domhoff, 2013). The process of unionization in the US is thus different from that of, for instance, German workers, who can simply join a union of their own volition–though these decisions are also informed by their material realities.

Bound by both class and racial subjectivities given the Black majority workforce, an organized effort was initiated for unionization in Bessemer in 2020 (Alimahomed-Wilson and Reese, 2021). This labor struggle dragged out until 2022 and continues, as RWDSU complained of unfair labor practices to the National Labor Relations Board (NLRB) after not winning the majority union ballot vote (RWDSU, 2021). Amazon organized a counterstrategy, including installing a mailbox outside of the warehouse in a tent plastered with "Vote No" or hiring anti-union consultants for US$10,000 a day. Above all, it has been holding mandatory captive audience meetings that spread misinformation about union dues, although these are prohibited in Alabama (Logan, 2021; Gurley, 2022b). Though the NLRB ruled that Amazon had violated labor law and workers had a renewed chance of an election, as a result of interrelated factors, workers two years later continue to struggle for union recognition. These tactics of Amazon were echoed to varying degrees during the organizing campaign at JFK8.

Workers were confronted with similar captive meetings and anti-union material, for which Global Strategy Group, a consultancy and polling firm, had been hired. In the process, Amazon has been retaliating against workers and union organizers: at one event organizers were arrested for trespassing as they distributed food to workers. Amazon's efforts amounted in 2021 to them spending over US$4 million on anti-union consultants (New York Times, 2022; Palmer, 2022; Kassem, 2023). Amazon continued to invest in challenging these ALU union results to the NLRB, which a labor official has concluded to "be set aside and Amazon Labor Union be certified to represent workers at the warehouse" (Scheiber, 2022).

There had been previous attempts to mobilize associational power, ranging from the call center in Seattle that got shut down for just attempting to organize or previous efforts by the RWDSU and International Brotherhood of Teamsters. Other instances include the Minnesota walkouts or the movement against Amazon establishing its second headquarters in New York City. Both RWDSU and Teamsters continue their general organizing efforts of Amazon warehouse workers. Yet the organizational drives in 2020–22 have been setting a precedent at Amazon, because of their scale, and having a ripple effect across the US labor market, given that Amazon is the second largest public company employer, coming only second to Walmart.[13] From traditional unions to more novel grassroot ones, Amazon's anti-union tactics in the US against these efforts explain the reputation it has gained as a union-buster, which it has exported beyond its US borders. These indicate the terrain workers have had to and continue to navigate to assume their associational power in growing organized drives (Kassem, 2023).

As "[a]t its core, capital is global [and] [a]s a rule, labour is local" (Castells, 1996: 506), it is important for workers to organize transnationally, because of Amazon's transnational character. The formation of transnational solidarity and mobilization is, however, directly tied to underlying national contexts and problems – including differing union memberships and representations, resources, industrial relations, linguistic obstacles and racialized and gendered material realities and subjectivities of workers. Workers must navigate their different terrains to overcome their divisions to collectively struggle for their common interests through a transnational associational power as embodied for instance in the Amazon Global Alliance. What was initiated by UNI Global Union (UNI) as an Amazon Working Group in 2014 to plan joint campaigns across Europe and quickly expanded to coordinating meetings since 2015 among for instance ver.di, GMB, Solidarność, Italy's Confederazione Generale Italiana del Lavoro (CGIL), France's Confédération Générale du Travail (CGT) and Spain's Comisiones Obreras (CCOO). The alliance of unions has continued to grow, amounting in December 2019 to 23 unions across 19 countries and even beyond Europe, and has invited researchers and institutions such as the International Trade Union Confederation (ITUC).

In their bi-annual meetings, predominantly full-time trade union secretaries along with some shop stewards primarily exchange country reports on obstacles and accomplishments. They also discuss past and future transnational industrial action on peak days such as Prime Day or Black Friday. While UNI sparked an effort to create a European Works Council, which led to its establishment in 2022 (UNI Europa, 2022), it has recognized the importance of strong local and national foundations for achieving stronger transnational impacts. It thus focuses its resources on increasing membership, which translates into associational power, and on mobilization, which translates into workplace power. Rather than competing with shop floor efforts, these are meant to complement coordination of solidarity and industrial action, though each union anchored in its own national context expresses these in its own nationally legally permitted ways. Thus, transnational action may not be identical, but has been motivated both prior and during COVID-19 by similar concerns over better and safer working conditions or collective bargaining agreements, while sharing central messages of warehouse workers, such as "Amazon, we are not robots" (GMB Union, 2018b; UNI and ITUC, 2019). A growing transnational associational power co-evolves alongside growing national ones and is in turn bound to magnify mobilizations of workplace power.

The associational power of Amazon workers extends beyond a traditional union structure, as exemplified by the wider political movement fighting capitalist and intersectional inequalities, the Transnational Social Strike (TSS) and its Amazon Workers International (AWI). AWI organizes its own bi-annual meetings between the US and France, Germany, Italy, Slovakia, Spain and Poland in its expanding network. It stands, however, in stark contrast to UNI, with its more grassroots 'from below' orientation, aiming to be inclusive across race, sex, contract status and sectors and overlapping subjectivities and solidarities (Heikkilä, 2020a). Dating back to 2015 with the previously mentioned first communication and industrial action between German and Polish workers, AWI presents a less traditional and more alternative form of associational power. It too organizes its own (digital) rank-and-file meetings to struggle for better working conditions, wages and contracts, aiming to slow down and possibly disrupt the valorization of capital both before and during the pandemic. Given the centrality of the disruptive power, AWI focuses on prioritizing actions including slowdowns, assemblies and picket lines to strike collectively for their common interests against Amazon, their binding employer (AMWORKERS, 2019). This form of associational power is characterized by its transnational nature, ultimately underlining that the "biggest challenge is to gain more power and to organize a majority of the Amazon workers worldwide. We have to overcome the idea, that this struggle can be won on a local base" (Barthel, 2019; Krähling, 2019: 17).

In an era in which technology is linked to the wider socio and political–economic fabric, it is important to highlight the additional potential of the digital sphere. A similar, less formal and institutional example of an attempt to organize the geographically, temporally and dimensionally dispersed Amazon labor force has been Former And Current Employees (FACE) of Amazon. Created by anonymous former Amazon employees in response to a 2015 *New York Times* article exposing Amazon's alienating corporate culture, FACE shares posts on personal grievances from Amazon workers regardless of which platform they work for and where they are located (Kantor and Streitfeld, 2015; Kim, 2016). FACE of Amazon has additionally attempted to organize the associational power through its Amazon Employees Internationally Organized Union, according to US labor law. Coupling this effort with the growing workplace power covering various platforms, FACE of Amazon directed an open letter to Bezos stating: "[i]f you choose to ignore us and continue to deny the clear facts of what is going on in your company, we will initiate a labor movement to regain our rights through unionization as was necessary for generations of mistreated employees before us."[14]

Unlike UNI's Global Alliance and AWI's current efforts, FACE of Amazon instrumentalizes the Internet to transcend temporal and spatial boundaries to form transnational cross-platform solidarity. There appear, however, no known cooperation between FACE of Amazon and the other associations. In contrast, the Make Amazon Pay campaign and now coalition, which supports global strikes, actions and protests, has brought UNI and AWI together. These join dozens of unions, social or environmental organizations, watchdogs and activists, including the Progressive International movement in the attempt to "Make Amazon Pay", stating "Amazon is everywhere, involved in almost every step of the global economy, but we are too" (Progressive International, 2021).[15] While cross-coordination of associational power is restricted to navigating different national contexts and union strategies, magnifying the impact of (trans)national coordination of those strategies proves crucial in view of the growing dimensions of Amazon's expansion.

Just as Amazon strategically counters the structural power of workers, so too does it undermine the associational power, earning itself a reputation for being "fundamentally unwilling to cooperate with trade unions on regulating working conditions" (Boewe and Schulten, 2019: 12). The implications of fixed contracts, of the vulnerabilities of precarious workers and of a reserve army of labor extend to the associational power. This explains, for instance, why many workers in Germany join a union only after receiving a permanent contract, despite that right being legally protected. The additional speed at which Amazon is opening warehouses and its revolving door of precarious, contracted or seasonal workers make it difficult for unions to maintain their membership and degree of organization with their limited resources. This is especially crucial when these overlap with peak times and the largest potential for disruptive power (Barthel, 2019). Unions must therefore navigate the terrain that Amazon creates through the organization of its platform, which essentially ruptures the mobilization of such power resources.

Where workers claim their associational power, Amazon actively aims to weaken or even block these. It does this by intimidating supervisory one-on-one talks to warn workers of the consequences of striking and unionizing, and by targeting union members with unpopular tasks or aligning anti-union campaigns with union strikes (Apicella, 2016; Boewe and Schulten, 2019). It comes as no surprise then that when Bezos visited Berlin in 2018 to receive the Axel Springer Award for business innovation and social responsibility, he stated:

> I am very proud of our working conditions and I am very proud of the wages that we pay. In Germany, we employ 16,000 people, we pay at the high range of any comparable work. We have workers councils, of course, and we have very good communications with our employees — so we don't believe we need a union to be an intermediary between our employees. (Schwär, 2018)

If this is Amazon's stance in countries where unions are part of the social partnership and institutional fabric, the cases from the US, on the other hand, underline the extent of union-busting tactics aimed at defeating unionization where in some cases even the NLRB has deemed these in violation of the law. As Amazon aims to manage the threat of associational power that it regards as unnecessary in the first place, 2020 has shown us how far it is willing to go to defeat these. This has ranged from posting a job that included in its description investigating threatening organized labor (Kollewe, 2020), to the leak that it had turned to Pinkerton operatives. This is a detective agency with a notorious record of union-infiltrating and busting, aiding Amazon in its efforts of spying on workers, especially during the peak season (Jones, 2018; Gurley, 2020). When discussing the agency of Amazon workers in their traditional, alternative, transnational and digital expressions, we must therefore put it in perspective not just in view of their weak marketplace power, but also in view of Amazon's systematic efforts to rupture and extinguish any efforts to mobilize workplace power and to form associational power given their co-evolving and strengthening dynamics. The lengths Amazon goes to to create fear are closely related once again to the platform's organization and national context, which more often than not favor Amazon.

## The institutional power of workers

While institutional power, rooted in cooperation and concessions between workers and capital, is reformist in nature, workers can still mobilize it to make gains depending on their context. Industrial relations and the organization of the platform can limit the spaces to be navigated, but these can, as the German case exemplifies, support the general pursuit for institutional representation through works councils and shop steward structures. Ver.di has been organizing shop stewards called *Vertrauensleute*, who are union members elected by the rest of the workers to act as a link between them and the union. These listen to workers' grievances regarding, for example, performance pressures or strategize industrial actions supporting the desired collective bargaining agreement. They also play an essential role in announcing strikes, and essentially in mobilizing workplace power (Boewe and Schulten, 2019). Such structures in the warehouses underline within this context the interconnectedness of the different power resources and structures in support of labor's struggles.

The German Works Constitution Act entitles workers to co-determination on two levels: first, the 'level of the establishment' at any 'private sector establishment' with at least five workers; and second, the 'board level' constituting equal numbers of worker and shareholder representatives wherever 2,000 or more workers are employed (The Federal Ministry of Labour and Social Affairs, 2019). Consisting of both pro-employer Amazon members and more class-conscious union members, works councils have achieved some successes for German workers such as modest wage increases or decentralized break rooms. In Bad Hersfeld it was even able to abolish the dreaded mandatory supervisory feedback talks. While Amazon may present accomplishments in start-meetings as being generously provided by the corporation, co-determination can act as a motivator for workers to mobilize for their institutional representation (Cattero and D'Onoforio, 2018; Apicella and Hildebrandt, 2019; Boewe and Schulten, 2019; Kassem, 2023). As the nature of the platform is bound by the national context and industrial relations where such expressions of institutional power may be possible as in Germany, workers in other contexts may need to struggle for their collective interests outside of the institutional setup. In contrast, the time-wage, determined by the conditions and length of the contract, can impact the extent to which workers partake in these struggles or benefit from their outcomes.

Since the corporation cannot prohibit the creation and presence of works councils in Germany, Amazon attempts to make these as divided and ineffective as possible by, for instance, supporting pro-employer lists and offering to print flyers or information at its cost. When interviewed, workers said that Amazon uses further tactics such as withholding information and extending the discriminatory treatment that it utilizes for those striking or unionized to works council members. A works council need not be necessarily pro-union or pro-labor, especially in newer warehouses without a history of labor dispute or organization.

Amazon also attempts to curb the institutional power by circumventing possibilities for group/central works councils. By establishing its European headquarters in Luxembourg it does not just benefit from tax advantages but Luxembourg's laws are also applied to the corporation, which do not include the representation of workers at corporate group levels. Amazon can dodge the creation of group/central works councils by organizing warehouses within its supply chain as "'profit centers' and subsidiaries" for Amazon EU Sarl in Luxembourg (Boewe and Schulten, 2019: 21). Amazon additionally attempts to eliminate any possibility for co-determination at board level by deliberately keeping the number of workers in a warehouse to under 2,000, as at its Graben warehouse, where the workforce dropped from the initial 5,000 to under 2,000. The only exception has been Bad Hersfeld, with its 3,500 workers, though these had to apply pressure for co-determination even though it should have been granted automatically (ver.di, 2014; Boewe and Schulten, 2019). While Amazon attempts to limit the institutional power of workers in Germany, there is potentially more possibility for this in some other national contexts.

Amazon's approach to institutional power can be understood as making as few concessions as necessary, limiting institutional powers to what is legally mandated and navigating industrial relations to its advantage. Central to this has been the pursuit of a collective bargaining agreement, which would result in an improvement of wages and working conditions. While I discussed the pursuit for the German collective bargaining agreement by ver.di in the associational power, it would represent a larger manifestation of the institutional power for the union and the workers. In fact, as reflected in a previous quote from Bezos, Amazon appears to use the institutional power of having works councils that are regarded as employee participation to dismiss this form of institutional power in Germany (Kassem, 2023). Amazon thus far rejects a collective bargaining agreement for the German retail industry and does not need to consider one in the US, at least until a formal associational power is officially achieved. It cannot, however, escape France's obligatory industry-level collective bargaining agreement for the entire non-food retail industry or the successful negotiation by Italian Filcam-CGIL, the retail section of CGIL, for the first workplace collective agreement in 2018. However, both of these are meant as a starting point and foundation stone to build on (Cattero and D'Onoforio, 2018). It also remains to be seen what the role of the newly established European Works Council will be and how this will translate into the possible strengthening of transnational power resources. Once again, the concrete manifestation of these powers can only be understood as arising from the specific configuration of the organization of the platform and the history of labor struggle within this constellation.

## The societal power of workers

While the discussion on the power resources paints a complex terrain that workers must navigate, our current moment appears to be conducive to their societal power. As more and more people come to rely on Amazon and its growing empire, only to be exacerbated by COVID-19, it continues to make headlines from the perspective of capital for its newest expansions, inventions and technologies, booming valuation or stories about Jeff Bezos. These appear to be increasingly countered by the working realities of workers, thereby strengthening their growing discursive power. Workers underline the importance of making their grievances public through the media as a means to tarnish Amazon's image, given how much it prides itself on being the most customer-centric company. While the nature of the platform allowed undercover documentaries to expose its catastrophic working conditions as seen in BBC's *Amazon – The Truth Behind the Click* and ARD's *Ausgeliefert! Leiharbeiter bei Amazon*, these efforts have since been complemented by anonymous reports by workers, especially during the peak season. The media can strengthen not only the societal power of workers to influence the public but can also increase and strengthen workers' other power resources, especially in relation to traditional and grassroots union organizing, as well as other forms of collective organization and ultimately their overall labor struggle.

While the discursive power is essential to their struggle, so too is their power to create coalitions, as workers underline the importance of further instrumentalizing this moment to gain the support of politicians and social and solidarity movements. Such an instance presented itself at the strikes in protest against Bezos receiving the previously mentioned Axel Springer award, in which ver.di took to the streets alongside other unions and Make Amazon Pay. The latter can in fact be regarded precisely as a manifestation of coalitional power, bringing together over 70 (global) labor, social, technological or environmental organizations and activists. In addition to those previously mentioned, it also includes Oxfam, IndustriALL, Data 4 Black Lives, 350.org and Amazon Employees for Climate Justice. While it aligns its common demands with protecting universal labor rights and aims to hold Amazon accountable in environmental and economic terms, it has also called for global actions, such as protests at Amazon's corporate EU headquarters. Supported by some Members of the European Parliament, this further underlines how such efforts can expand the coalitional, workplace and associational power (UNI Europa, 2021a).

Unions too, through their direct associational power, have further cultivated the coalitional power by expanding the scope of the Amazon labor struggle as embodied in UNI's global symposium organized along with the ITUC. Entitled *Symposium on the Unchecked Power of Amazon in Today's*

*Economy and Society*, and coinciding with Cyber Monday in December 2019, its participants included activists, researchers, NGOs and politicians to problematize the corporation's growing digital, economic, political and societal power as well as its environmental carbon footprint. It encouraged in many ways cross-platform and transnational solidarity (UNI and ITUC, 2019). Not just the economic dimension but also the political dimension of the labor struggle have been previously highlighted by politicians such as Elizabeth Warren and Bernie Sanders, who have underlined the importance of breaking Amazon up; Sanders was also a strong supporter of increasing Amazon's minimum wage to US$15. Other instances have included Ilhan Omar's show of solidarity with the workers in Minnesota or Alexandria Ocasio-Cortez's support for the movement against HQ2 in New York City (Hamilton, 2018; Lieber, 2018; Rosenberg, 2019).

On the other side of the Atlantic, concrete coalitional power manifestations are attempting to "Europeanise Amazon", as the European Trade Union Confederation (ETUC) underlines Amazon's attempts at "undermining the European social model" regarding collective bargaining, working conditions and labor rights and tax avoidance (ETUC, 2021). While these efforts culminated in a hearing at the Committee on Employment and Social Affairs of the European Parliament, Amazon declined to attend this altogether. As UNI's Hoffman states, "Amazon had $44 billion in sales in Europe and paid no corporate taxes. The fact that they are failing to appear to answer questions from duly elected members of the European Parliament is a slap in the face to Europe and reflects Amazon's general contempt for democracy" (UNI Europa, 2021b). The expansions of this corporation, spanning continents, sectors and industries, not only poses a wide array of threats to these but also allows for various points for workers to gain public and political support. It also allows for the creation of a solidary network and movement from various societal sources. The networks and labor struggles expand, magnify and co-evolve along with Amazon's exponential growth.

Amazon counters societal power by continuously constructing itself in a positive light as an employer that is tolerant and embraces diversity within its warehouses, the same warehouses that are open for public. All one needs to do is to sign up for one of its 'Fulfillment Center Tours', where visitors can see workers laboring and ask any questions they may have. These tours allow Amazon to underline its commitment to transparency and dismiss reports on poor working conditions. These tours are now even offered virtually, making these even more accessible, no longer tied to cost of traveling to the warehouse. It has also created its own blog 'day one' – and uses it along with articles written by 'Amazon staff' to inform those interested in its newest developments, post its own videos featuring workers with positive perceptions of work or to respond to media attacks.[16] Amazon additionally has had active Twitter ambassadors, essentially "[an a]rmy of fulfillment center employees [who] jump to [the] company's defense online when it faces a barrage of bad press" (Tynan, 2018a). These various tactics demonstrate how Amazon quickly, repeatedly and strategically distances itself from any negative press and image-tarnishing efforts. It diverts attention away from its workers and their labor realities and more toward employee and customer satisfaction, technological developments and capital gains – all of which mask the huge ongoing economic inequalities within the corporation. If it features any workers, these appear as happy and satisfied. Our current moment and growing attention around the platform economy in general, and Amazon in specific, appear to be strengthening possibilities for solidarity, resistance and organization.

What appears to the customer behind the screen as a human-less process is based on the exploitation of warehouse workers in these factory-like lines of circulation. Examining the relations of alienation demonstrates the ways in which a location-based platform estranges and robotizes its workers and reduces them to a number, whilst the time-wage masks the exploitative UPH regime. Though this may individualize and fragment workers, they are not mere appendages of the machine. They can consciously struggle for their collective class interests bound by the various facets of their material, racialized and gendered subjectivities and solidarity. Amazon's location-based nature allows it to exploit the wider contextual conditions and precarious contractual agreements to further fragment and intimidate workers from mobilizing their power resources. While acts of individual resistance are complicated in the times of digital Taylorism and increased precarity, workers may navigate their material obstacles and Amazon's counterstrategies to instrumentalize their workplace and disruptive power derived from their assembly within warehouses. As labor organizations support associational and institutional powers (trans)nationally and digitally to improve their working conditions and fight back against the various facets of alienation, workers are increasingly gaining momentum in organizing themselves and making their movement intrinsic to the wider public debate. It is crucial to continue to cultivate these power resources holistically, given how these co-evolve. In doing so, they are claiming their agency and conceiving of it in broader terms of a possible transnational, inter-platform and inter-sectoral movement. As Awood's Abdirahman Muse highlights, as Amazon continues to adapt, so too must the labor movement.[17]

8

# "Artificial Artificial Intelligence": Gigging on Amazon Mechanical Turk

"I can work when I want
and not work when I want."

MTurk worker

As a second-generation platform, MTurk exemplifies how capitalism continues to evolve. While all platforms assume, regardless of their nature, the digital dimension of the Internet to mediate, web-based platforms additionally instrumentalize this infrastructure to organize and mediate all the capital–labor relations. In stark contrast to warehouse workers, MTurk workers are organized on a web-based platform to complete piecework, which is increasingly normalized and reproduced beyond the platform economy. They share in that regard the nature of the work with the larger gig economy, which I return to in Chapter 10. As "technology has the potential to be leveraged by capital to capture and alienate labour power in quite novel ways" (Bergvall-Kåreborn and Howcroft, 2014: 221), I now investigate how MTurk systematically alienates workers. These labor atomistically without ever encountering either capital that employs them or other workers on MTurk's Application Programming Interface (API).

## Alienation from the labor activity

To study this fundamental relation of alienation, it is important to begin with the triangular relationship between Amazon, requesters and workers (Figure 8.1). While requesters and workers access MTurk through two different interfaces (one for posting tasks and one for laboring), their relationship is facilitated by accepting MTurk's "Participation Agreement", which functions like a contractual agreement.

**Figure 8.1:** Mediation between Amazon, requesters and workers

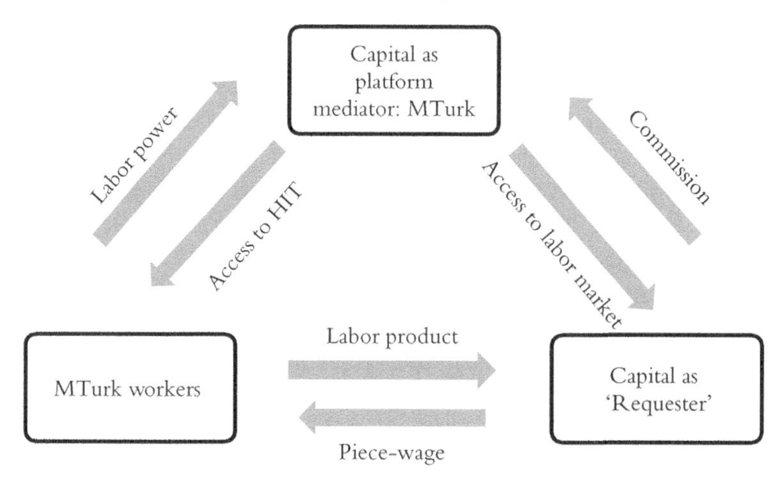


In a seemingly contradictory manner, MTurk extracts itself from capital–labor relations yet lays out its terms, which is characteristic of the platform economy. Amazon presents itself as merely facilitating the exchange of labor through its infrastructure, for which it receives 20 percent commission and an additional 20 percent for tasks requiring more than ten workers.[1] As the infrastructure provider, labor mediator and financial intermediator with the power to cancel accounts and deprive workers of wages, Amazon removes itself from extending rights to workers or any legal disputes. Instead, it classifies workers who do "work made for hire" as independent contractors, "not as an employee of a Requester or Amazon Mechanical Turk or our affiliates" despite referring to them as "Workers" in its requesters guide (Amazon Mechanical Turk, 2020).[2] I approach those laboring on MTurk as workers, bearing in mind their precarious classification which denies them the rights granted in a traditional employment relationship. I use the terms 'web-based labor' or 'workers laboring digitally' to not separate them from their material conditions.

Alienation from the labor activity on MTurk is premised upon the anonymized relationship between workers and requesters. Workers on the platform are assigned an alphanumeric worker ID that appears merely as a line of code: a sequence of letters and numbers. While this ID can help reduce discrimination based on sex and race, it de facto dehumanizes workers from the very beginning, initially from themselves as they appear as an ID code on their screen, but also dehumanized from the platform and requester (Berinsky et al, 2012). Just as workers are anonymized to themselves and to capital, which appears once as Amazon and once as the requester, so too does the requester appear by and large anonymous to workers. The name with which these post microtasks is not necessarily telling, as they can also anonymize themselves on the platform. Researchers classify requesters into three larger groups, the first of which stems from the academic or research community for surveys, for instance. These may need to clearly indicate their identities for ethical approvals of studies and review boards. This category has been, however, substantially critiqued for questions of representativeness, reliability and validity but especially ethical concerns regarding low pay and unequal power dynamics between those who employ labor and those laboring (Berinsky et al, 2012; Buhrmester et al, 2018; Samuel, 2018). The two other groups include both small-scale companies and start-ups with limited resources and low operating costs, as well as larger ones that directly or indirectly through consultancy firms access MTurk, such as Walmart, Coca-Cola, the US Army, P&G, Pinterest or YouTube (Bergvall-Kåreborn and Howcroft, 2014; Reese and Heath, 2016). All these requesters essentially turn to MTurk to access "a global, on-demand, 24x7 workforce".[3] MTurk can be regarded then as premised on the anonymization and de facto dehumanization of capital–labor relations.

The alienation from their labor activity is further magnified, as workers own much of the means of production. As with all labor, workers represent variable capital through their labor power. Given that these workers are located in the production process, they create surplus value in addition to their own value. Workers also own much of the constant capital, which constitutes the means of production, "i.e. the raw material, the auxiliary material and the instruments of labour, [that] does not undergo any quantitative alteration of value in the process of production" (Marx, 1977: 317). While Amazon owns the platform's physical and digital infrastructure, the remaining constant capital is sourced directly from workers, because of the hyperoutsourcing model on which the larger gig economy is based.

Workers access the platform through their own devices, such as computers, laptops or mobile phones with an Internet connection. They must also hold a level of computer literacy and usually English proficiency. As such, they do not receive any training from MTurk or requesters, which further reduces costs for capital. The burden of cost is not eliminated altogether but shifted onto the workers, where their socio-economic status can play a crucial role, especially in the Global South (Gupta et al, 2014; Gray and Suri, 2019). From capital's perspective, this hyperoutsourcing model is complemented by hiring workers as independent contractors to do piecework. This allows capital to dodge minimum wage regulations and benefits, as web-based platforms operate outside of legal frameworks because of how work has become deterritorialized (Ettlinger, 2017). As the "sun never sets on Amazon's technology platform" (Irani, 2013: 726), MTurk can thereby offer requesters access to a large, efficient, inexpensive and global workforce, who only incur the costs of commission.

Unlike Amazon warehouse workers, who circulate value, workers on MTurk are located in the production process of what are termed Human

Intelligence Tasks (HITs), which underlines the dependence on humans for these (Kassem, 2022). By accepting the Participation Agreement, workers must agree not to "use robots, scripts, or other automated methods as a substitute for your [their] human intelligence or independent judgment to perform Tasks" (Amazon Mechanical Turk, 2020). These microtasks, essentially complex tasks broken down into their elementary components, cannot yet be carried out by machines. They range from digital transcription tasks of scanned documents such as receipts and answering surveys to tagging images and identifying or classifying emotions. The requester sets the required labor time as the time allotted, the piece-wage as the "reward" and the number of workers translates to number of HITs. As workers "accept & work" tasks they produce value, as well as surplus value, which is ensured by the low wages. Digital piecework shares many similarities with industrial piecework – though pushed to new dimensions via the web-based nature of the platform, where workers do not communicate directly with requesters but rather the interface (Bucher and Fieseler, 2017).

Given contemporary technological conditions, it is important to conceptualize MTurk's web-based labor, like those in Amazon warehouses, as algorithmically managed. As each microtask indicates the necessary time needed to complete it, the interface measures the time workers take down to the minute and seconds. Upon completing the task within the allotted time, the worker submits their labor product, which the requester receives along with the exact time taken to complete it. The requester has then a 30-day window to review the task and decide whether to approve or reject it. The worker is only paid the piece-wage if the task is approved. Rejecting a task means workers are denied their piece-wage despite their submitted labor products. The API of MTurk allows all these processes from accessing the workforce, posting tasks, evaluating and rewarding or rejecting piece-wages to be automated, as requesters can either humanly or algorithmically evaluate labor products. Though Amazon states that work should not be rejected "without good cause" (Amazon Mechanical Turk, 2020) – requesters do not need to justify such actions to Amazon or the workers (Scholz, 2015). Should it be rejected, the worker's "approval rate" will drop in the same manner that an approved task would improve it (see Figure 8.2). One requester defends this efficiency model, stating, "You cannot spend time exchanging email. The time you spent looking at the email costs more than what you paid them. This has to function on autopilot as an algorithmic system … and integrated with your business processes" (Irani, 2013: 727). What is to capital an efficient process can result for the worker in wage theft, not just tolerated but also normalized by MTurk.

The approval rate, de facto the productivity rate, acts here as the mechanism by which workers are digitally measured, disciplined and sometimes

**Figure 8.2:** Labor process for MTurk workers

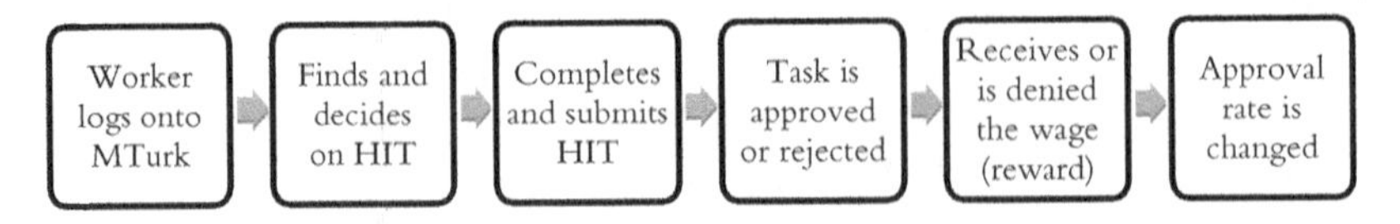


rewarded through additional payments. Given the way the API is designed to mechanically oversee the labor process, technology can be instrumentalized to replace direct human supervision or management. Workers interact "with a 'system' rather than humans" (Berg et al, 2018: 9). Given also the power of the approval rate, workers have internalized it and are disciplined by it, while requesters can filter out workers based on their approval rate or other factors such as geographical location or additional MTurk qualifications. As Amazon can request a higher commission rate for accessing the labor pool with various "Masters Qualifications" for which higher paid tasks are opened up, it is not clear how workers obtain these (Ellmer, 2015). MTurk merely states that this is awarded to workers who have "demonstrated excellence across a wide range of HITs".[4]

From the worker's perspective MTurk is characterized by this lack of transparency, which makes it difficult for workers successfully to challenge the denial of their wage. They also pay the price for glitches and breakdowns that further impact their approval rate. Gray and Suri adopt Eric Meyer's concept of "algorithmic cruelty" to underline the repercussions of the lack of empathy and accountability in "essentially thoughtless" algorithms (2019: 68). While MTurk only allowed workers to see additional information about requesters such as their HIT approval rates in 2019 (Amazon Mechanical Turk, 2019), which can influence workers' decisions to accept tasks, there is a clear asymmetry of power within the relationship between workers and requester. With no direct supervisor in place, as has been historically part of laboring, algorithms become increasingly embedded within capital–labor relations in web-based platforms and the larger gig economy.

The worker is further alienated not just by the invisibility of the capital–labor relation but also by their assigned function as 'artificial artificial intelligence'. Referring to the 18th-century automaton, MTurk's API masks the web-based human laboring and social relations. In the process, it "render[s] workers invisible, redirecting focus to the innovation of human computation as a field of technological achievement" (Irani and Silberman, 2013: 613). Essentially, workers are hired based on their human intelligence, cognition, judgment and labor for HITs. The produced data can be further used to train machine-learning algorithms for Artificial Intelligence (AI). Given the growing centrality of AI, the data labeling market was estimated to be US$500 million in 2018, and was projected in 2019 to reach US$1.2

billion in 2023 (Metz, 2019). MTurk workers are often confronted with tasks that build such datasets to tag images later used, for instance, to train self-driving cars to recognize objects and people. As such datasets allow computer systems to draw conclusions by detecting patterns, such microwork has become essential to the tech industry concerned with advancing machine learning (Reese and Heath, 2016; Schwartz, 2019). In an interesting twist, workers are essentially training not just the machine but the very machine meant to replace and displace them once it can perform these tasks without them. As the next relation of alienation underlines, while workers are managed by algorithms, they also contribute to their creation and development. It will be interesting to see how the centrality of AI changes and develops for (microtasking) platforms over time.

Laboring on MTurk further estranges workers through the multifold division of labor. MTurk first contributes to the reproduction of a division between high- and low-skilled labor. While MTurk focuses on what is considered low-skilled labor producing data, high-skilled labor elsewhere configures such data into machine-learning algorithms for AI. Second, microtasking needs to be imagined as various parallel digital assembly lines mediated via the Internet. Subdividing tasks as such cheapens the labor power and allows for higher extraction of surplus value and ultimately profits. Numerous workers perform the same microtasks to produce larger data sets, possible because of what MTurk names a "scalable workforce" that allows requesters to expand or minimize tasks as they see fit, whether that is "100 tasks one day and 10,000 the next".[5] Workers find themselves constantly jumping between assembly lines in which they do not know which line or what stage they are on, further atomizing the labor activity. Finally, MTurk creates a hierarchy among globally competitive workers based on approval rates and possible Masters qualifications, which acts as a mechanism to divide workers and constantly push them to be productive.

This division of labor of a digital nature translates into hypertaylorized virtual assembly lines of geographically and temporally dispersed labor activities that cannot be fully visible or known to any one worker. While workers may be aware of academic, market or scientific purposes behind surveys, the concrete purpose and contribution of piecework for machine learning and AI remains largely a mystery, as the next section exemplifies. In fragmenting the labor process into individual steps, the overall project becomes obscured to the workers (Braverman, 1974). Pushing what is known from factory work into new dimensions of atomized and displaced digital production lines, the platform's digital piecework nature comes to anonymize capital–labor relations and render the worker and their labor activity invisible behind the shadows of technology and algorithms. Amidst it, the worker is left estranged from the very activity of laboring despite owning most of the means of production.

## Alienation from the product of labor

Unlike workers who circulate products, MTurk workers are located within the sphere of production. Yet the labor product resulting from their own activity also appears as alien to them, because of the larger virtual assembly line. To grasp the microtasking nature of laboring, Kristy Milland, former MTurk worker and activist, gives the example of a text that is to be translated, where every sentence is broken down into one microtask. It would take a mere six minutes to translate an article of 1,000 sentences, costing a total of only US$20 (Milland, 2019). MTurk classifies its microtasks into four larger groups: image/video processing (for example, tagging and classifying), data verification and clean-up (identifying duplicates, verifying data), information gathering (such as taking surveys) and data processing (for example, transcribing audio and content such as receipts).[6] Workers decide on which tasks to accept by weighing the kind of task in relation to pay, the requester (should they be identifiable) and, lastly, the time allotted for the task. Consequently, workers are more likely to divert away from incredibly low paid tasks of transcription, especially of receipts, which are perceived as "boring", and flock more towards the better-paid ones like surveys and video-related tasks perceived as "interesting". By laboring on MTurk, workers agree to forfeit all ownership, as they "waive all moral or other proprietary rights" and their labor product becomes the private property of capital "for the benefit of the Requester" (Amazon Mechanical Turk, 2020).

While the nature of HITs may differ on MTurk, their essence is of the same digital and immaterial nature: data, a product that is part and parcel of the platform economy. Increasingly understood to be a commodity, data "spawns a lucrative, fast-growing industry ... [considered to be] the oil of the digital era" (*The Economist*, 2017). In contrast to oil, data does not exist externally to human labor, but only comes into existence because of it; it needs to be generated, classified and analyzed. While other web-based digital labor platforms focus on macro-tasks to create, for example, videos, graphic design or content, MTurk workers are hired less for their creativity than for their ability to gather, generate and analyze data on the basis of human cognition and intelligence (Gonzalez, 2019).

This can mean differentiating between colors and animals, objects and subjects in an image of a street, or tracing specific objects to grasp their different 2D/3D dimensions. Other microtasks can focus on identifying human opinions, tastes, perceptions, judgments and emotions, as machines cannot yet interpret human behavior or emotions such as differentiating between happiness and anger. Workers may also review the labor products of previous workers to evaluate to what extent they reflect accurate human cognition, perception and opinion. The use-value of HITs lies then not in the individual labor product but in the amassed totality of data in datasets.

Only when a dataset entails thousands of labeled dog and cat photos can the algorithm learn to differentiate between the two. In doing so, microwork platforms can attract more financial capital by selling themselves not as labor but as technology platforms (Irani, 2013; Milland, 2019).

While workers may recognize their labor products as data, the concrete use-value remains unknown because of the highly taylorized, fragmented virtual production lines that span across geographical and temporal zones. This is further amplified by the fact that workers in many cases do not know who the requester is. Milland (2019) explains, for example, that data derived from receipt transcriptions could be further sold to, for instance, P&G and Johnson & Johnson's research and marketing departments. Another MTurk worker, Rochelle La Plante, further states that "[you] could be tagging faces in a crowd, but maybe something is being built for a malicious purpose or something ... You don't know what you're doing, exactly, because there's no information" (Reese and Heath, 2016). Even if the general use-value of machine-learning algorithms for the training of AI is known, it is impossible for the worker, whose labor product is just a micro-component of a larger digital assembly line, to infer and discern its concrete use within capital's value chain.

In contrast, exchange-values of HITs, meaning piece-wages, are clearly stated alongside the microtask – though it does not account for both unpaid labor time and rejected labor products. MTurk initially masks the wage by referring to it as a 'reward'; just as capital 'requests' labor, so it 'rewards' workers. MTurk workers, who already provide constant and variable capital, can see piece-wages priced as low as possibly conceivable, at US$0.01, and may not exceed a few US$. Given that MTurk workers de facto labor as independent contractors, their wages can fluctuate. Any calculation of the median wage needs to include unpaid labor and time that goes into searching for well-paid, interesting tasks, those rejected by requesters and those that could not be submitted because of technical glitches. Task rejection translates into wage theft by withholding the piece-wage but retaining the ability to use the labor product. According to a 2016 International Labour Organization (ILO) survey, 94 percent of MTurk and former Crowdflower workers had experienced this (Berg, 2016). While requesters may, depending on location, pay on average more than US$11 an hour, requesters with minimum-paying tasks flood the digital labor market, ultimately pushing for a race to the bottom. The ILO estimates in 2017 the US median hourly wage to have been US$7.5 accounting only for paid work and US$5.63 for paid and unpaid work, while the Indian hourly wages were US$2.14 and US$1.67 (Berg et al, 2018; Hara et al, 2018). The exchange-values of these labor products do not account for these factors or the relations of uneven geographies behind them. Such piece-wages clearly undervalue human labor, not always translating into an average livable wage.

The processes of exploitation are further magnified by two facts. First, while the worker must complete the HIT within a given time frame, requesters have 30 days to evaluate the labor product, accept and pay or reject it altogether.[7] As an independent contractor, the worker can never actually know when or if they will receive the piece-wage. Such web-based platforms operate in the digital sphere thus far outside of national labor regulations and traditional employment that encompass labor rights, protections and benefits such as sick leave, retirement and insurance. Capital, as is increasingly common in neoliberal times, exploits these conditions to pay workers by the task and only by the task, thereby dodging other rights and benefits granted elsewhere in the labor market. What is damaging is that such labor and the larger gig economy normalize this form of work, which increasingly subsumes more and more tasks that could be performed by other industries (De Stefano, 2016; Casilli, 2017). While classifying workers as independent contractors is reproduced in both location- and web-based labor platforms, in the concrete case of the MTurk workers it is the result of *both* the nature of their piecework *and* the web-based nature of the platform. Second, should workers successfully receive a piece-wage, it can only be transferred to a US or Indian US bank account, while all others are thus far paid in a different form of currency, namely through a transfer to their Amazon.com gift card balance, explaining why work is most desirable in the US and India (Bergvall-Kåreborn and Howcroft, 2014). As the financial mediator, it appears Amazon can in some cases keep the money within its own circulation.

Once the dialectical relation between use-value and exchange-value is considered holistically, it becomes apparent that the worker is alienated from their own labor product as a result of the fetishized nature of commodities. Workers, who are situated in their own material contexts, are hired for their ability to conduct Human Intelligence Tasks, yet they are meant to produce an output of data that is devoid of their humanity, their data as devoid of any social relations of exploitation. These microwork platforms appear as mysterious "digital black box labor" both to workers who cannot know for what and whom they are laboring and to capital, to whom these workers are rendered invisible (Scholz, 2015). Algorithmically managed workers perplexingly participate in the creation and development of algorithms which could ultimately be instrumentalized by capital to further manage and oversee labor processes even beyond the platform economy, thereby contributing to the reproduction of alienating working conditions.

## Alienation from species-being

The web-based nature of the platform leads to the collapse of what has been traditionally known as a physical workplace, such as the factory or an office, and other non-work-related spaces. Melissa Gregg (2011) argues that increasingly normalized forms of virtual and remote work result in the general encroachment of labor into homes. As a fixed workplace is no precondition for such remote laboring, workers can be located and deliver work from anywhere as long as they have access to an Internet connection and a device by which to access it (Webster and Randle, 2016). In the case of MTurk, much web-based work appears to be done from the confines of the home, as workers report the ability to work from home as one of the main reasons to join these digital labor platforms. This muddling of the boundaries of work and non-work can prove detrimental, as Marx states that workers feel "at home when he is [they are] not working" and vice versa (Marx, 1844). It is necessary to emphasize, however, that the home has not historically been a site immune to the encroachment of labor. Previously largely reserved for unpaid and at times paid reproductive labor, the home becomes a space absorbed by additional forms of paid labor expanding both working time and space beyond concrete bounds.

Within neoliberal times the ability to labor remotely, virtually and easily are hailed as empowering workers. The promise of flexibility appears attractive to workers who may be restricted in their ability to take on more traditional nine-to-five jobs, those wanting to avoid toxic work cultures and workplace discriminations or those with restrictions in mobility and additional responsibilities in reproductive labor. This also explains the gendered dimension of digital laboring, as women may balance microtasking with their reproductive laboring and care work (Gerber, 2022). While statistics from a decade ago showed that there was a gender imbalance with MTurk workers predominantly identified as women in the US and men in India, there seems more of a balance today, though women are thought to balance laboring with their care work (Ross et al, 2010; Berg et al, 2018; Berg and Rani, 2021). The web-based nature and relatively low entry into the digital labor market can be understood as empowering historically marginalized workers who have been forced out of the formal labor market and can now take control of their own laboring to achieve some financial independence (Gray and Suri, 2019).

As such workers are assumed to gain autonomy, while enjoying being part of a project, developing and training skills such as language translation, transcription and computer literacy. Within this context, MTurk workers list the ability to learn something new on a daily basis while working from home and choosing their own hours as among the advantages of laboring on the platform. When I asked workers on my surveys to choose between describing the work as 'liberating' or 'isolating' – the majority opted for 'liberating'. One worker noted, "This may actually be the future of 'work'. Data and data science and similar things are quite saleable and MTurk workers are valuable employees. So, I feel valuable and I put effort in and respond honestly and thoughtfully and get a somewhat reasonable compensation." Workers repeatedly emphasize their appreciation of MTurk's flexibility, which allows them to be in control of their work schedule and work-life balance, laboring "independently, out of the system" and "as little or as much as you want" from the confines of their home, "with no supervisor or staff to attend to" and "[n]o boss looking over my shoulder". The promise of flexibility makes MTurk in many ways attractive to those who want to work without obvious physical supervision, in an enforced space or working time.

The nature of the platform and work thereby extend the working day, a reality that has become increasingly clear in the context of COVID-19 and rise of remote work. While it is yet to be seen how this reality has skewed laboring on such digital labor platforms both in gendered and racialized terms, we can generally understand the working time spent on these platforms as standing in close relation to how much it is relied on for subsistence, being a primary or complementary source of income. As of 2016, the ILO measured 49 percent of Indian MTurk workers as being fully dependent on MTurk and 38 percent of US MTurk workers – of whom a proportion reports to be working seven days a week (Berg, 2016). Increased precarity translates into workers also laboring for complementary piece-wages, with many workers laboring on MTurk during the working hours of their other job or after their job (Berg and De Stefano, 2017; Berg et al, 2018). The political–economic landscape of stagnating wages and rising inequalities in the neoliberal era, magnified by COVID-19, pushes workers to embrace remote laboring, which comes with lower wages and working conditions with the classification of being independent contractors. Referring to the last economic crisis, "[i]t is no coincidence that these online, on-demand businesses gained major traction during the deepest economic downturn in nearly a century, when unemployment was in double digits and the condition of the most vulnerable workers put downward pressure on all workers" (Hill, 2018).

The length of the working day fluctuates in relation to the time needed to complete enough microtasks for piece-wages, which can come to consume the worker and leave little space for leisure. Unlike those laboring for additional piece-wages who argue that MTurk does not interfere with their social life, the reality seems somewhat different for those for whom this is a main source of income. They note that it is difficult to relax when the wage is not guaranteed, as they feel the necessity to labor on every available task. One worker notes their "[s]ocial life is very limited because I have to work 14 hours a day to make ends meet". The reasons for laboring do not, however, negate the flexibility that workers underline, considering that MTurk still provides labor within constricting material conditions.

The precarity of the MTurk work and its invasive nature are not perceived then uniformly across workers. Some labor to sustain themselves and perceive it as an actual job and some work for additional income, while others state "[i]t doesn't feel like a job. If anything, it feels like a hobby or something I do every now and then to kill time." For these workers it is about conducting interesting and fun tasks while earning a piece-wage. One need not exclude the other. In fact, most of my surveyed workers attributed more positive adjectives to describing the work on MTurk than negative ones, with words such as 'interesting', 'fun' and 'exciting' more common than 'tedious', 'boring' and 'annoying'. The reason workers choose surveys over transcription tasks is not just because the latter are low-paid and possibly rejected en masse but also because they are perceived as being boring and tedious compared to more exciting and interesting tasks such as surveys. Workers mention that they get some form of fulfillment, making them feel "valuable" and "contributing to society and getting compensated for it at the same time". Others underline the sense of concrete fulfillment that comes with "work[ing] on extremely interesting studies" and "contributing to a scientific body of data/evidence". Some workers attribute also some social value to their labor. To what extent the act of laboring is perceived in this way can then further magnify a worker's alienation, should they regard their own work as devoid of any exploitation.

The extension of the working day is closely related to the geographically and temporally dispersed and displaced nature of work because of the nature of the platform. While the demand for labor by capital "is relatively geographically concentrated", the supply of labor "is relatively geographically diffuse" (Graham et al, 2017: 142). The repercussions of these uneven geographies are twofold. For one, it means that capital mainly in the Global North dictates the working day where workers need to be on alert for tasks, thereby putting in question the true bounds of flexibility. Miranda Hall (2017), who studied how refugees in Lebanon's Shatila Camp labor digitally, points out that "digital workers' bodies are no less regimented to the demands of capital than their industrial counterparts". Workers, depending on their location, must "adjust their sleeping patterns to the demands of (western) capital".

The second consequence is that workers face high competition among themselves to snatch up especially high-paying tasks as soon as they are posted. Some set up alerts and "drop everything and do it. I'm literally chained to my computer. If this is how you feed your children, you don't leave" (Reese and Heath, 2016). The international division of labor and the reserve army of labor ensure that there is always pressure to labor. As one MTurk worker notes, it is "first come first serve". Given that most MTurk workers are either located in the US or India, workers in India may be more vulnerable to bigger time differences considering that capital is by and large located in the Global North. Work on web-based digital labor platforms can therefore be both gendered and racialized. With the days of some MTurk workers becoming structured by laboring opportunities, the platform and general context of imperialist capitalism further factor into the intermeshing of work and time used for other activities.

While many appreciate laboring on MTurk for its flexibility and independence, for others it becomes their only means of subsistence and cannot be understood outside of the wider political–economic conditions that make such work "less flexible". The organization of the platform allows the labor activity to assume new dimensions of time and place, further muddling work and non-work activities. This is magnified by the effects it can have on workers' mental states, considering that some microtasks may include tagging violent and graphic images and content. While this work can help remove such content from platforms, it can prove traumatic for those workers (Reese and Heath, 2016; Metz, 2019; Milland, 2019). Such trauma-inducing labor can consequently affect the worker and their mental state, which ultimately additionally alienates workers from their species-being and social relations.

## Alienation from fellow humans

As MTurk workers do not convene within a physical space and labor atomistically, they do not encounter one another on the platform. Web-based laboring disrupts traditional capital–labor relations, as it "renders the physical collectivity of the traditional workplace, where workers are brought together under one roof, increasingly obsolete" (Webster, 2016: 58). The MTurk platform is set up in ways to essentially fragment and compartmentalize the workforce, as each worker labors individually on the workers' API. It is as though they log onto atomized and dispersed digital workspaces with no ways to connect across them. Not only is the worker anonymized and rendered invisible behind their alphanumerical ID, but other workers cannot see this ID, rendering them additionally invisible to one another.

The very fabric of the digital labor platform is one that is individual and excludes the possibility of coming together to form a collective on the API, while the classification of independent contractors considers them not to belong to the workforce at all. This explains why many workers regard themselves as laboring independently rather than identifying as part of a workforce. One worker highlights that "MTurk likes it that way. If I left a job, that workplace would be impacted. If I left Turk … it would not." Considering contemporary technological and political–economic conditions, it appears that web-based piece-laboring "is the logical outcome of a long-term process of work fragmentation and the physical disconnection of workers that was initiated by Adam Smith, Charles Babbage, and Frederick Taylor in nineteenth-century manufacturing" (Webster, 2016: 59). If there is any perception of other workers via MTurk, it is to the extent that these represent competition extended across spatial and temporal zones and

**Table 8.1:** Four relations of alienation of MTurk workers

| | **Appearance for worker** |
|---|---|
| **Alienation from the labor activity** | • Anonymization of capital–labor relations, 'artificial artificial intelligence'<br>• Digital hyperoutsourcing of invisibilized assembly lines<br>• Division of labor across geographical/temporal boundaries<br>• Productivity measured through approval rating<br>• Algorithmically managed labor process |
| **Alienation from the product of labor** | • Production line of microtasks as data<br>• Fetishistic nature of commodities: exchange-value as piece-wages mask use-value of data and machine-learning algorithms<br>• Workers paradoxically produce algorithms that may manage or displace them |
| **Alienation from species-being** | • Flexibility and autonomy hailed as work encroaches into home<br>• Home as also the space of reproductive labor<br>• Labor not always perceived as labor<br>• Extension of the working day: concentrated capital, geographically distributed workers |
| **Alienation from fellow humans** | • Individual, isolating nature of web-based microtask laboring<br>• Fellow workers: competition within the international division of labor and reserve army of labor |

exacerbated by increasing precarity, the global availability of workers, the international division of labor and the reserve army of labor. The competition appears accentuated in relation to one's position within the labor market in the Global North and Global South, not immune to racialized and gendered dimensions and capital's race to the bottom. In comparison with what are regarded as traditional workplaces, web-based workers could be assumed as having fewer bonds and less power within their (digital) space – which is further explored in the next chapter.

From the premises of anonymity on MTurk and production of data largely for the sake of machine-learning algorithms to the encroachment of labor beyond temporal and spatial limits, MTurk leaves workers estranged and atomized across all dimensions (Table 8.1). The thousands of workers laboring from behind their screen are reminiscent of the 18th-century Mechanical Turk, rendered invisible in the webs of the algorithms. This investigation of alienation on MTurk reflects the evolving nature of capitalism, by which exploitation takes on new dimensions through technological development to the benefit of capital. While capital dodges regulation, minimum working conditions and wages, costs are shifted onto the shoulders of globally dispersed and competing workers denied their classification as workers altogether.

9

# Instrumentalizing Technology: Digital Solidarity with and among MTurk Workers

Just as not all Amazon warehouse workers are compliant and some may resist in different ways, so it is important not just to study the alienation of MTurk workers but also how they may organize. They too are exposed to different relative and general capitalist conditions that may affect their class consciousness – though it is a process that is complicated for MTurk workers. While the labor process can bring about the social organization of workers, the nature of the platform and the nature of the work rupture this very process. The division of labor, which both alienates and in contradictory fashion brings about their cooperation, is obstructed as spatially and temporally displaced web-based workers do not assemble or interact within a physical or same digital space on the platform. Second, the gig nature of the work ensures workers labor on each task isolated from one another, further atomizing them from their collective labor and from an understanding of the overall labor process. The social organization of workers is further inhibited by their geographical dispersal across the Global North and Global South with different class-based, gendered and racialized dimensions, exposing them to different political–economic conditions, industrial relations, labor histories and organization. Workers are not necessarily confronted with identical working realities and substantially differ in demographics from age and sex to educational background. Given, however, the general capitalist conditions, it can be assumed that MTurk workers are conscious of the precarious labor market, the international division and the reserve army of labor. When delving into the agency of MTurk workers, it is important to bear in mind that they do not labor outside of material conditions but are located within time and space. As one worker notes, "We are real people with real needs trying to make a living."

If class consciousness is understood as a process and not a dichotomy, then the investigation of MTurk workers demonstrates certain indications of common class interests – though, as Marx writes, a class in itself is not yet a class for itself. Workers are conscious of the capital–labor relation mediated by the platform regardless of their motivation to labor on MTurk. As my analysis of the power resources demonstrates, workers in my surveys implicitly and even explicitly reject Amazon's assigned classification of independent contractor as stated in the Participation Agreement and identify instead as a worker or a 'Turker' (MTurk worker). As they recognize themselves as workers, they perceive capital twice: once as Amazon, the platform mediator, setting the general terms and conditions for the digital labor market that could set a minimum wage, and once as the requester who sets the concrete working conditions for the Human Intelligence Task (HIT).

I look at class interests further in my coming analysis, but many workers appear aware of the unbalanced power relation between them and capital, characterized by opacity, invisibility and lack of communication. Contrary to the surveyed workers who describe the work as fun, others critique their alienating working conditions as "demeaning, low-paying" or "exhausting, frustrating, and time-consuming". A main concern is the absence of a guaranteed living wage, as one worker puts it: "We are taking time out of our days and using our own equipment. If you brought workers into a computer lab to do the same work, you would end up having to pay much more." While workers may attribute positive adjectives and appreciate MTurk as an additional source of income, they may still be conscious of the exploitation on MTurk. To summarize this experience, another worker states:

> MTurk is like a roller coaster. It has its ups and downs, highs and lows. There are moments of frustration and moments of joy and fulfillment. Every day can be a new learning experience. I do feel replaceable and interchangeable at times. But all work tends to have that same vibe. I would say I see myself as a faceless cog in a machine when using MTurk. I am my worker ID number.

While merely focusing on alienation paints an image of submissive workers laboring in their individualistic virtual cubicle, the discussion of their power resources is integral in detecting instances across the Internet in which workers form solidarity within their own collectivities. It is important to approach this within the bounds in which MTurk workers labor, which tend to be less emancipatory, given their material and precarious conditions, and more reformist, aiming at improving working conditions, given their dependence on MTurk for income. When confronted with my survey question, "Would you rather see it [MTurk] being improved or replaced?", workers unanimously responded with "improved". Second, it is important to conceptualize different forms of collective action and resistance beyond traditional understandings of unions and national responses. Just as work is not traditionally organized here, so too workers express themselves in ways that would not have been possible a few decades ago. The specific organization of platform and wider political–economic, social and technological conditions translate into obstacles, but also possible opportunities, for workers. Though their hands are tied on MTurk, workers navigate and in varying ways reclaim the very infrastructure of the Internet, by which they are exploited, to create spaces for collective expressions and solidarity (Table 9.1). In this regard the very technology that alienates workers, disciplines them and impedes their collective organization can be empowering when instrumentalized and repurposed by workers according to their interests. Studying the case of the MTurk workers, who form part of the ever-growing gig economy, can shed light on the repercussions of precarization for their agency within and beyond the platform economy, as well as potentialities for collective organization.

**Table 9.1:** Power resources of MTurk workers vis-à-vis inimical conditions

| | **Inimical political–economic and technological conditions** | **Workers' expressions and manifestations of powers** |
|---|---|---|
| **Structural power** | • No physical workplace<br>• International reserve army of labor<br>• Precarious labor as 'independent contractor' outside of industrial relations | • Shared class position and interests<br>• Transnational, geographically and temporally dispersed workforce<br>• Possibilities through Internet |
| **Associational power** | • Workforce is anonymous<br>• No physical representation or financial/ organizational resources<br>• Not bound by any industrial relations | Not in the traditional sense:<br>• Internet used by workers to organize<br>• Workers' Forums, Turkopticon, Dynamo, Daemo, Fair Crowd Work |
| **Institutional power** | • Right to organize and collectively bargain denied based on status<br>• Who represents the employer/ capital?<br>• Question of legal jurisdiction, lack of applicability of industrial relations | Largely non-existent with efforts to evaluate and regulate platforms:<br>• Frankfurt Paper<br>• FairWork Foundation<br>• European Commission's proposed directive |
| **Societal power** | • Workers are invisible to society, laboring as artificial artificial intelligence | Growing discursive power through academics and media<br>Growing coalitional power through academics, unions, organizations |

## The structural power of MTurk workers

When we contextualize MTurk workers within their political–economic and technological conditions in relation to the organization of the platform, it presents at first a rather grim picture in terms of their marketplace and workplace power. Yet MTurk workers demonstrate that these very conditions, which can prove to be obstacles, can be a source of power when instrumentalized by them.

The weak marketplace power of MTurk workers is bound to the ever-growing supply of labor on the digital outsourcing market, which has only further magnified with COVID-19 and the larger shift to the 'digital' (Kassem, 2022). As one worker notes, "MTurk is all about supply and demand"; another states that "[t]he pandemic has made [M]Turk more competitive". The Internet, instrumentalized to digitally mediate labor, reproduces an international division of labor, overlapping with "racialized and gendered marginality and Internet based labor in the Global South" (Casilli, 2017: 3940). Unlike macrotasking platforms for specialized skills for larger projects such as graphic design, microtasking platforms like MTurk are integral to what is considered a low-skilled digital market. This market merely necessitates "human judgment and intelligence". As MTurk states, "[a]nyone can submit virtually any task that can be completed using a computing device connected to the Internet."[1] The entry requirements to this gig labor market are essentially reduced to being a human able to connect to the platform by accessing a device once MTurk approves your account. While the piecework nature ensures that capital does not need to invest in the people it hires, the web-based nature of the platform ensures that an ever-growing number of workers can compete on the virtual labor market within the race to the bottom.

These requirements may be regarded as minimal, especially in the Global North, but one should bear in mind that the nature of work as 'independent contractors' shifts the costs of a stable Internet connection and device onto the workers. There are also additional costs associated with laboring from home such as electricity costs or different ones if laboring from a café. Yet the relatively lower barrier to this labor market opens the door to a global workforce, a door one could regard as furthering the deskilling of workers, considering that these workers generally hold a higher level in education, from university degrees or some exposure to college. In relative terms more 'crowdworkers' hold a postgraduate and college degree in the Global South, amounting to 72 percent, while this number is 48 percent in the Global North. Only 12 percent in the Global South and 19 percent in the Global North hold only a high school diploma or lower qualification (Berg et al, 2018; Berg and Rani, 2021).

In the case of MTurk, as only workers in the US and India (for now) receive their piece-wages in their bank accounts, it comes as no surprise that studies show the majority of workers as located in these two countries. This is reflective of an imperialist asymmetric relationship of power in which the Global South, such as the Philippines or India, provides labor for the Global North, such as the US, Canada, UK and Australia, because the former is cheaper to hire (Graham et al, 2017; Difallah et al, 2018). This general shift to web-based digital labor platforms has been accelerated by the pandemic, where online tasks initially declined but picked up as more capital shifted work online. In the process, the pool of workers grew as both inactive workers and new ones flocked to such digital labor platforms for additional piece-wages (Simonite, 2020; Stephany et al, 2020; Kassem, 2022). These factors ultimately reflect the precarious conditions in the labor market and political–economic and technological conditions pushing such workers, considered in the labor market as 'skillful' to accept 'low-skilled' work – ultimately weakening their marketplace power.

The web-based piecework nature also diminishes the workplace power of workers. Because of the minimal entry requirements and the precarious conditions, MTurk is characterized by its revolving door of workers. A leading researcher on MTurk demographics, Panos Ipeirotis (2018), estimates that half of the entire worker's population changes on average every 12 to 18 months. As quickly as one can join the platform, one can leave it willingly or unwillingly by being deleted or blacklisted. While some workers may just labor on it for few days or weeks, others labor on it for months and years. A workforce that is temporally in flux, changing and dispersed globally poses direct challenges for its organization and mobilization. If "[a]s a general rule, workers cannot co-operate without being brought together" (Marx, 1977: 447), then both the nature of MTurk's work and the nature of the platform fundamentally inhibit the socialization of labor and impede cooperation. MTurk renders workers invisible not just from capital but also from each other as they log on their own Application Programming Interface behind their screens. It is difficult to know who is on the platform, let alone to coordinate, organize and mobilize. Unlike large-scale industry, which historically brings workers together, the decentralized Internet isolates workers from each other and from those employing them.

While the cooperation of MTurk workers is fundamentally disrupted by the nature of the platform, the nature of the work leaves them vulnerable to the dictates of the market and in fear of unionizing and organizing. Historically, time-wage laborers have been the focus of organized labor. In contrast, what is considered in capitalist economy 'unskilled' piece-laboring and contracted laboring escaped regulations time and time again, becoming an additional way for capital to exploit workers, who bear the cost of flexibility. The technological and political-economic conditions of the platform economy, and of the gig economy more specifically, allow it to reproduce this trend of casualization in the labor market, which denies workers their social rights, benefits, protection and insurance. Workers may thus fear the consequences of collective action for better working conditions.

While this may be regarded to "drive the requesters away" by some workers, there is also a fear among others of "Amazon closing the platform" and workers being replaced, undercut and 're-outsourced' through the virtual revolving door of global precarious labor. MTurk appears designed to exclude ethical concerns from its capital–labor relations, all while requesters "see themselves as builders of innovative technologies, rather than employers concerned with working conditions" (Irani and Silberman, 2013: 613; Salehi et al, 2015). As the precarious nature of the work is related in this case to the digital labor platform's web-based nature, MTurk can bypass and operate outside of any national contexts governed by laws, industrial relations, certain bargaining powers and protections. The Internet allows "digital work platforms and practices to be presented as not just unregulated, but also unregulatable" and to escape any accountability (Graham et al, 2017: 153). Accordingly, the organization of the platform weakens both the marketplace and the workplace power of MTurk workers.

The contrasting political–economic and technological conditions of MTurk make historically possible smaller acts of resistance almost impossible to detect and identify. The platform's web-based nature allows for micro-surveillance of the entire labor process as algorithms come to replace the social eye of management and assume the task of tracking, rewarding, disciplining and punishing workers. This is coupled with the gig nature, which limits any opportunities to reduce productivity to disrupt the circuit of capital by slowing down, as the micro-surveillance ensures workers are only possibly paid if the task is submitted within the allotted time. Reducing the productivity would mean a lower approval rating, limiting in turn accessible tasks. Other acts of resistance such as providing incorrect answers for tasks would be quickly filtered manually or by algorithmic tests for correct answers, which would further reject the task and payment. It would equally not benefit the worker or have disruptive force if they left the platform completely, considering how interchangeable workers are and the labor surplus on the digital labor market (Irani and Silberman, 2013). If fundamental acts of individual resistance related to productivity are largely eliminated, so too are the possibilities of resisting by distancing from, for instance, the work culture. This directly results from MTurk's nature of work that does not consider workers as part of a collective workforce. MTurk's platform organization appears as directly hindering historically important individual acts of resistance, emphasizing the necessity for collective acts.

With a bleak workplace and marketplace power and in the absence of individual forms of resistance, it becomes difficult to conceive how MTurk workers can collectively struggle to instrumentalize what is traditionally regarded as location-based industrial action and disruptive power based on solidarity across geographical zones (Graham et al, 2017; Vandaele, 2018). Instead of dismissing possibilities and understanding the conditions fatalistically, it is important to reconceptualize resistance beyond the parameters needed to navigate the inimical conditions. By looking more closely, it appears that MTurk workers recognize their shared class position, first, through solidarity for and with fellow workers, and second, in opposition to capital by seeking an improvement in their working conditions – whether they do so implicitly or explicitly. Despite the isolating and alienating conditions, some MTurk workers perceive themselves as "part of a workforce and can communicate with other[s]" to "help one another". MTurk workers recognize that requesters not only hold full intellectual property over labor products but also determine working time, piece-wages and ultimately whether to pay these.

Although the MTurk platform allows workers to contact the requester, these are not required by Amazon to respond. Meanwhile workers cannot pursue any legal action against them. This frustration projects itself onto the platform mediator, Amazon, who is disguised behind the veil of flexibility in order not to assume any responsibility. According to some workers, Amazon "simply ignor[es] the fact that without workers, nothing would be done", and it "will take requesters' money but not manage, oversee, or mediate the problems and injustices on their site" (Irani and Silberman, 2013: 615). Without overromanticizing and overstating the class consciousness of all MTurk workers, we can observe a degree of collective interests among them to improve the working conditions of the gig platform despite the competitive nature of the digital labor market. This expresses itself in their associational power through various manifestations of solidarity despite inimical material conditions within their own spaces.

Unlike requesters, who may be geographically concentrated, MTurk workers are dispersed and clearly outnumber requesters, though it proves difficult to obtain up-to-date numbers as these are not directly tracked. Already prior to the pandemic, Amazon had listed that "500,000 Workers in 190 countries" labor on the platform.[2] Although researchers in 2018 argued that the number may be more accurately around 100,000–200,000, Ipeirotis has estimated that around 2,000–5,000 workers are active in any one moment on MTurk, amounting to 10,000–25,000 full-time workers (Difallah et al, 2018; Ipeirotis, 2018). Considering that at least half of workers do not work full-time, the total number can be assumed to be higher – especially in light of COVID-19, when more workers may have turned to MTurk during times of lockdown and remote work (Kassem, 2022). An application named OTTO by the worker forum Our Hit Stop, which as a Chrome extension helps workers find higher-paying HITs to match their criteria and pay, detected a 20–30 percent increase in user memberships (Simonite, 2020). This can be understood as reflecting higher activity on MTurk itself. A larger and growing MTurk workforce, resulting from the platform organization, can dialectically become the source of their workplace power even if it does not manifest itself in direct industrial action.

The hostile conditions within both the organization of the labor process and the larger workings of the platform severely limit the disruptive power foundational to structural power. Virtual picket lines are in that regard difficult to coordinate and to imagine and the withdrawal of labor would likely not have any impact. Thus it is helpful to think of the agency of these workers as taking on alternative appearances within certain parameters, thereby neither equating it to the traditional appearances of the four power resources but also not dismissing activity and potentialities altogether. While workers cannot convene on MTurk, the Internet can be used to coordinate collective action through its decentralized nature connecting these very workers from across the world. It is important to remember that "it is not the digital infrastructure – the digital means by which firms hire workers and workers find work – that is exploitative, but rather, the way it is governed and organised" (Ettlinger, 2017: 30). Understanding the current capitalist moment dialectically, historically and holistically also entails rethinking the ways by which we conceptualize workers, their organization and resistance.

## The associational power of MTurk workers

MTurk's platform organization and wider context severely complicate more traditional understandings of associations and call instead for an analysis of alternative forms. While MTurk's web-based nature limits the possibilities for anonymized workers to interact, communicate and form associations and collectives through the platform itself, its gig nature impacts their physical representation and organization through traditional unions when workers are considered independent contractors. This is complicated by MTurk's virtual revolving door of workers, who come and go and may also be laboring on multiple platforms simultaneously. Unions appear to have only recently developed an interest in organizing gig workers at all, recognizing that the gig economy risks normalizing precarious conditions in the name of flexibility, thereby threatening to retract previously acquired rights by organized labor (Berg and De Stefano, 2017; Harmon and Silberman, 2019). Workers may lack the time, financial, organizational and technical resources to initiate such efforts.

An additional obstacle to forming associations in the traditional sense, referring here to unions, comes from the workers themselves, who do not identify with traditional unions and are, in fact, quite critical of them. Given the dynamics, discussed above, workers are often uninterested and consider unions "inherently impractical in this environment" (Salehi et al, 2015: 1624). When asked in my survey whether workers would consider joining a union, interestingly enough more workers answered 'No' prior to the pandemic. One could speculate that this is affected by the fact that these surveys were two years apart or by the larger more precarious environment amidst the pandemic in which workers more generally regard unions as providing protection. It would require though a larger investigative effort and surveys to understand this further and grasp possible changing perceptions of unions in the (digital) labor market. In the specific case of my surveys, in both rounds it is evident, however, that a large portion of these workers perceive unions as posing a direct threat to their flexibility and even being inimical to digital laboring. One worker went so far as to state:

> I have no need for the protections of benefits provided by a union. Anything that erodes my ability to work and act independently is an impedance and I will not be involved in it. I make far more than the average worker and have no interest in things like collective bargaining for fair wages for inane tasks like receipt transcriptions and the usual mind-numbing, ridiculously low paying tasks that the majority of workers toil away at daily.

While such statements appear individualistically oriented and portray unions as largely "unnecessary", diverting time away from working, for others there is a fear of "getting banned" from MTurk altogether for joining a union. There appears therefore a degree of mistrust toward unions, an understanding that these do not represent those who labor digitally in the 21st century even if some workers recognize some of the benefits that could be gained. A rejection of unions by such workers should not be equated to an absence of collective interests, but instead needs to redirect the attention to how MTurk workers identify their own bottom-up structures through which they form collectivities and solidarities, and how they consequently may not see additional benefits from joining a top-down union.

Workers integrate the Internet, by which their labor relations are organized, into their struggle to organize amongst each other. Initiatives range from creating tools for workers to rate and review requesters through Turkopticon and organizing through forums, to former 'quasi-unions', such as Dynamo, and some attempts by unions to support workers, such as Fair Crowd Work. The browser extension Turkopticon was developed by scholars Irani and Silberman (2013) seeking to strengthen the position of workers and their common interests. Turkopticon aims implicitly, if not explicitly, to counter the workforce's alienation, invisibility and individualization and instead to coordinate action, build solidarity and mobilize on the platform. Its function is reflected in its name, a play on MTurk and Michel Foucault's analysis of Bentham's concept of the panopticon (Foucault, 1995). The panopticon refers to a specific kind of prison system with a central tower allowing the prison guard to watch prisoners without them seeing the guard. This places prisoners effectively under constant surveillance, with the result that they self-discipline.

Rather than surveilling MTurk's workers, Turkopticon turns the panopticon around to allow workers to review and rate requesters (Ettlinger, 2017).

Considering the disparity and asymmetrical power relationship between workers and requesters, Turkopticon is an essential tool for workers. By posting MTurk surveys asking workers to formulate a "Worker's Bill of Rights", Irani and Silberman were able to identify workers' central concerns and interests to ultimately review according to *communicativity* with requesters, *generosity* in piece-wages relative to working time, *fairness* of requesters in evaluating tasks and *promptness* of payment. By partially obscuring the email addresses of workers, they protected them from retaliation. Turkopticon was, therefore, created as "a means of association people whose common cause was their work on AMT [MTurk] but who lack the technical skills to build infrastructures of assembly" (Irani and Silberman, 2013: 616). While workers do not directly challenge Amazon or requesters on Turkopticon, it offers them a way to resist which (re)configures the power relationship. Workers are able to review those who discipline them with an extensive reach across the workforce. These reviews, accompanied by comments, are made available to workers who can directly look up a specific requester. They could be regarded as acts of solidarity, given the common interest to spare other workers requesters likely to reject tasks and deny piece-wages. In the same manner, they direct workers to those likely to pay (higher) piece-wages. Workers thereby counter the de facto normalization of wage theft on MTurk.

Turkopticon is known to and used by many workers, thereby building on the far-reaching geographical reach of the structural power afforded by the web-based nature of platform. As of April 2018, over 60,000 requesters were evaluated by 430,000 workers' reviews (Berg et al, 2018). Because this number is connected to the users on MTurk, it is bound to have increased in recent years during the pandemic as workers continue to turn to Turkopticon (Kassem, 2022). These reviews are crucial because they directly relate not just to piece-wages, but also a worker's approval rating and, therefore, to future access to microtasks and piece-wages. One worker notes: "If I had to [give] one tip to a beginner[,] it would be to check the requester and their acceptance rate [rather] than the pay." Although MTurk workers did not create the infrastructure of Turkopticon itself, it cannot be understood without their participation. Far from being a top-down approach to organizing workers, workers have been at its core: from relying on them for its creation to its dependence on the continued mobilization of their structural power. It can only sustain itself through the continuous reviews and continuous use *by* workers. Though it legitimizes MTurk's existence rather than emancipating workers, it offers "workers a way to dissent, holding requesters accountable and offering one another mutual aid" (Irani and Silberman, 2013: 614). It has become an essential tool which workers have come to rely on, creating a sense of community for them.

Turkopticon is not the only digital space where workers create solidarity and organize collectively. Among the most central platforms and forums for communication are Reddit and subreddit threads with specific topics (see: /r/TurkerNation, /r/mturk, /r/HITsWorthTurkingFor, r/mturkgrind). As such, workers also make use of already existing platforms to create their own spaces for association, using also Facebook or WhatsApp groups and chats. Additional useful platforms include the once famous Turker Nation, which created its own subreddit and Slack Channel with 24/7 chat communications. But MTurk workers have also established new platforms, such as MTurk Forum Turkerview or Our Hit Stop. Workers essentially use the decentralized structure of the Internet to interact, exchange perspectives on the nature of work and share their subjective experiences to counter the opacity of the platform and become "part of a community of fellow workers". Workers may ask specific questions and generally advise new workers, who must initially labor at low-paying tasks, on difficulties and obstacles. These forums can provide structures of support, information and knowledge exchange on how to navigate the platform and find higher-paying HITs or which requesters are prone to denying payment. In some cases, workers even engage in smaller-scale collective actions to raise funds for fellow workers in times of need (Martin et al, 2014; Salehi et al, 2015). As many workers join MTurk precisely because of recommendations by friends and family or come across it in these forums and online searches, they tend already to have an existing knowledge of navigating such spaces for online communities or encounter these relatively quickly. Such efforts demonstrate how members of an invisible, atomized and alienated workforce can become visible to one another.

In contrast, the 'quasi-union' platform of Dynamo sought to push solidarities into collective action aimed at more directly challenging and confronting MTurk and requesters. Its creators, who had been both requesters and workers on MTurk, investigated the barriers to collective action for web-based labor in light of the absence of face-to-face interactions and a decision-making and -enforcing body. Bearing in mind the distrust of MTurk workers toward unions, Dynamo was created as an alternative digital space to allow workers to mobilize around issues they deemed important. Workers could communicate through pseudonyms within what was meant to be a trusting environment and pitch ideas within 140 characters to be voted up or down by others. With 25 votes an idea could become a campaign to be discussed, disseminated and possibly acted upon. Rather than gaining the attention of all MTurk workers, the goal here was to attract an active group of workers to become an action-oriented alternative to unions. Compared with Turkopticon, six months after its creation a lower number of 470 workers had registered along with 5,800 visitors. The number of views had amounted, however, to more than 32,000 (Salehi et al, 2015). Though it no longer appears to be active, Dynamo is a notable attempt to grasp additional possibilities when the virtual picket line and withdrawal of labor through the mobilization of workplace power become severely complicated.

Among the alternative collective efforts was, for instance, the idea of creating a worker-run alternative to MTurk (such as the initially beta-launched Daemo). These are similar to what Scholz (2016) highlights as platform cooperatives, meaning platforms run by the workers themselves. These may, however, be more difficult and less successful for web-based labor than location-based labor, given that work can continue to be outsourced elsewhere in the world. There are nonetheless two specific Dynamo ideas worth mentioning that turned into larger campaigns. The first was the creation of "Guidelines for Academic Requesters", consisting of ethical research guidelines, including fair wages, and respect, for MTurk workers.[3] This is important in view of the wide use of MTurk by academic communities and the implied ethical concerns. In contrast, in the "Letter Writing Campaign", meant for Bezos, workers aimed to move away from their media portrayal as parts of a machine and instead to humanize themselves in order to be treated fairly (Harris, 2014). This eventually played a crucial role in Indian workers receiving wages in the form not (as previously) of Amazon gift certificates but of bank transfers (Reese and Heath, 2016). Dynamo's associational power dwindled away, however, as Amazon shut down the account from which tasks were posted on MTurk to verify that members were indeed MTurk workers. However, Dynamo was not just meant to create an associative space, something in and of itself crucial for web-based workers, but also showed how collective organization and action can take place despite digital challenges and the gig nature of the work.

As workers assume their associational power through digital spaces, unions appear to be increasingly grasping the importance of organizing these workers in view of current debates on digitalization, the future of work and gig economy. Given that increasing economic inequalities relate to the bargaining power of workers, it is vital for unions to turn their attention to these workers before essential rights struggled for by previous labor movements disappear altogether. A concrete transnational effort of unions is exemplified by Fair Crowd Work – a project of the German union IG Metall in collaboration with the Austrian Trade Union Confederation, the Austrian Chamber of Labor and the Swedish Unionen. It supports workers on web-based digital labor platforms, such as MTurk, Upwork or Clickworker, through informative sections on rights and unions by creating an overview of these platforms. Allowing for a side-by-side comparison of their working conditions, each section expands to one on background information, one of workers' reviews along a five-star system and one reviewing official Terms of Service by union lawyers.[4] Fair Crowd Work seems more like a portal and to be less interactive than Turkopticon,

Dynamo and MTurk worker forums. Although it is a product of unions, the unions do not speak for the workers but instead utilize financial and organizational resources to support them and raise awareness. It, therefore, serves not merely as a supporting pillar to the associational power of workers but also, as stated later, the societal power.

Consequently, it is apparent that MTurk's specific platform organization extends new challenges to the associational power of workers, confronting them with a terrain of working conditions and inimical conditions quite different from the terrain of traditionally employed and location-based workers. While workers have been largely ignored by unions for some time, these are becoming increasingly important to organize as the gig economy continues to expand, both in location- and web-based contexts, where "the workers themselves do not understand what rights they have left" (Dewhurst, 2017: 23). One could argue that this is increasingly changing with the growing labor organization and efforts of platform workers and, of relevance here, gig workers as highlighted in Chapter 11. MTurk workers have then been among those who have instrumentalized the digital terrain in forming their own collectivities for their interests and offering solidarity and hopes of collective action, crucial to understanding contemporary labor activity and organization. It is important to note that these spaces for associations and collectivities lack one fundamental right usually granted to unions, namely, the right to collectively bargain, as the next section outlines. Rather than emphasizing one form of associational power over the other, here alternative versus traditional, it is important then to underline how these complement each other, as "labor advocates need to adopt new strategies to ensure that the 21st century digital economy does not return labor markets to the conditions of the 19th century" (Hill, 2018).

## The institutional power of MTurk workers

If associational power is traditionally expressed via unionization, then institutional power is the outcome of capital–labor concessions such as collective bargaining and works councils. With this in mind, it is clear that institutional power is incompatible with web-based piece laboring in its current form, as such a power is not just weak but largely nonexistent for MTurk workers. It is important to underline initial attempts to reclassify these workers, including the most recent 2021 European Commission proposal, which may eventually supplement the associational power of web-based gig workers in the future and in the long run possibly lead to an institutional power, at least for some of them.

The first main obstacle to institutionalized power arises directly from the questions of which association would represent workers' interests in such web-based digital labor platforms, with whom is one to negotiate and according to whose laws and industrial relations. While the examples of associational power discussed here help workers navigate platforms and build solidarity, they do not represent workers and cannot collectively bargain vis-à-vis Amazon. The classification of MTurk workers as independent contractors directly jeopardizes the right of workers to organize and collectively bargain (De Stefano, 2016; Silberman, 2017). The institutionalized power of workers is further complicated by the question of who represents the employer with whom one is to collectively bargain. Amazon constructs itself as the platform mediator and not as the employer of workers – while requesters only hire workers per task as independent contractors. Interestingly enough, the majority of workers in my surveys understood Amazon and not the requester as the employer, perhaps precisely as the former is the platform mediator and would thereby have the right to set the conditions, although this would jeopardize its business model. Amazon does not dictate specific conditions, such as setting an hourly wage, to requesters. The latter do, however, play a crucial role in gig work, exposing MTurk workers to different conditions depending on the nature of task and requester. Essentially, this also implies that workers have several requesters as employers.

The obscurity of the employer especially on web-based platforms proves to be a drawback, as "[u]nions cannot collectively bargain with an algorithm, they can't appeal to a platform, and they can't negotiate with an equation" (Gearhart, 2017: 13). However, even with the presence of a union that could collectively bargain with Amazon or a requester, the web-based nature of the platform still raises fundamental questions. If institutionalized power is linked to specific industrial relations and a specific context, then which industrial relations apply to the Internet for geographically dispersed capital and workers? How can these be regulated and enforced? With no formal workers' association, capital operates via the 'jurisdictionless Internet', in which no body currently regulates such platforms, proving inimical to the existence of any institutional power.

In the absence of such a legal foundation, it is helpful to recognize efforts to protect workers' rights and possibly regulate capital in the platform economy, which appear to be gaining ground in the last years. In the concrete case of MTurk, the 2016 position paper "Frankfurt Paper on Platform-Based Work" presents an initial attempt at transnational union cooperation that further suggests that various actors, including platforms, workers and policymakers, should work together. It engages with central issues regarding worker status, the unbalanced power relation and the need to comply with national law and international principles. Referring to the "Universal Declaration of Human Rights" and the International Labour Organization's (ILO's) "Declaration of Fundamental Principles and Rights at Work", it emphasizes the right to organize and the right of access to social protections. It also suggests that web-mediated wages should comply with national minimum wages within the worker's jurisdiction (Frankfurt Paper on Platform-Based Work, 2016). Similar points were echoed across the ILO's 2018 report, putting forward a list of criteria to guarantee "decent work" to strengthen workers, underlining the crucial point of reclassification of workers and protection of their rights to association and collective bargaining (Berg et al, 2018). These efforts may translate into strengthening the associational, as well as, potentially extending to the institutional power of platform workers by, for instance, supporting the fair representation of workers or ensuring national minimum wages.

The struggle for fairer working conditions has also been supported by the efforts of Fairwork, which ranks platforms based on desk research and interviews according to five main principles of fair pay, conditions, contracts, management and representation, each containing two thresholds, to score and rank platforms out of ten points. With growing case studies across the Global North and Global South, as well as of cloudwork platforms, including MTurk, as a category in themselves, these efforts can help strengthen the power resources of workers.[5] By evaluating essential facets of their institutional and associational rights, these could possibly lead to platforms improving their working conditions in relation to the rankings.

As gig work on digital labor platforms, both location- and web-based, expands across the EU and risks undoing historically acquired rights, the European Commission proposes a directive along with guidelines to regulate more closely the employment relationship of gig workers and improve their working conditions (COM(2021) 762 final). Given how capital–labor relations are mediated on these platforms and given that less than half of all workers – 45 percent, to be precise – earn a net hourly minimum wage, this directive supports establishing one where nationally possible as well as prioritizing protection from algorithmic management (European Commission, 2021a, 2021b). We had already seen in 2021, crucial rulings in Europe to reclassify gig workers that could be regarded as setting precedents: Uber drivers in the UK (Satariano, 2021) and food delivery workers in Spain (Faus and Carreño, 2021) and the first reclassification case of a Glovo food delivery rider Italy in 2020 (Aloisi, 2021). This proposed directive of the European Commission would go a step further in the range of workers covered: both geographically, as it would apply a set of common EU rules and emphasizes the cooperation of the national level, as well as in terms of the gig work it targets, including web-based workers (Aloisi and De Stefano, 2022; Aloisi and Potocka-Sionek, 2022). These efforts can be regarded then as instrumental steps both in reclassifying workers, a step which has been thus far contradictory to the nature of work, and include digital labor platforms regardless of whether the platform is web- or location-based.

If such efforts materialize and are enforced, these are bound to provide the essential, foundational setting for institutional power. Considering how interrelated power resources are, this would strengthen associational and workplace power as these proposals support workers' labor rights, benefits and protections. All these efforts ultimately highlight that, in a context where the premise of the platform is inimical to institutional power, it is important to create mechanisms and regulations. One should bear in mind, however, that this could accelerate a race to the bottom when it comes to web-based platforms, as these could escape such regulations by more systematically targeting workers located outside of the Global North (should other countries follow suit) and focus on the Global South. It remains to be seen how these efforts may seep over into national contexts where gig work merely joins the precarity of large informal economies and where traditional employment relationships do not constitute the norm for the majority of their populations.

## The societal power of MTurk workers

The broader labor struggle of MTurk workers can be strengthened through the societal power, both in discursive terms through the media and academics, and also in coalitional terms through cooperation across society to build solidarity. The first challenge is rooted in the fact that MTurk workers are rendered invisible to wider society by the nature of the platform. As these workers contribute to data more generally and also powering technology in the form of machine-learning algorithms for artificial intelligence (AI) such platforms mask their human labor behind technological developments. Unlike platform workers in location-based platforms such as Uber, MTurk workers neither interact face-to-face with those who employ them nor are they visible to the public. Thus, unlike Uber, for instance, MTurk can evade the scrutiny of the public for its working conditions and can slip under the radar (Katz, 2017; Gent, 2019). If the workforce is not known to the public and if users interact with the very technology to which MTurk workers contribute without acknowledging their labor or existence, then it makes it difficult to build and mobilize a societal power.

Despite these obstacles, it is apparent that the discursive power of MTurk workers is increasingly growing, as it is tied to all other power resources. For one, the working conditions of workers have become known because of the forums and platforms discussed in relation to the associational power. Similarly, workers created the "Letter Writing Campaign" meant for Bezos on Dynamo to humanize themselves. These stories and experiences of workers – by some regarded as laboring in a "digital sweatshop" (Zittrain, 2009) – continue to be picked up by the media, ranging from the BBC and *New York Times* to *Wired* and *TechRepublic*. Such journalistic work contributes directly to a growing understanding of the workforce behind the screen. This is especially important within our current moment, in which AI becomes more and more relevant and part and parcel of specific debates on the future of work and also wider debates of society. As the media bring the labor realities to the public, it further supports their associational and institutional power by reporting on the efforts to improve their conditions such as Turkopticon and Fair Crowd Work or the newest developments in reclassification in Europe (Brandom, 2013; *The Economist*, 2018).

The discursive power is not just tied to efforts of the media, but academics and researchers appear to have especially played a role. The cheap labor power that attracted academic and research communities to MTurk for surveys has also attracted critical engagement with MTurk's working conditions and supporting workers' associational and potential institutional power. Such examples range from Turkopticon, the direct product of engaged academics Irani and Silberman and Fair Crowd Work to which Silberman has contributed, to Fairwork, which originated from the Oxford Internet Institute and the growing international collaborations. These continue to expand in the context of COVID-19, where Savage and Jarrahi (2020) created system architecture as a Chrome extension meant to support location-based gig workers that navigated to web-based gig laboring given the changing dynamics of the labor market during the pandemic. Based on 'Solidarity Brokers' meant to efficiently optimize support among workers through machine-learning algorithms via a plugin, workers can leave micro-advice for each other to be later up- or downvoted based on usefulness (Kassem, 2022). Thus, the support coming from the research and academic community continues to evolve alongside political–economic and technological conditions. The growing research on platform cooperatives and institutes, such as the New School's Institute for the Cooperative Digital Economy or the Platform Cooperativism Consortium, can indirectly complement the societal power by presenting what fairer conditions in cooperatives look like in contrast to the capitalist platform economy.[6] There is an ever-growing scholarly effort not just to humanize but also to support workers through alternative platforms and potentially push for regulation of the platform economy.

The societal power is also bound to the coalitional power which grows out of these networked and collaborative efforts with academics and researchers, the ILO, unions, journalists, policymakers and regulators. However, possible concrete regulation of the platform economy, as sketched out, does not just need the attention of policymakers and legislators, as seen through Fair Crowd Work, but also needs to be enforced to ultimately strengthen labor's position (Silberman, 2017). While different members of society have helped formulate essential criteria for a fairer gig economy, it is up to regulators and policy makers to follow through with these. We have seen some efforts, ranging from court rulings in the UK, Spain and Italy to the European Commission's most recent proposed directive on platform work. It is yet to be seen how these are implemented and enforced both by national actors and possibly by civil society and what their possible impact and implications will be for web-based gig workers. Consequently, while the very premise of web-based labor platforms is one that mystifies workers to themselves, capital and society, these instances illustrate growing efforts within society to counter these in view of the rate at which more generally gig labor is growing. Various actors appear to play a different role for the societal power and larger labor struggle.

These workers of MTurk, meant to function in a way similar to the Mechanical Turk of the 18th century, have indeed become integral to digital outsourcing as well as the development of AI through the production of an immense wealth of data. The nature of the platform and of the work fundamentally rupture cooperation between workers as they labor atomistically and are managed by algorithms across the virtual assembly line. At first the political–economic and technological conditions manifested in the platform's organization appear to obstruct all socialization among workers and pose material obstacles to their power resources. Although web-based digital labor platforms fulfill "the neoliberal fantasy of a dispersed, decontextualised, deterritorialised, and Taylorised global labour market" (Ettlinger, 2017: 30), it appears that workers – with different degrees of class consciousness – instrumentalize the very infrastructure by which they are alienated and anonymized from one another.

Despite a weak marketplace and workplace power, they have grasped alternative spaces of online associations and collectivities beyond traditional unions to form solidarity and potentially dissent. Given the novelty of such platforms within the capitalist trajectory, the agency of workers must also be conceived of in novel ways. This potential for associational power is not accompanied, however, by an institutional power for MTurk workers, as their precarious status leaves them outside of any governing legal and industrial relations framework. We are, however, potentially seeing initial efforts to more generally reclassify workers and to improve their condition, thereby also strengthening their societal power. As technology becomes integral to the foundation of the platform economy and increasingly to contemporary capitalism, it is crucial to grasp the new ways by which workers are organizing themselves precisely by instrumentalizing that very technology without abstracting them from the material context to which they are bound.

10

# Alienation across Amazon and the Platform Economy

When looking at the two Amazon platforms, it appears that the platform economy may contain some peculiarities, but ultimately (re)produces current capitalist trends towards algorithmic management of labor processes, hypertaylorization of work, fragmentation of the workforce and precarization of the labor market. The Amazon warehouses illustrate, on the one hand, the historical continuation of traditional time-wage laboring, in which the workforce is assembled in the same physical space within the platform economy, sharing similarities to other platforms such as Facebook and Google. The case of MTurk, on the other hand, sheds light on a different historical continuation, namely of piecework adopted by capital into the new dimension of the digital. While even time-wage laboring platforms such as Facebook and Google are known to contract labor and depend on ghost work of entities such as MTurk, the MTurk case is meant, first and foremost, to give insights into the significance of laboring remotely through the web and also of piecework. The gig economy is founded precisely on the latter, constituting an essential part of the platform economy. This chapter compares the two Amazon workforces first in terms of their alienation, before, in the next chapter, looking at their agency. Rather than presenting the platform economy dichotomously as consisting of either location-based time-wage labor or web-based piece-wage labor, this chapter contextualizes the cases in the larger platform economy. It, therefore, also includes location-based gig platforms like Uber.

## Alienation from the labor activity

All platforms, regardless of their function, are characterized by their mediating nature by which they represent capital. While the infrastructure of the Internet is central to this function, capital–labor relations, and the composition of labor, are always bound to material contexts in which they are located. These reflect to differing degrees wider racialized and gendered labor markets and are not abstract to them. While Amazon mediates e-commerce through the circulation of commodities for which it relies on manual labor, MTurk mediates outsourced labor power for digital 'human intelligence' microtasks. Amazon's role as the platform mediator is fundamentally different in this case, however, because of the nature of the work. Workers in Amazon warehouses, like those in some location-based platforms such as Google, Amazon Web Services (AWS) and Facebook, stand in what can be understood as a traditional relationship to their platform mediator. The platform sets general working hours and guarantees them a time-wage, accompanied by rights and benefits. This appears to be more common in first- and second-generation platforms. As capital seeks to increase its profits, it also cuts its spending on labor. It comes as no surprise that, for instance, Google consisted, as of 2019, of 54 percent temps, vendors and contractors (Wong, 2019). Traditional time-wage relations at these platforms should not be understood as devoid of precarious short-term contracts and (sub) contractors, who are not valued equally to directly hired staff, leaving the former stripped of an equal wage, rights and benefits.

In contrast, the reality of MTurk workers is characterized by piecework and these workers are by default classified as independent contractors who confront capital, first, as the platform mediator and, second, as the requester of the task. This capital–labor relation is advantageous for capital, saving on costs by hyperoutsourcing most of the constant and variable capital to the worker. This allows capital, both Amazon and requester, to escape any responsibility from being the employer, de facto stripping workers of benefits and labor rights attained by previous labor movements. MTurk forms part of the gig economy as a digital labor platform of the second generation. Third-generation location-based platforms, which have expanded existing kinds of digital labor platforms, such as Uber and Deliveroo are, however, also part and parcel of the gig economy. They have become renowned for this employment relationship.[1] The nature of such work reflects the larger neoliberal trend towards precarization of the labor market (Collier et al, 2017). It is important to note that labor on these platforms, like the two Amazon case studies, is not immune to the wider racialized and gendered dimensions of the labor market, but is in fact a reflection of it. Migration and migrant labor play a crucial role in powering the gig economy and such third generation platforms (Van Doorn, 2017; Van Doorn and Vijay, 2021; Van Doorn et al, 2022). The employment relation and different material contexts pose in turn repercussions for both capital–labor relations and possibilities for resistance. It remains to be seen how the rulings in countries such as the UK, Spain and Italy, as well as the European Commission's proposed directive, may redefine these and the gig economy.

In contrast, the nature of the platform informs the degree to which the worker is aware of their employer and of other workers. While location-based platforms entail a dimension of physical location, the way by which labor and capital confront one another differs. Location-based traditional time workers, such as those in Amazon warehouses, encounter one another and their managers, whereas location-based gig workers, like those of TaskRabbit assembling IKEA furniture, encounter the person requesting and paying their labor power rather than the platform mediator. Unlike the former, location-based gig workers are geographically distributed and do not encounter other workers while laboring their specific task per se (unless for instance a food delivery worker runs into another in a restaurant or on the street). In that regard, location-based gig workers have similarities to web-based workers in terms of the nature of their work which atomizes them in that regard. But they also have at least some similarities to location-based ones because of the same nature of the platform. In contrast, the case of MTurk demonstrates that the configuration of web-based gig platforms removes the possibility of encountering either capital or labor in their physical form, as these are spatially and temporally detached from one another.

While platforms, like all other capital, are founded upon workers' exploitation and alienation from their labor activity, the platform economy appears to be a forerunner in framing these positively. First-generation and some second-generation platforms, with the forerunner of Google, have been hailed for their jobs, widely ranking as the best place to work. Amazon warehouse workers are confronted with their work mantra of "Work hard. Have fun. Make history", while Amazonian work culture constructs a community for workers at the workplace. In contrast, work in the gig economy is glamorized, precisely by framing precarity in terms of 'flexibility' as its biggest selling point. Given the hyperoutsourcing model and fetishization of the labor process, one becomes one's own boss, decides one's own working hours, as demonstrated with the MTurk case. Consequently, the gig economy perversely constructs itself not as alienating, although workers own both most of the constant and the variable capital, but as *empowering* workers. Scholars highlight and critique how the discourse around 'crowdwork' has even gone so far as to frame it as "a 'silver bullet' for development and for fighting poverty", as it presents "opportunities for non-specialists to access the labour market" – especially in the Global South (Berg et al, 2018: 88).

Beneath the positive construction of laboring in the platform economy lies its division of labor and hypertaylorized labor process. While Amazon warehouse workers are subdivided along the circulation line and are pressurized by different Units Per Hour (UPH) rates, MTurk workers form part of a digital production line in which they face competition from global workers. The nature of the platform alienates workers from their labor activity differently, to the extent that Amazon warehouse workers are familiar with the totality of the circulation line, as they can be shifted around. Workers in location-based platforms generally have an understanding of at least part of the production/circulation line, which becomes crucial for their socialization. This also applies to location-based gig workers who labor for digital labor platforms offering services, be it a ride or delivering a product, and are familiar to an extent of the function of their labor. One Deliveroo worker describes their work as "alienating – for example, if you are picking something up from a restaurant because someone is too lazy to walk a minute down the road. ... At times like that you think: what am I doing? That this is like late capitalism" (Khaleeli, 2016). Web-based workers differ here by laboring from behind their screens, unable to grasp the entirety of the production line, while falling under the umbrella of human computation whose labor is meant to appear as a humanless process. This can differ for macrotask platforms when workers accept a project from a certain person or account with a certain degree of contact and exchange. The repercussions of the hypertaylorization process across the platform economy appear then closely related to the nature of the platform and the work.

Intrinsic to its fabric are capital's dependence upon technology for the mediating role of platforms, but also the way technology is instrumentalized for algorithmic management. Workers are alienated from their labor activity by not only performing as machines, but in fact being increasingly supervised and disciplined by them. At the heart of this process is the way by which capital can grasp and translate the productivity rate of a worker in quantitative terms: the UPH rate of the Amazon warehouse workers and approval rating of the MTurk workers. Workers are "monitored and supervised by robots", as a leaked Amazon document from 2019 stated that workers' productivity rate "automatically generates any warnings or terminations regarding quality or productivity without input from supervisors", though according to Amazon those can be overridden by those in supervisory functions (Lecher, 2019). The algorithmically calculated and monitored UPH rate of such warehouse workers is an example of how technology can be used in a location-based platform, in addition to social surveillance by management, to evaluate workers' performances. This is rather unsurprising, given that platforms are not just at the core of technological developments but are also forerunners in their application through the quantification of work and algorithmic management of workers.

This is even more evident in the gig economy, as the exchange of labor and labor activity is exclusively mediated via the Application Programming Interface (API) for both its location- and its web-based laborers. Through an array of tracking processes across their platforms, these workers are essentially quantified (Moore, 2018; Moore and Joyce, 2020). In the case of Uber, algorithms match the closest logged-on driver with a ride requester, giving them 15 seconds to accept the task. The algorithm further calculates the price for the ride, of which a portion represents the driver's piece-wage based on the supply of drivers, demand of rides and fare prices, including surge prices. At a final step of the labor process the driver, like other gig workers, is evaluated through a rating system that essentially ensures competition by tracking the performance of workers. If the average rating of an Uber driver drops below 4.6 out of a possible 5 stars, then their accounts can be deactivated, resulting in de facto termination of the gig worker (Cook, 2015; Lee et al, 2015). Unlike Amazon warehouse workers, who are additionally under the surveillance of their supervisors, location-based gig workers have their entire labor activity structured by algorithms. There have been scandals about how racially and gendered biased algorithms play a role in the (non-) hiring of certain workers – such as Amazon's now dropped sexist Artificial Intelligence (AI) recruitment tool (Dastin, 2018; Bogen, 2019). The gig economy alienates its workers by scrapping the main human personification of capital that hires them and steers the labor activity altogether. Workers can be both hired and fired all by algorithms.

This is pushed to additional limits for web-based workers, especially those completing microtasks like MTurk workers, who have no possibility of encountering the capital that employs them. For those laboring in a largely opaque system in which activity is tracked, tasks approved or rejected by algorithms and productivity measured by approval ratings, human interaction is thereby not just reduced but eliminated altogether. The approval rating, rooted in algorithmic management of the labor process, is instrumentalized to ensure competition and performance pressure among these geographically and temporally distributed gig workers. Other web-based platforms have been reported to surveil every moment of the labor activity. One of Facebook's contracted content moderators states they "have to clock in and clock out even when going to the toilet and explain the reason why they were delayed, which is embarrassing and humiliating", while another highlights that they are only "allowed four or five mistakes a month – a 2% failure rate, 98% quality score" (Gilbert, 2020). Upwork tracks their workers differently, as those opting to be paid by the hour are confronted with its "Work Diary", where the platform takes several screenshots per hour to ensure workers are laboring on the task for the full hour.[2] It also tracks mouse clicks and keystrokes and possibly even takes their photo via a webcam – though workers can deny permission for that. Interestingly enough, workers may reproduce and normalize such surveillance to justify their (higher) hourly wage (Schmidt, 2017). Algorithmic management appears, therefore, to be fundamental to the platform economy and the alienation of workers, though its bounds too differ depending on the organization of the platform.

Leaving some workers feeling like interchangeable cogs, the hypertaylorized division of labor simultaneously structures and fragments the labor activity while producing a hierarchy within and among platforms. First and foremost, both cases of Amazon warehouse workers who circulate commodities as manual labor, as well as MTurk workers to whom work is digitally outsourced, represent what the labor market considers 'low-skilled' labor. These stand in stark contrast to the directly hired engineers and programmers of AWS and Google, who are considered to be 'high-skilled'. These too reflect larger racialized and gendered dynamics in the labor market, though these platforms have aimed to become more diverse.[3] Having said that, the dependence of Amazon's growing e-commerce on manual workers and the dependence of the machine-learning and AI market on (MTurk) workers point to a larger trend toward deskilling where an army of 'low-skilled' workers power the growth of the platform economy. This is only magnified when one considers how so-called low-skilled gig workers, ranging from Uber and Deliveroo to web-based microtask workers, dominate the overall workforce of the platform economy in quantitative terms. Platforms thereby reproduce both a division of labor and hierarchy across its different workers, who are ultimately not all valued equally.

Platforms additionally create a division of labor within their own platform and for workers within the same position. In Amazon warehouses the manual workers called "warehouse associates" are at the bottom of the hierarchy with the leads and various managers in higher and more strategic positions. However, even the warehouse workers find themselves in a hierarchy in their position: quantitatively through productivity rates as some become 'top-performers' and others 'low-performers', and qualitatively based on their different contracts (fixed or temporary contract, contracted labor, seasonal and so on). Google has equally created an "artificial class system" by assigning different colored badges which grant different levels of access: from the white one for full-timers to red for contractors, green for interns and yellow for low-skilled workers who may scan books for Google Books (Barrett, 2011). Such a hierarchy takes on a further dimension for MTurk workers because of their gig nature, where their performance measured by approval rating and possible additional qualifications can make tasks (in)visible for workers. This further impacts platforms such as Airbnb, where the host of the space is evaluated by visitor reviews and can gain titles such as Super Host. Uber drivers are in turn disciplined by the ride requester's rating and their vehicle, which opens up different options from the cheapest and most common ride of UberX to the more expensive luxury cars of UberLUX (Helling, 2022). A fundamental difference between time-wage traditional workers, like Amazon warehouse workers, and gig workers is that the quantified evaluation of their labor activity is not just algorithmically managed but is relevant to finding future gigs. This is only exacerbated by the competing supply of workers.

When it comes to the role of technology in the platform economy, it is important to emphasize how it can come to replace and displace workers. The automation of labor activity can pose a contradiction to the inner workings of capitalism, as it seeks to increase profits by cutting the cost of labor – its source of surplus value. In the case of Amazon's e-commerce, it seeks to automatize its circulation line and realization of surplus value. This would enable it to push productivity even further and potentially do away with workers: from its Amazon Robotics, which simplifies the picking step to its first roll-out of automating the packing step in 2019 (Dastin, 2019). Amazon is not unique, as millions were invested into developing Uber's self-driving cars, a part of its business that it sold in 2020 to the start-up Aurora (Metz and Conger, 2020). While MTurk workers are meant to labor as artificial artificial intelligence, they are essentially contributing to the development of algorithmic management to train AI that may in a general sense come to replace and displace them. MTurk is also not unique to this, as Appen, which acquired Figure 8, formerly Crowdflower, states that it "combines human intelligence from over one million people all over the world with cutting-edge models to create the highest-quality training data for your ML projects".[4] The automatization and fragmentation of labor steps, all under the umbrella of algorithmic management, increasingly characterize the different alienating labor activities of 21st-century capitalism. The specific organization of the platform plays a fundamental role in how this expresses itself in capital–labor relations.

## Alienation from the product of labor

The platform economy is no different from other parts of the larger economy in which laboring can take place in the sphere of production as well as circulation. The appearance of the labor product, closely tied to the previous relation of alienation, varies depending on the function of the platform: advertising through data commodification via Google or Facebook, accommodation via Airbnb, rides via Uber or Lyft or digital laboring via MTurk. To grasp the different ways in which workers confront the labor product, it is constructive to differentiate here first between traditional time-wage location-based platforms and all other platforms on the basis of forming part of the gig economy.

Workers in the platform economy increasingly find their laboring reduced to metrics, where the (im)material products of their laboring confront them as fetishisms. As Amazon warehouse workers circulate labor products, rather than produce them – the nature of this commodity and the social relations by which it was produced become irrelevant. The contact of any one worker to the commodity is only relevant to the extent that it represents one quantitative unit of the UPH rate that needs to be achieved, though this is not uniform within or across warehouses (see the German UPH to Polish UPH). Such a variation according to national labor markets and working conditions is not unique to Amazon warehouse workers and is determined by the material context. Similarly, Facebook content moderators in Europe may have to see 150 pieces of content a day, which are deemed of more graphic nature, while workers in Thailand and the Philippines may have to review 1,000 (Gilbert, 2020). Even though Amazon workers receive a traditional time-wage and are not paid by piece rate, the relation of the worker both to their labor activity and the labor product is reduced to quantitative appearances.

If such time-wage laborers illustrate how the qualitative essence of the product of labor is obscured through its quantitative relation to the worker, this relation is magnified for gig workers. Like Amazon warehouse workers, location-based gig workers are likely to know the use-value of their labor product. For the latter their labor power represents a service – whether it is, for instance, delivering a meal or driving someone to their destination. As independent contractors in the gig economy, workers' subsistence directly relates to the quantity of their labor products and their exchange-value: a Deliveroo workers needs to deliver as many orders as possible, the Uber driver as many rides as possible. How much is labored plays an additional role for drivers such as Uber workers, who use their piece-wages for extra expenses in terms of constant capital to maintain their cars, pay for gas and insurance given the gig's economy hyperoutsourcing model. These piece-wages can drastically change according to the platform. In a *Guardian* article published in 2016, an ex-Uber driver notes how it took a toll on workers when Uber dropped its "fees from £1.30 a mile and 15p a minute to £1 a mile and 10p a minute … Once you minus your expenses, it worked out at about 30p a mile" (Khaleeli, 2016). While platforms continue to develop and change the schemes by which they pay for gigs, this example from 2016 exemplifies what the cost calculation can look like for these workers. This may also differ in national contexts where Uber is more regulated similar to the taxi industry such as Germany or the UK, which has since then ruled to treat its drivers as employees in 2021 who are now entitled to a minimum wage (Satariano, 2021). Having said that, at least until a national minimum wage is applied across platforms and contexts, gig workers continue to be strongly dependent on the number of gigs they can complete whether they receive a gig time-wage or a gig piece-wage.

The alienation from the labor product is magnified for web-based platform workers, as the MTurk case exemplifies. Like location-based gig workers, web-based ones are assigned the status of independent contractors and therefore depend on the number of gigs they complete. While each gig factors into their approval rating and is an additional wage, the latter is never constant or guaranteed since the requester can reject the task while retaining rights over the product. Furthermore, MTurk workers, like other gig workers, bear the cost of the constant capital to compete in the labor market, from the device, Internet connection to any additional training or qualifications beyond the platform. Unlike with location-based workers, the web-based nature of the platform additionally estranges gig workers from the use-value of their labor. While they may be aware of its general nature for largely machine-learning algorithms for AI or for academic studies, the concrete use-value can be unclear because of anonymity and virtually displaced production lines. As digital immaterial labor products, meant to possibly manage and displace them, their labor products appear as devoid of any social relations and human interaction altogether. Thus, while the platform economy is not unique in alienating workers from the products of their labor, it takes on different appearances depending on the nature of work and platform.

## Alienation from species-being

In the discussion on the different realities of platform workers, it is important to point out what appear to be larger capitalist developments and what is particular to platforms. While location-based platforms ensure that work is predominately dependent on a certain location, though emails can nevertheless be checked 24/7, their time-wage nature theoretically defines temporal boundaries for work and thereby also for non-work activities. These platforms may frame the working day as fun, while capitalizing on workers' creativity. Amazon, for one, calculates the working day at the start-meeting and not from the moment of entering the warehouse, while it encourages workers to submit *kaizens*. Continuous rotating shifts, combined with performance and productivity pressures which are difficult to escape, leave workers with little time and energy to pursue activities outside of work. Amazon is not unique in this regard – either in the platform economy or beyond it. Google has become renowned for pushing the working day to its limits by offering workers all sorts of meals, additional activities and services at the workplace. Google, like Amazon, absorbs the creativity of workers by patenting their ideas (Yang, 2017).

What has come as a novelty with the platform economy, however, is the ability to work by logging onto an interface, through which labor is mediated. This is characteristic of all gig work and thus the rest of location-based and web-based platforms. Location-based gig workers may find limits set to their working day: for example, Uber has a 12-hour continuous driving time limit that can only be reset with depending on location, a six to eight hour time break, from the app (Uber Blog, 2018).[5] Because of the gig nature, workers find their working day pushed to additional limits as a result of their dependence on the piece-wage. This precisely defines what the gig economy is about: the unfixing of the temporal bounds of the working day. Within the illusory webs of flexible and autonomous laboring of the gig economy, which promises workers they can labor as much or as little as they want, workers are bound to the desires of the market. They seek work in surge times during which their labor power becomes higher in value given the increased demand, such as for rides. Considering that workers are paid not for the time in which they search for work but solely for the tasks they complete, workers find themselves spending additional time of their day laboring. Given the competition between the supply of workers on these platforms and the precarious situations in which workers find themselves as independent contractors, the worker's day becomes structured by the opportunities to labor, meaning the availability of gigs.

While the piecework nature of the work plays a similar role in estranging MTurk workers, it is magnified because of the nature of the platform. Web-based workers can work not just at any time but also from any place, as long as they have a device and Internet access. Unlike Uber drivers, who must get into the car to labor, MTurk workers present an additional contemporary example of paid labor making it into the confines of the home, a space that has been historically for unpaid reproductive labor. For many, the ability of working from home is embraced by workers who value their ability to choose their working hours and space – which appears to have only intensified in the context of COVID-19. A platform like MTurk has generally proven especially beneficial for those not mobile for health reasons, for marginalized workers who face difficulties in entering the labor market and for workers, especially women and women of color, who must simultaneously undertake care labor while laboring digitally. Like location-based gig workers, web-based workers are not paid for the time they spend undertaking additional qualifications and searching for tasks. Though workers may appear at first to have complete flexibility, they too are bound by the concentration of those seeking digital labor in the Global North. Web-based platforms have both temporally unfixed the working day and spatially unfixed work altogether. Unlike Uber drivers, who compete with other drivers within a physical space of a city, for instance, the digital mediation of MTurk workers translates into a global labor market where competition extends across geographical and temporal zones. The gig economy fetishizes and blurs the line between work and non-work, which cannot be detached from the larger political–economic context.

Finally, the function of the work can further alienate workers. Not only does the stress leave workers mentally and physically exhausted after such laborious days, but it can also seriously interfere with their mental state. While Amazon warehouse workers find it difficult to leave behind the performance pressures experienced at work, MTurk workers may experience trauma related to the content they must review. This leads to some workers suffering from Post-Traumatic Stress Disorder, which has also been expressed by Facebook content moderators, as one has filed a lawsuit in Ireland over the "psychological trauma" resulting from reviewing graphic material (Newton, 2019; Gilbert, 2020). As platforms reproduce generalist capitalist trends to extend the working day, they blur the temporal and spatial limits and confines of work, while some platform work can additionally take a toll on the mental wellbeing of workers and their general fulfillment.

## Alienation from fellow humans

The platform economy demonstrates not only how workers are alienated in their individuality in the 21st century within the labor process and beyond the workplace, but additionally in their collectivity. This is most dominantly, intrinsically, tied to the atomization and fragmentation of workers and their collective consciousness. Location-based platforms that may pay a traditional time-wage, such as Facebook, Google and Amazon, have created a fetishized work culture that creates a sense of community, unity, inclusivity and diversity among workers. Amazon warehouse workers are presented with events, T-shirts and slogans such as "Work hard. Have fun. Make history", while other Amazon employees are presented with their own leadership principles.[6] Platforms construct an image of a diversified workforce, from workers of various racial backgrounds and sexes to military veterans.

The work culture is meant to lift morale and build a sense of community, given the nature of the platform: workers convene within the same location and interact with one another. Yet Amazon is not unique in using its corporate culture to blur the inequalities and material differences between workers, who are hierarchized based on individual performance and contract status. Such a hierarchy also hides behind the veil of Google's work culture: Google been repeatedly judged the best place to work as it offers "freedom to be creative" in a "fun environment" characterized by "true flexibility", "constant innovation", "shared values across organization" with free meals and onsite recreational facilities and services (Forbes Technology Council, 2018). Such work cultures in the platform economy, and beyond it, obscure the very different material realities of workers laboring under the same roof. The extent to which a platform is keen on constructing a work culture characterized by diversity and unity yet rooted in individual metrics and competition, is intrinsically linked to the organization of the platform.

If the gig economy amplifies the alienation of workers across the previous relations, then it needs to be understood as not fragmenting its workforce but as going even a step further. While initial efforts and possible changes are taking place to re-classify them, the status of independent contracts is a de facto denial of the status of the worker. Workers are atomized and left to their individuality with no workforce to turn to. This is generally the case for both the location-based gig workers of Uber (with possible exceptions such as the UK) and the web-based ones of MTurk. While it is difficult for

**Table 10.1:** Comparison of relations of alienation

| | | Differences | | Similarities |
|---|---|---|---|---|
| | | *Amazon warehouse workers* | *MTurk workers* | |
| **Alienation from the labor activity** | ***Nature of platform*** | Visualization of assembly lines and hierarchy | Digital infrastructure: anonymizes capital–labor relation and obscures the assembly line | • Labor activity presented positively<br>• Hypertaylorized assembly line<br>• Algorithmically managed labor process that surveils and disciplines productivity<br>• Division of labor: 'low skilled'<br>• Technology replacing the worker |
| | ***Nature of work*** | Different relationship to capital | • Precarious piece-wage through hyperoutsourcing (gig economy)<br>• Double appearance of capital | |
| **Alienation from the product of labor** | ***Nature of platform*** | Circulation of material products | Production of immaterial digital data; concrete use-value unknown | Commodity fetishism: quantitative character of metrics masks social relations |
| | ***Nature of work*** | Time-wage obscures relation to piecework | Microtasks as gigs | |
| **Alienation from species-being** | ***Nature of platform*** | Absorption of creativity, rotating shifts, performance pressures, limits by workspace | Flexibility hailed, work encroaches into home and dimension of reproductive labor, global competition | • The bounds of working time are extended to different degrees<br>• Different performance pressures and stress beyond the working day<br>• Additional dimension of reproductive labor, though to varying extents |
| | ***Nature of work*** | Temporal limits to the working day/ working hours | Autonomy hailed, working day extended through gig nature and location of capital | |
| **Alienation from fellow humans** | ***Nature of platform*** | Fetishistic Amazonian work culture | Individual and isolating digital nature | Competition ruled by individual metrics |
| | ***Nature of work*** | | No work culture as independent contractor | |

location-based gig workers to identify their co-workers, workers are rendered invisible on web-based platforms such as MTurk, where they labor from their API behind their screens. The difficulty is magnified therefore for the latter because of the digital nature of the platform. Not only do gig workers not encounter each other, but they also represent direct competition to one another in the gig market. Though the neoliberal discourse frames the gig economy as empowering workers, it is important to underline how the status of the independent contractor – at its core – normalizes the precarization of the labor market and the denial of labor rights and benefits, ultimately reflecting wider capitalist tendencies. Unlike with Google or Amazon, there is no need here to construct a work culture to gain the loyalty of workers and to motivate them if the precarious material conditions and wider political–economic context push them to labor whenever possible.

The platform economy, founded upon technology to increasingly mediate and manage workers, ultimately appears intrinsically to alienate them in their individuality and collectivity, both within and beyond the confines of work (Table 10.1). While the division of labor, fragmentation and atomization of workers and their algorithmic management are characteristics common to all platforms, the extent to which these happen varies and can be more magnified for gig workers. The web-based nature of the platform such as MTurk pushes the alienation of workers to additional bounds through its digital mediation of labor, in which one worker only ever interacts with their interface, never encountering a personification of either capital or labor. Workers generally find themselves alienated then from fellow humans; if they do encounter or perceive other workers, it is on the basis of competition based on individual metrics. While traditional time-wage platforms such as Amazon can mask this through their fetishistic work cultures, it is precisely the pillar on which the gig economy, including MTurk, rests. In the latter, workers are by and large denied their status as workers completely, as the gig economy bulldozes over their rights. This proves especially detrimental to larger capital–labor relations and the labor movement considering that the gig economy represents the majority of work in the platform economy. It is important to remember, however, that this platform economy has not evolved in a vacuum but is in every way grounded in the current neoliberal moment, in which the interest of capital comes at the price of labor. As a result it further (re)produces capitalist tendencies that celebrate individuality and aim to rupture a sense of collectivity and labor's organization.

11

# The Power of Amazon Workers and Platform Workers

While platforms systematically organize work and workers in ways that alienate them, the different Amazon workforces demonstrate that such alienation, while it has implications for the larger fragmentation of workers, is not all-encompassing. In some cases, Amazon warehouse workers may indeed show no interest in collective organization, identify with Amazon and perceive the workplace surveillance as legitimate and labor organization in fact as illegitimate. Meanwhile, MTurk workers celebrate their flexibility and freedoms, some not even perceiving their labor as work at all. Yet if we analyze how these workers mobilize their power resources, these cases are among many contemporary examples that demonstrate that workers *do* claim their agency, dismissing the passive portrayals of what Taylor and Smith regarded as a "trained gorilla". Amazon warehouse workers and MTurk workers show that the formation of class consciousness and conducive material conditions are essential for workers to mobilize their different powers. I have only touched upon the complex process of class consciousness and solidarity, to which gender and race can be integral, forming and reforming differently through interacting general capitalist conditions. These include the intensification of exploitation, crises and unemployment – and relative conditions – such as the degree of socialization of the labor process, exposure to unions, labor history and personal experiences. The broad differences in these conditions make it difficult to generalize across the platform economy, both in terms of the different organizations of platforms but also in terms of the different material conditions that workers are confronted with. The realities of globally distributed workers of the same platform, let alone across different platforms, can strongly vary.

What can, however, be inferred regarding the platform organization is the different degrees of socialization of the labor process that bring about the cooperation of workers within their relations of production. The case of Amazon warehouse workers, reminiscent of more historical organization of workers in factories, underlines the importance of assembling workers within a physical space to bring about their social organization. It is only ever their collective labor that ensures the circulation of products to the customer. The very division of labor, which alienates workers, can be their source of disruptive power once it is collectively instrumentalized to struggle for their interests. In contrast, this process is impeded in the case of MTurk, as any conception of collective labor is distorted. Web-based gig work translates into the inability of workers to identify their location along the geographically and temporally dispersed invisible production line, with no (digital) space that assembles all workers while laboring. Location-based gig workers appear closer to MTurk workers based on the atomistic gig nature of work with no space that assembles them. The gig economy appears, therefore, to be predominantly organized in ways that rupture the social organization of labor.

The social organization is not the only crucial condition but interacts with other relative and general ones. Amazon warehouse workers have different labor histories, contracts, legal and material conditions, which can have a significant impact on the extent to which they are compliant or vocal about their class interests. Such relative conditions are even more magnified on MTurk, where workers are at opposite ends of the globe. These appear, however, to grasp the general capitalist conditions, considering that gig workers only ever labor in a precarious world of work characterized by competition. Workers show initial indications, as they recognize the importance of solidarity and their collective interests in less traditional ways. While this by no means presents a systematic analysis of the processes of class consciousness formation, it is important to underline that it is a complex process that develops to varying degrees in our current moment and is central to resistance. This becomes even more so important within our current moment of exacerbated inequalities, especially in light of the COVID-19 pandemic, as the inner contradictions of capitalism and its unsustainability are laid bare. As precarity intensifies and its implications are felt, so too do class interests intensify. These can be further intertwined with their racialized and gendered subjectivities, experiences and their material contexts, which become intrinsic to the fabric of their solidarity within their labor struggle, prior to and taking on new dimensions since the COVID-19 pandemic.

Both case studies demonstrate that, when workers come to express their agency, it is in opposition to their alienation and to the labor process, which strips them of their humanity in which they are meant to labor as machines. As workers of Amazon warehouses state, "I am not a robot"; MTurk workers note that they "are real people with real needs". Navigating the capitalist world and considering the dependence on jobs and wages for their livelihoods and possibly even their status, these labor struggles appear less emancipatory, and are more oriented to improve working conditions. These vary from better health and safety and collective bargaining agreements in Amazon warehouses to more transparency, minimum wages and the reclassification of MTurk workers. These workers essentially strive for more regulation, and protection of rights and wages, and do not want to jeopardize their source of income. This is once again telling not just of the platform economy but of the larger political–economic context characterized precisely by increased precarity, replacement and displacement of labor.

It is now important to integrate the wider material conditions to contrast the power resources of platform workers in relation to the organization of platforms. As the ability of workers to act is both contextually and materially bound, these can provide obstacles for their organization even if this is what the workers want. While Amazon continues to counteract and weaken any attempts by workers to mobilize, such efforts are not needed at MTurk because the platform organization undermines workers' agency altogether. Yet, just as capital evolves in relation to the political–economic, social, and technological conditions, so too must the understanding of the agency of workers. Amazon warehouse workers show parallels in their powers to workers in other sectors beyond the platform economy, and MTurk workers shed light on the novel and less traditional ways by which organization becomes possible via the Internet. As capital increasingly moves away from traditional time-wage laboring and embraces the gig economy, these cases further underline the implications of the normalization of increased precarity both for working conditions and labor rights, but also generally weakening of power resources of workers across the board (Table 11.1). The analysis illustrates the differences across platform workers in light of the diversity in platform organization, but also hints at the potentials. This is especially the case for their growing societal power, which has reached a new level within times of crisis and during a pandemic, recognizing the indispensability of these workers, many of whom are left vulnerable and unprotected, only deepening and exacerbating inequalities in our current day and age.

**Table 11.1:** Comparison of strength of power resources

| | | **Amazon warehouse workers** | **MTurk workers** |
|---|---|---|---|
| **Structural power** | **Marketplace** | Weak | Weak |
| | **Workplace** | Strong | Weak |
| **Associational power** | | Country-dependent, gaining strength | Weak in traditional terms, vibrant in alternative forms |
| **Institutional power** | | Country dependent | Largely non-existent |
| **Societal power** | **Discursive** | Strong | Gaining strength |
| | **Coalitional** | Strong | Gaining strength |

## Structural power of platform workers

The structural power of workers, which forms the basis for collective action, appears in its marketplace component as relatively weak for what is considered to be 'low-skilled' platform labor. A crucial difference lies, however, in the workplace power, with Amazon warehouse workers having a clear advantage over both location-based gig workers and web-based workers in digital labor platforms.

What essentially ruptures marketplace power is that these platforms provide opportunities for whoever is willing to work on the labor market, characterized by low entry requirements and no required work experience. In both Amazon cases, workers are hired on the basis of being human: for one for their physical labor in warehouses, for the other for their basic mental labor as long as they have an Internet-equipped device. This weak marketplace power is further undermined by the fact that both these workforces can easily be replaced: for one the traditional time-wage contracts and their benefits appear attractive for workers, especially when Amazon opens its warehouses in areas with a relatively high unemployment rate. This can be further undermined by the different durations and terms of contracts, varying from a seasonal hire to a direct fixed hire. The competition can even transcend borders, as demonstrated with the Polish workers in relation to the German market. The marketplace of MTurk workers in contrast is further diluted because of the web-based nature of their work, which ensures that they are replaceable as independent contractors on the global digital labor market.

The platform economy reproduces global divisions of labor and a hierarchy between workers that could be regarded as contributing to a larger trend of deskilling. While 'high-skilled' workers at Google and Amazon Web Services (AWS) that perform technical labor have a higher marketplace power, as they are also instrumental to profitmaking in the platform economy, the majority of platform workers, who are gig workers, share a weak marketplace power. Take, for instance, the Uber driver or the Deliveroo rider: while the Uber driver needs to have access to a car and additional constant capital, they only need to drive it, while the Deliveroo rider is considered to need only to know how to, for instance, ride a bike and deliver the food. While these workers, unlike web-based workers are not confronted by a global reserve army of labor and competition, they are confronted by their own local reserve armies which easily enter the marketplace, considering the low entry requirements, making labor (re)outsource-able.

As previously stated, this is closely tied to and reflective of general gendered and racialized compositions, precarious trends and dynamics within the labor market and the legal status of the worker. In many cases these can be filled by migrant students and workers even more dependent on these jobs and left vulnerable to the whims of the market and their residence status, which can dictate their employment possibilities within the country (Van Doorn et al, 2022). The platform economy, therefore, is built by and large on the weak marketplace power of its workers, which poses obstacles for them should they seek to organize, as they are easily replaceable, given the revolving door of workers. It will be interesting to see how this develops in the future and whether platforms will always have guaranteed access to workers. Amazon for one stated in a leaked internal memo of 2021, viewed and published by *Recode* in June 2022, that "If we continue business as usual, Amazon will deplete the available labor supply in the US network by 2024" for its warehouses given their turnover rates (Del Rey, 2022). Not only would this potentially have implications for capital and impact the platform's business model, but it could also impact labor's power resources that would co-evolve with these larger political–economic conditions in the labor market. Amidst different waves of 2022 layoffs in the platform economy, it also remains to be seen how these power resources will develop when platforms can no longer sustain their levels of growth experienced during the pandemic and in moments of crisis.

In contrast to the marketplace power, the workplace power in the platform economy appears less grim, as it is based on the potential collective strength of workers that can be mobilized for their interests. Accordingly, workers *may* mobilize despite their vulnerable positions and material contexts. Both Amazon manual workers and MTurk workers outnumber the capital that employs them – albeit one within the confined space of the warehouse, the other across the globe. To put it another way, Amazon cannot, for now, exist without its workers – both the manual labor to circulate commodities, and the mental labor needed to produce data to be later used for Artificial Intelligence (AI). The specific organization of the platform and the wider context interact, however, in fundamentally different ways when it comes to the mobilization of said structural power.

The real strength that Amazon warehouse workers have over MTurk workers is precisely the nature of their platform, as it seems that location-based time-wage laborers have the strongest workplace power within the platform economy. Warehouse workers convene daily under one roof, which can facilitate their social organization, cooperation and ultimately organization – though this can be undermined through the different contracts and degree of precarity among the workforce and their legal status within a national context. MTurk workers as web-based laborers have no physical, or even digital, space that brings them together or interact on MTurk, as the Application Programming Interface atomizes workers and renders them invisible from one another. The piecework nature not just of MTurk but of the gig economy at large weakens the workplace power, as workers are only ever hired per task, making it difficult to grasp who constitutes the workforce to begin with. The fact that the labor relations for location-based gig workers are mediated by an app further atomizes labor, as the workers do not assemble within a space either. These workers stand, therefore, in strong contrast to one another because of the way the platform organizes them.

The interplay of the two dimensions of the nature of the work and the nature of the platform severely complicate the ability to resist through smaller everyday acts which has historically played a crucial role in expanding resistance beyond the record of visible collective action. Within our current day and age these possibilities are increasingly limited by the growth and function of algorithmic management. As the analysis of the relations of alienation demonstrates, platforms instrumentalize technology for the micro-surveillance of the labor process and the worker. Workers are no longer confronted by just the surveillance of the social eye of their managers. As Amazon tracks the log of workers' (in)activity and keeps track of their productivity via the quantified Units Per Hour (UPH) rate, resisting by working at a slower pace to reduce productivity becomes detrimental to the worker and can result in their (in)direct termination. The same logic applies to the possibility of reducing work time through additional bathroom breaks – given the reports of workers having no time to use the bathroom in the first place (Liao, 2018; Gilbert, 2020). While workers can resist from a distance by ridiculing Amazon's work culture, this does not disrupt Amazon's circuit.

If individual acts of resistance are severely complicated within location-based traditional time-laboring platforms, they appear paradoxical in the existence of the gig economy as a whole. Workers cannot resist by laboring more slowly or reducing their productivity if they are hired per task. Whether it is a food delivery worker or one on Upwork, where their screenshots are captured, the worker cannot afford to deliver more slowly without directly impacting their performance. For an MTurk worker this is detrimental, as it would lead to a drop in their approval rating and rejection of the task, thereby resulting in wage theft. If one gig worker does not perform the task, another will. Web-based laborers are additionally confronted with not just a local but a global workforce. The independent contractor status further complicates any act of individual resistance as the question arises of who these can be directed against when the lines of capital are so blurred between those sourcing the labor and the platform itself. An MTurk worker has nothing to gain from giving incorrect answers to the requester, which are filtered out, or, from leaving the platform of Amazon altogether. Unlike the warehouse workers, gig workers such as those of MTurk have no option of resisting from a distance, when their premise is based on being excluded from a workforce. The digital infrastructure in which workers labor, the intrinsic surveillance, precarious gig nature and capital's twofold appearance are obstacles to the possibilities of individual resistance for gig workers.

Given the technological and political–economic conditions, it is more fruitful for workers to turn their attention to the collective struggle for their interests. Location-based platforms, with traditional time-wage agreements, facilitate the creation of solidarity by bringing workers together within a single space, while the nature of the work facilitates possibilities for disruptive action such as striking. Location-based platforms more generally, where workers encounter and perceive one another, can be ground for further solidarity based not just on their material realities, but those related to their gendered and racialized experiences, material conditions and subjectivities. As these, depending on context, overlap, workers may form trust to one another and mobilize on that basis within their local contexts. Accordingly, the nature of the platform also relates to the formation of the fabric of solidarity itself. Their social organization is therefore the source of the disruptive power of Amazon warehouse workers, who are stretched across the hypertaylorized circulation line. This power can be magnified temporally, by disrupting Amazon's peak season of orders and profits, and spatially, by cross-sectoral coordination and (trans)national action. Given the different material conditions of contracts and industrial relations, workers demonstrate a wide range of tactics that can be employed, from blockades and unannounced walkouts to (general) strikes. Industrial action intensified globally in light of the COVID-19, as workers ranging from the US and India to France, Italy and Germany walked off the job in response to the lack of health and safety precautions in the warehouses. Despite their weak marketplace power, Amazon warehouse workers demonstrate the potentialities for workplace power given their platform organization (Kassem, 2022).

The mobilization of the workplace power of location-based platform workers is generally increasingly gaining momentum. In November 2018 a total of 20,000 Google workers from 40 offices from across the globe – reaching from Tokyo and Singapore to Dublin and San Francisco – staged the "Google Walkout for Real Change", in protest against "sexual harassment, gender inequality and systematic racism". As one worker states, "I'm not at my desk because I'm walking out in solidarity with other Googlers and contractors to protest [against] sexual harassment, misconduct, lack of transparency and a workplace culture that's not working for everyone" (Weaver et al, 2018). While such a walkout was framed differently from those at Amazon, it is a clear example of workers' mobilization and solidarity sparked by gendered and racialized material realities and bound to these subjectivities. The growing interest in the collective power of 'tech workers' is also embodied in the Tech Workers Coalition (TWC): "guided by our vision for an inclusive & equitable tech industry, TWC organizes to build worker power through rank & file self-organization and education."[1] The outcomes of such actions include not just raised awareness but also increased pressure in labor's interests and an increase in their power.

Location-based platforms can make it difficult to instrumentalize the nature of the platform when it comes to gig workers, given the isolated atomistic laboring of Uber drivers or Deliveroo riders. Thus, the political–economic and technological conditions appear at first to inhibit the possibilities of mobilizing a structural power for these workers. However, on 8 May 2019, Uber and Lyft drivers from several countries, such as the US, UK and Australia, organized a strike from the app in light of Uber's Initial Public Offering (IPO) to shed light on their working conditions (Bergfeld, 2019; Sainato and Paul, 2019). This was not an exception, as Uber and Taxify workers elsewhere, such as South Africa, have at different times gone 'offline' on the apps as a form of strike for a similar cause (IOL, 2018). Deliveroo workers are among the delivery workers who have equally staged strikes time and time again, in the case of Deliveroo over plans of changing its payment structure in the past from time-wages to exclusively piece-wages. Such a work stoppage by 'logging out' of the platform results, however, in algorithms managing the platform setting higher rates because of the lower supply of workers, which can undermine such collective action (Osborne and Farrell, 2016; Vandaele, 2018).

While the mobilization of this form of structural power may be difficult to translate into the de facto disruption of a platform (Joyce et al, 2022), workers are increasingly organizing – at times through different traditional and/or more grassroots unions or own informal groups with the potential to affect regulation (Dubal, 2022b). Such attempts are, however, more difficult for web-based workers such as those of MTurk, who additionally cannot easily form (digital) picket lines. Yet the location-based gig workers demonstrate, as becomes clear for the associational power also of MTurk workers, the ability to instrumentalize the Internet's decentralized nature. The Internet is thereby used to connect in alternative ways through digital spaces to form solidarity, disrupt digitally or physically and alter the asymmetric capital–labor relation. Such a discussion of the structural power of platform workers sheds further light on how the interlocking of the nature of the platform and the nature of the work relates dialectically to the challenges and possibilities of expressing different forms of workplace power despite a relatively weak marketplace power.

## Associational power of platform workers

The hostile conditions to the structural power of platform workers extend to their associational power, though workers have found their own ways to instrumentalize these and form traditional and alternative associations. The different industrial relations play a crucial role here, as they may to different extents facilitate or support the establishment of associations or hinder this process. While the associational power of Amazon warehouse workers is context-bound, this power resource for MTurk workers is relatively weak in traditional terms but demonstrates a vibrant landscape when it comes to cultivating solidarities in alternative ways.

Given that associational power is traditionally expressed through unions, it comes as no surprise that these are more likely to be present in traditional laboring in location-based platforms – especially ones organized like factories with a history of labor struggle. While the Basic Law, Germany's constitution, known as the *Grundgesetz*, guarantees the right to association, where ver.di began to organize workers in 2013, industrial relations differ depending on the country. Such a right may not always be guaranteed in the same manner. In the US, the right to unionize can be accomplished only through a majority vote, which is difficult but not impossible to obtain at the union-buster Amazon, as the labor struggles in Bessemer or Staten Island prove. These cases also shed light both on traditional and more grassroots natures of unions, as well as the formation of solidarity among racialized workers for their labor struggles. This is further complicated when workers are on different contracts within a warehouse, let alone across warehouses and borders.

Despite the difficult political–economic terrain to navigate and Amazon being a union-buster, its warehouse workers show diverse efforts to claim their disruptive power through the coordination of the manifestations of their associational power. This has transcended national borders – from the efforts of UNI's Amazon Global Alliance and the political movement of Transnational Social Strike (TSS), which established Amazon Workers International (AWI), to digital associations such as the FACE (Former And Current Employees) of Amazon. In comparison with other location-based platforms, Amazon warehouse workers appear to be one of the most organized in associations in the traditional sense through (trans)national unions and wider movements – though the playing field is closely bound by political–economic conditions, industrial relations and precarious material conditions.

In the current momentum of growing labor organization, there have been wider attempts to form associations in other location-based platforms where workers too are facing union-busting efforts. In June 2019, 2,000 workers in Zürich attempted to organize an event over labor organization, unionization and labor rights. This event was eventually cancelled "at the request of Google's leadership team" (Gallagher, 2019b). Despite the pushback, Google workers went ahead with a similar but much smaller event in October 2019, where members of the Swiss labor union Syndicom were invited to speak. While Google management attempted to block such an event (Gallagher, 2019b), in 2021 we saw Google workers found their own union, named Alphabet Workers Union.[2] Though still small in size, it is growing and demonstrates a crucial attempt by workers to assume their associational power at the often rated "best place to work".

The growing potentials of organization for these platform workers are met with attempts by capital to break these up, making headlines for spying and firing workers who speak out or organize. Amazon, for one, has terminated the contracts of Emily Cunningham and Maren Costa from AWS, who formed collectivities under Amazon Employees for Climate Justice (AECJ), whose mission is to make Amazon accountable for its climate footprint and to develop a climate change plan (Weise, 2021). The case of AECJ demonstrates a crucial effort where workers in AWS, Amazon's most crucial branch of profit, have begun to organize, but also reflects that Amazon's union-busting behavior is not limited to the warehouses. It also touches upon solidarity beyond class, as AECJ addresses what it refers to as "Amazon's environmental racism", considering "[t]he fact that pollution disproportionately harms people of color is an effect of systematic racism" (Amazon Employees for Climate Justice, 2020). This is yet another example of the overlapping material, gendered and racialized realities and solidarities.

In this respect, Amazon is not unique in the platform economy, as the case of some Google workers demonstrate. They accused Google of a tool possibly implemented to surveil labor organization which sends out immediate alerts as soon as any calendar event is created exceeding ten rooms or 100 participants (Gallagher, 2019a). So the platform's control over technology extends not just to monitoring productivity but also any attempts at organization. These efforts appear to have culminated in its highly secret 'Project Vivian', lasting between the end of 2018 and the beginning of 2020, which explicitly targeted labor mobilization and organization and overlaps with previous labor activism and workplace unrest. The National Labor Relations Board lawsuit by previously fired employees revealed in early 2022 that Google's very own director of employment law described it "as an initiative 'to engage employees more positively and convince them that unions suck'". Apparently, there was even a proposal to find a "respected voice to publish an OpEd outlining what a unionized tech workplace would look like, and counseling employees of FB (Facebook), MSFT(Microsoft), Amazon, and google (sic) not to do it" (Gurley, 2022a). This more generally reflects not only how platforms attempt to fragment workers through the ways in which they organize their workforces, but also how they systematically attempt to undermine their agency and unionization, possibly seeing the latter as a threat across platforms. Despite these, workers in the platform economy are becoming increasingly active and outspoken even in the absence of labor protections, taking on various forms of associations in their own hands.

The situation appears initially daunting, however, when one considers, first, gig workers and, second, web-based gig workers like those working for MTurk. The general struggle for the right of association of gig workers is rooted in their classification as independent contractors, thereby denying them the status, benefits and rights of workers – such as the right to organize. Location-based gig workers have an advantage, however, over web-based workers in that they are based within certain national borders that allow them to fight their battle for recognition and reclassification. The legal sphere comes to play a crucial role in these struggles. We have seen such battles fought, such as Uber in California, and won, such as the delivery workers in Spain, Italy and the Netherlands and Uber drivers in the UK – with potentially the largest effort in scope thus far being manifested in the European Commission's proposed directive.

Additionally, we continue to see how the landscape of unionization is itself changing and experiencing in certain cases a shift to more grassroots unions and bottom-up forms of organization within the platform economy (Dubal, 2022b; Joyce et al, 2022). Take for instance the delivery platform workers in Berlin – such as those of Lieferando who set up "Lieferando Workers Collective" or those of Gorillas who organized the "Gorillas Workers Collective" (Eurofound, 2021). In other instances established unions have backed and supported workers' efforts as seen with ver.di in Germany, the Riders Union in Netherlands and the Federation of Dutch Trade Unions (FNV), or Deliveroo Riders Roovolt and the Independent Workers' union of Great Britain (IGWB) (Eurofound, 2022). These collectives, unions and grass-root efforts too face union-busting efforts from the platforms themselves, thus reflecting tactics of other platforms. The nature of the platform provides then a starting point for a struggle for their rights, including the right of association. This is of course closely bound to the context and which rights are protected under national law. This may vary from country to country in the Global North and Global South, especially when the majority of workers labor in the informal economy.

Web-based platforms operate outside of industrial relations and legal frameworks altogether, which goes to the root of the organization of web-based platforms. As the discussion on the institutional power underlines, MTurk workers are not just assigned the status of an independent contractor but are additionally confronted with the question of whose industrial relations and laws they should be regulated by. Workers have until recently been left outside of the organizing efforts of unions altogether, though the case of Fair Crowd Work demonstrates a union effort to support these workers. These workers have assumed their associational power more directly by using the Internet to form less conventional and traditional forms of association and solidarity to advise and support one another, even if they cannot hold capital accountable. MTurk workers have heavily relied on Turkopticon, forums and subReddits, and during its lifetime Dynamo too exerted grassroot efforts for collective action. As workers laboring digitally, they are familiar with how to instrumentalize and mobilize via the Internet for their interests. Ultimately it is the interplay of the various conditions, and the organization of the platform, that opens up or closes spaces for associational power – ones that may not necessarily translate into what are perceived as traditional unions. The increased tendency towards the use of gig workers in the unregulated (platform) economy sheds light on the implications of the independent contractor status which risks undoing historically attained rights, as well as the new forms of labor struggle, organization and mobilization.

## Institutional power of platform workers

Institutional power, understood as an expression of associational power through collective bargaining and works council gains, appears quite limited in the platform economy. This is generally reflective of a larger economic trend in national industrial relations and declining union power. The overall institutional power of Amazon warehouse workers is weak, though as location-based time-laborers, it shows potential, depending on country. This is fundamentally different for gig workers, especially web-based ones such as those of MTurk, whose institutional power is negligible because of their classification as independent contractors. While the European Commission proposed a directive on platform work that includes both web- and location-based workers, it remains to be seen how this will be translated into praxis in the future and by whom this will be implemented and monitored (Aloisi and De Stefano, 2022; Aloisi and Potocka-Sionek, 2022). This also raises questions as to its implications for the general gig economy, whose very fabric is defined by the precarious independent contractor status.

It is difficult to generalize about institutional power in the case of Amazon warehouse workers, because of varying industrial relations (i.e. different countries). However, they can be considered in some countries relatively speaking a forerunner in the larger platform economy, which is by and large characterized by weak institutional power. While ver.di in Germany has invested in shop floor steward structures and workers can additionally guard their right to a works council through which they push for additional benefits, they have not yet been able to secure the desired collective bargaining agreement. On the other hand, France has a sector-wide collective bargaining agreement that Amazon cannot escape, while Italy presents a unique example where workers negotiated a collective bargaining agreement. These countries are not, however, representative of the landscape of Amazon warehouses on a global scale, considering that a country like the US cannot safeguard the associational power of workers, let alone institutional power. Given the contemporary labor struggles at Amazon in the US, it will be interesting to see how these develop and how a possible associational power will be translated into an institutional power (Kassem, 2023). This appears to be more a phenomenon in Europe than across the Atlantic. If workers cannot become members of unions without their employment being terminated, it is rather difficult to talk about institutional power.

It does not take long to realize that it is difficult to conceptualize an institutional power for gig workers, location-based ones, but even more so detrimentally for web-based ones. Taken their status as independent contractors, capital excludes them from their workforce and thereby eliminates the possibility of developing an institutional power as long as they are classified as such. This underlines once again the importance of struggling for the reclassification of gig workers not as self-employed or as independent contractors but as workers. Unions and institutions are showing increasing interest in this struggle, given that such a status poses a real danger in threatening to strip workers of fundamental rights even outside of the platform economy. However, as all power resources co-evolve and are bound to their contexts, workers have also been their institutional power pursuing in different ways. In the case of Gorillas workers in Berlin, workers have elected their works council despite legal battles to get there (ver.di, 2021), while the FNV won a battle in the Netherlands by which workers of Deliveroo are to be "covered by the collective labor agreement for the transport of goods" (Eurofound, 2022). In the same manner, battles of reclassifications won elsewhere provide a starting ground for the pursuit of this power. Accordingly, it appears that here too workers are setting precedent by pursuing different labor and legal battles, which would result in a growing associational but also possibilities for institutional power.

This struggle for (web-based) gig workers is further complicated by the mediating role of platforms and the twofold appearance of capital, raising questions about who bears the responsibility. While the platform defines the employment relationship, the requester reproduces and normalizes it based on the hyperoutsourcing model. This becomes even more complex when one considers that web-based platforms fall outside of the jurisdiction and industrial relations of any one state. MTurk workers are not considered employees by Amazon, nor is their labor regulated in the maze of the Internet. The configuration of these platforms, such as MTurk, demonstrates that the nature of the platform and the nature of the work are fundamentally antithetical to institutional power. The proposed directive on platform work could potentially present a large-scale effort in countering this, at least in a part of the Global North. It could strengthen the associational power there, which might in turn seep over into the institutional power of these platform workers. Similarly, specific battles fought and won as in the UK or Spain could potentially lead to changes not just for the associational power of these workers, and potentially this power resource – though this too is yet to be seen.

Gig workers are thus increasingly included in debates on the future of work and regulation, given the dangers of the gig economy in normalizing precarious employment even beyond the platform economy. This is reflected in the International Labour Organization's (ILO's) report "Work for a Brighter Future", which formulates essential criteria for the future of work, echoing previously mentioned efforts. This includes generally protecting a living wage, collective representation and working hours and using technology to support decent work through a "human-in-command" approach (International Labour Organization, 2019). While such efforts would strongly facilitate the structural, associational and institutional powers of workers, it is, as with the European Commission's proposed directive, questionable how far they can be ratified, and how much they will be accepted, and kept to, by platforms. Given that institutional power is in many ways a translation and expression of a traditional associational power and that most platform workers cannot join unions without repercussions, it can be said to be relatively weak. We do see a potential shift, however, with the growing forms of more grassroots organizations, unions and collectives. Amazon warehouse workers have in some cases a certain terrain to navigate to strengthen their institutional power, depending on national industrial relations. It can be said, however, as the example of the MTurk demonstrates, that workers' institutional power remains largely weak and, in some cases, negligible within the current conditions of the platform economy.

## Societal power of platform workers

While previous power resources are more closely connected to the class position of workers themselves, other actors are instrumental in mobilizing this power resource to strengthen the larger labor movement in society, in turn strengthening the other power resources too. Our current moment presents a real opportunity to form a larger labor movement of the platform economy and strengthen both coalitional and discursive power across platforms.

Even though platforms do not employ the majority of the world's workforce, they have come under growing public attention and scrutiny because of their working conditions and largely unregulated exponential growth, for many even more so as a result of COVID-19. This ranges from Facebook's Cambridge Analytica scandal and Google's sexual harassment and misconduct lawsuits to Airbnb's detrimental effects on gentrification and the housing market and Uber's destruction of local taxi industries with drivers who often do not make ends meet. Amazon and Jeff Bezos – who has been regarded for decades as its physical embodiment – are no strangers to these headlines, in relation to the latest technological developments, working conditions and organizing effort, from Amazon warehouse workers to MTurk workers and AECJ. The efforts made by investigative journalism, academics and researchers play a critical role in directing attention to the voices and actions of workers, bringing their stories to the media, supporting and reconstructing them as an increasingly active workforce. These efforts legitimize the struggles of workers and are crucial in debunking the celebrated neoliberal platform economy, which until recently had been largely glamorized for its innovation, entrepreneurship, flexibility and autonomy of its workers.

The different natures of the various platforms and types of work play an important role vis-à-vis this power resource in so far as they relate to the relationship between these workers and the public. Location-based workers have had a stronger ground for their societal power, as they are more visible to the society who constitutes the user base of these very platforms. Because Amazon prides itself on being the most customer-centric company, workers recognize the importance of affecting its public image through first and foremost the efforts of investigative journalists. Location-based gig workers have a strong discursive power, as these platforms, such as Uber and Deliveroo, are quite popular in wider society. This is fundamentally different from web-based labor like MTurk workers, whose realities have remained largely invisible. A different form of effort had to be exerted just to humanize this workforce to the public. This effort does not just relate to the working conditions of such web-based labor and capital's trend in offshoring and outsourcing labor, but also seeps into debates on the future of AI, by virtue of the role of these workers in creating data for the purpose of training machine-learning algorithms. While journalists were able to bring these stories into headlines across the media, researchers and academics also contribute to the discursive power through their own systematic investigations and development of digital infrastructures such as Turkopticon or Fairwork. The platform economy demonstrates that the societal power of workers co-evolves in a dialectical relationship to the growing power of platform capital.

Contributing to the growing general interest has been the COVID-19 pandemic, which presents an additional instrumental moment for workers across platforms that has redefined some of these workers in the wider discourse as 'essential workers'. Amazon warehouse workers have been in headlines regarding health and safety in warehouses, strikes, cases of dismissals like that of Christian Smalls and the organized drive of the Amazon Labor Union (ALU). Bezos, one of the richest humans in the history of the planet, also continues to feature in the media, as in the summer of 2021, when he went into space for ten minutes, something he later thanked Amazon workers and customers for paying for. Similarly location-based gig workers have received additional attention ranging from Uber and Lyft drivers struggling for eligibility for unemployment pay, to places of support for gig workers and freelancers in these times. This was also a time that emphasized the vital role of food couriers in delivering food during the pandemic for those in quarantine and lockdown (Chaudhry, 2020; Scheiber, 2020; Simon, 2020). Web-based workers indirectly form part of these discussions by raising questions about the uncertainty of (online) jobs, their eligibility for benefits within their national contexts and generally questions around working from home. The context of COVID-19, which has intensified inequalities, has been crucial for platform workers, shedding light on their working conditions, their precarity and the implications of their legal status, whilst also illustrating their vital importance in times of crisis and their organizing efforts amidst these.

While it remains to be seen to what extent this context will strengthen their coalitional (and other) powers in the long run, it is important to illustrate the extent to which a coalitional power is forming. For one growing discursive power among actors in society leads to a coalition among these. Platform workers are cultivating their cooperation with wider political movements, unions, academics, organizations and policymakers to strengthen their labor struggle. Considering that Amazon has come to grow into a monopoly, seeking ever greater control of the supply chain, more actors in society are showing interest in regulating it and cooperating with unions. MTurk is in turn gaining the attention of unions and organizations because of the fear of the repercussions of gig work. The coalitional power of platform workers seems to grow along with their platforms, which not only reproduce trends (Collier et al, 2017), but are also forerunners and exporters of algorithmic management beyond the platform economy into the wider economy, politics and society.

Understanding the current moment and context both holistically and historically underlines the need to reconceptualize the labor movement away from a white male-dominated movement of traditional workers, and as one that also centralizes further racialized and gendered subjectivities and is more grassroots and bottom-up oriented. Workers have gained support from additional actors, bolstering their coalitional power in society precisely around issues of race and gender, further strengthening their class position and support from society. The East African Amazon warehouse workers in Minnesota, which were the first ever to go on strike in the US, grouped together and formed solidarity because of their shared racial background and experiences. The Awood Center has been central in supporting these. This is one of many examples where issues of race overlap with those of class, as capital continues to instrumentalize the intertwinings of class, race and gender in its pursuit of profit. These intersections are integral to contemporary labor struggles, as seen with the recent organized drives in Bessemer and JFK8 (Alimahomed-Wilson and Reese, 2021; Lee et al, 2022). Similarly, web-based digital labor platforms such as MTurk are built precisely on the global division of labor increasingly outsourced to the Global South while extending paid work into spaces most dominantly reserved to the unpaid reproductive labor of predominantly women, and women of color. In other words, the history and development of capitalism has always been intrinsically tied to distribution and division of labor along many racialized and gendered lines.

Apart from Amazon hiring migrant workers in the US and across the globe for what is considered its low-skilled labor, Google workers staged the Google Walkout in November of 2018 to protest against the handling of sexual harassment cases within the corporation. Google has additionally seen protests over the unequal employment and treatment of temporary workers, contractors and vendors, shedding light on the overlap of subjectivities and interests but also their power. Google has in fact reacted by extending certain benefits to these workers (Campbell 2019; Wong 2019). This overlap of subjectivities and realities was echoed once more after Google fired the co-lead of its AI Ethical Research Group, Timnit Gebru, who previously published on algorithmic bias and facial recognition, for her co-authored paper shedding light on the risks potentially resulting from large-scale language models (Schiffer, 2020). Across these examples and also those in third-generation platforms like Uber drivers and delivery workers, who depending on their local context can be predominantly migrant workers, it becomes clear: the labor movement needs to be understood intersectionally, integrating gender and race into its class fabric. Rather than undermining it, it can strengthen the labor movement and its very foundation of solidarity by mobilizing alongside other movements and organizations.

The societal power of workers can be regarded as extending solidarity beyond a single platform, and fostering the coalitional power of workers across platforms and borders. This sheds light on the potential of such a 21st-century labor movement, precisely for groups of workers who have been largely dismissed as passive. UNI's Amazon symposium in December 2019 discussing various facets of Amazon's political, economic and environmental power and repercussions, included not only union secretaries but also key figures from, for instance, the Awood Center or AECJ. These underline how one part of the larger Amazon workforce is not isolated from the other, as workers expressed solidarity with and for one another. Support from AWS workers is not just critical for mobilizing tech workers, but additionally presents an opportunity for warehouse workers, given that the former have a stronger structural power to leverage Amazon because of their profit-making function (UNI and ITUC, 2019). Location-based gig workers have equally not just expressed but also demonstrated cross-platform solidarity, as previously highlighted with Uber and Lyft drivers. Interestingly enough, cross-platform solidarity is accounted for in the digital associations of web-based workers. With the exception of Turkopticon and Dynamo, digital spaces such as forums do not exist merely for the workers of MTurk. These are used more generally by web-based workers for a wide array of reasons and platforms. Web-laborers such as MTurk workers in many cases already labor on multiple platforms. Accordingly, workers can strongly benefit from the current moment in which we are living and mobilize the growing societal power resulting from the wide-ranging political–economic, societal, technological and environmental effects of platforms.

Workers' societal power, when taken as a whole and in combination with the other manifestations of power, sheds lights on their ability to claim their

**Table 11.2:** Comparison of four powers

| | | | Differences | | Similarities |
|---|---|---|---|---|---|
| | | | *Amazon warehouse workers* | *MTurk workers* | |
| **Structural power** | **Marketplace power** | *Nature of platform* | • confronted by a local and/or cross-national reserve army of labor | • confronted by a global reserve army of labor | Low marketplace power: low/no entry requirements as 'low-skilled' labor and revolving door of the reserve army of labor |
| | | *Nature of work* | • different contracts can be attractive to workers and undermine their power | • even more undermining, because workers are left no bargaining leverage<br>• workers need to be in possession of constant capital | |
| | **Workplace power** | *Nature of platform* | • little possibility for individual resistance<br>• possibilities of disrupting circuit of capital: spatial and temporal dimensions | • no possibility for individual resistance<br>• no possibility for disruptive power<br>• source of strength when instrumentalized by workers | |
| | | *Nature of work* | • different rights according to different contracts | • independent contractor status further weakens this; no overview of workforce | |
| **Associational power** | *Nature of platform* | | Varying political–economic conditions and industrial relations<br>• (trans)national unions, TSS and FACE of Amazon | • no traditional possibility for unions<br>• decentralized nature of Internet allows for alternative and novel possibilities | New potentials can be grasped by workers through technology and the very infrastructure that alienates and mediates them |
| | *Nature of work* | | Different contracts, different rights | • as independent contractors, rights of association stripped | |

**Table 11.2:** Comparison of four powers (continued)

| | | | **Differences** | | **Similarities** |
|---|---|---|---|---|---|
| | | | ***Amazon warehouse workers*** | ***MTurk workers*** | |
| **Institutional power** | ***Nature of platform*** | | • various industrial relations and differing laws | • no industrial relations by which to regulate the Internet | Weakened by the overall neoliberal trends |
| | ***Nature of work*** | | • in certain circumstances: possibilities for works councils and collective bargaining | • not considered part of a workforce at all or as having rights, it remains to be seen how contemporary regulations may seep over | |
| **Societal power** | **Discursive power** | ***Nature of platform*** | • society more likely to interact and know of these workers | • initially invisiblized workers<br>• support from media, unions, ILO and academics | Capitalist moment, COVID-19, economic insecurity and precarity |
| | | ***Nature of work*** | • recent growth in reports on working conditions and Bezos | | |
| | **Coalitional power** | ***Nature of platform*** | • cooperation with social movements, solidarity groups, organizations and media | • increased support form unions and academics, labor rights advocates given the dangers of independent contractor status in undoing achievements of labor struggles | |
| | | ***Nature of work*** | | | |

agency and express their class-conscious, gendered and racialized subjectivities. Workers in the platform economy, whose agency had previously been largely dismissed and whose conditions of work seriously fragment and alienate them, are forming solidarities and organizing often by instrumentalizing technology – not just intra- but even inter-platform. Workers from across the platform economy mobilize their powers and increasingly make headlines for their "tech activism" (Nedzhvetskaya and Tan, 2019) in pursuit of rights, interests and organization of (digital) action. In doing so, they must navigate the specific interplay of both the nature of their work and the nature of the platform within their larger material context. As individual resistance becomes difficult, because of capital's algorithmic management of the labor process and the gig nature of much of the platform economy, it becomes even more important to mobilize collective power. The landscape for the collective organization of labor is becoming more and more vibrant in the platform economy, but also beyond it, as we are witnessing workers navigating their wider conditions to organize on their own terms – from within the walls of Amazon warehouses to the streets of delivery riders and Uber drivers. Their power resources are continously evolving given their interdependencies and ongoing political–economic, technological and social conditions and developments.

As workers of the platform economy demonstrate the possibilities for solidarity and resistance even in contexts where capital systematically cracks down on labor's collective efforts, these developments must also be accompanied by a widening conceptualization of the contemporary labor movement. Much of the labor organization in the platform economy is very different from traditional portrayals, as it increasingly represents bottom-up unionization and grassroots organization, all whilst raising more broadly social awareness of what goes on behind the (digital) walls of their platforms. Traditional time laborers such as Amazon warehouse workers have mobilized their growing workplace and associational power, and show signs of an institutional power. Such location-based workers, including gig ones, hold an advantage over web-based workers when it comes to forming solidarity through different subjectivities but also regarding their larger societal power. Whereas the former are in a way visible or known to society because of their platform's popularity, the latter have until recently been largely unknown to the public. Yet gig workers, like those of the web-based platform MTurk, have demonstrated alternative ways by which to form solidarity and digital collectives, instrumentalizing the very technology that is meant to drive a wedge between them (Table 11.2). Within this growing momentum of platform workers, we must recognize the ongoing potentialities and (alternative) actions of workers across their power resources to humanize themselves against their alienating working conditions. The case of the platform economy demonstrates that, as capital evolves and renegotiates its relation to labor, so too do the subjectivities of workers and their actions co-evolve to renegotiate these for their interests.

# 12

# Conclusion

This book has in essence been about the ability to act and struggle in the hope of bringing about change in a system designed in the interests of the few and at the cost of the many. Workers in the platform economy constitute one of countless contemporary examples that shed light on the complexity of agency within our current capitalist moment, as they face hostile material conditions that aim to restrain and impede their labor organization. As platforms continue to grow in economic, political, social and technological power, which has become even clearer in light of COVID-19, it is crucial to delve into the exploitative social relations between capital and labor at the heart of the platform economy. I avoid fetishistic understandings that paint technology as devoid of all materiality and humanity, and deterministic understandings that paint workers as devoid of all subjectivity and agency, which normalize and eternalize capitalism. I see this as crucial in order to understand current developments and inequalities not as inevitable and preordained, thus opening up the possibility of conceptualizing change and transformation.

Amazon has become representative of trends and developments in the platform economy with other corporations looking to 'Amazonify' their business model in terms of capital and their workforces. Amazon's ecosystem has long evolved beyond the initial online sale of books and now stretches across commodities, technologies and services. Considering that platforms do not organize workers uniformly along the same working conditions or contexts, it has been important to examine two contrasting case studies: the Amazon warehouse workers and MTurk workers. The interaction between the nature of the platform and the nature of the work appears at first to alienate workers in different ways and to frustrate possible expressions of their agency. Examining each dimension, from traditional location-based laboring and its time-wages to the novelty of web-based laboring and traditional piecework, sheds light on their larger repercussions for the working conditions and labor's struggle within the platform economy and possibly beyond it. Rejecting a capitalist deterministic perspective, this book has argued that workers may be conscious of their alienation and strive to organize and foster solidarity around their class interests – for which political–economic and technological conditions can provide obstacles but also opportunities. While Amazon warehouse workers must navigate the alienating circulation line, Amazon's union-busting culture and the larger political–economic context, MTurk demonstrates how gig work both magnifies the alienation of workers and weakens their overall power resources. This is further exacerbated for those laboring remotely via an unregulated Internet. Yet workers claim their agency within the possible parameters, mobilizing their power resources to organize across the turbulent terrain of the platform economy. They do so in both traditional and alternative ways through their own grassroots and bottom-up efforts and structures and by instrumentalizing according to their interests the very infrastructure by which they are mediated and alienated. In what appears to be an increasingly vibrant terrain of labor struggles, platform workers are pushing back, organizing and cultivating their different power resources. These resources are to be regarded holistically, as they form different facets to their labor struggle.

By investigating two case studies that stand in a stark contrast to one another in terms of the nature of their platforms and nature of of their work, it is possible to underline the parallels and diversities of platforms, as well as the ways by which platforms both reproduce trends and produce novel ones in the larger labor market. Alienating working conditions characterized by algorithmic management have seeped into the labor market, proving to have grave consequences when workers are not just meant to labor as part of the machine but also to be monitored, controlled and disciplined by it. Algorithms come to dehumanize the capital-labor relation, increasingly removing the possibility for workers to challenge capital as they cannot struggle per se against an application or interface. The possibility to challenge capital at all becomes further threatened by the very foundation upon which class relations are organized, which is meant to fundamentally oppose, limit and break up labor organization. The platform economy, through its gig economy, deliberately reproduces and normalizes precarity in the labor market under the banner of the independent contractor, which endangers labor rights and workers' collective organization. Although the platform economy does not in relative terms currently employ the largest number of workers on a sectoral and global scale, it continues to expand and interweave itself into the fabrics of our day-to-day life, our social relations and labor relations.

The investigation of the platform economy, as a widely celebrated contemporary capitalist development, is one of several that illuminates the course of the current labor market, which in its current shape and form is evidently not to the benefit or serve the interest of the workers. In this debate, I have centered class and class consciousness and only briefly touched upon race and gender, and how these relate to agency. Recognizing their importance and the bounds of this research within the moment it was pursued, further investigation is needed to grasp these complexities and gain an even more holistic understanding. With ongoing scholarly efforts (see Van Doorn, 2017; Reese, 2020; Alimahomed-Wilson and Reese, 2021; Van Doorn and Vijay, 2021; Dubal 2022a) it is crucial therefore to examine more closely the interactions of class, race and gender, and how systemic inequalities and visa regimes further project themselves onto their material conditions and the organization of work and workers. Such research is crucial in further understanding how these inform the different subjectivities of workers and are claimed for solidarity, agency and a more intersectional labor movement. In the same manner, it will be integral to continue to analyze these in relation to the wider political–economic, social and technological context, which is bound to continue to evolve – ranging from COVID-19, ongoing wars and rising inflation, all of which have further intensified inequalities.

## The digital social fabric and the future of workers

As digital platforms increasingly become part of our daily lives and interweave themselves into our social fabric, our usage of these remains by and large a personal choice. Some of us may order on Amazon for its convenience or book an Airbnb when on holidays, while others may choose to navigate around them or boycott at least some digital platforms altogether. Some may want to support alternatives in the form of platform cooperatives and place orders on Fairmondo and book their holiday on Fairbnb. These cooperatives stand in opposition to capitalist platforms to provide instead an alternative model where workers have a stake in the ownership and collectively and democratically participate in organizing fairer working conditions (Scholz, 2016). While platform cooperatives present an alternative, they are confined by capitalist conditions and competition from other platforms. Rosa Luxemburg underlines the contradiction facing cooperatives more generally, as workers "are obliged to take toward themselves the role of capitalist entrepreneur – a contradiction ... [in] which [they] either become pure capitalist enterprises or, if the workers' interests continue to predominate, end by dissolving" (Luxemburg, 1900: n.p.). Cooperatives are growing and should by no means be dismissed. They must be acknowledged for their efforts to create alternatives. They are not, however, currently the size of the capitalist enterprises, which look as though they are ever-present. We may therefore still find ourselves navigating towards capitalist ones in our contemporary moment.

My hope is that this book contributes to the growing scholarly efforts to examine what unfolds at the (digital) shopfloor level and in the world of the workers to grasp the repercussions of the platform economy, based on which readers and consumers can make their conscious decisions, whatever these may be. As members of society there are many ways to support these workers and increase their societal power, and more specifically discursive power, from evaluating consumer choices or simply discussing platforms with others. Some of us may want to raise awareness, sign petitions and join mobilizations to tax such corporations, or pressure governments in their decision-making roles. Workers across interviews recognize and underline the crucial role the public plays in their labor struggle, given that society at large are their very consumers and clients. While workers power the platforms through their labor, consumers and clients keep them alive by using these platforms and additionally producing data integral to their network effects and platform models. They might even be investing financial capital into platforms. Yet regardless of what one chooses for oneself, whether it is an occasional or regular use of platforms, it is important neither to individualize the responsibility nor to project it onto the consumers, especially as platforms become ever-present. Instead, we must redirect our attention to the regulators.

This book looks at the world of these workers to humanize them not as objects of analysis but as subjects with agency. Research can piece together experiences and struggles to contextualize and analyze these, but the aim of this book has never been to speak *for* the workers. What we can do is contribute to the strengthening of their societal power and support their power resources more generally by advocating for their associational and institutional rights or even creating (digital) spaces like Turkopticon. But it is *the workers* who have time and time again proven in their labor struggles that they know best how to navigate platforms. Whether it is the Amazon warehouse workers conscious of Amazon's different tactics and strategies, MTurk workers responding to the very first surveys for Turkopticon and turning to forums or Uber drivers and food delivery workers who log off their alienating apps and stage a collective strike. We can support them precisely based on their efforts to mobilize to improve their working conditions despite their precarious positions. Depending on the organization of their platform and their material contexts, workers may have a weaker structural power and feel more exposed to the whims of the market and fearful of retaliation and losing their jobs. These risks are important to recognize in order neither to project all responsibility onto the workers nor to dismiss the very real material contexts that they must navigate on a day-to-day basis. Yet amidst this all, we have also seen workers finding ways by to strengthen their power resources, from industrial action to opening up during interviews despite the risks and their vulnerabilities. Whether it is then by laboring day in and day out to sustain their livelihoods or the array of ways by which they express their agency in traditional and alternative terms, workers are playing their part, and I hope with such efforts we can continue to support them.

We must not forget how many of the rights we have today have been precisely the result of previous struggles. Historically, unions have played an essential role in these, and social movements have been instrumental and a mobilizing force. These have, however, initially directed less attention and resources to organizing workers in the platform economy. This could be understood in relation to the overall weakening of unions in the neoliberal context over the last decades and because the exponential growth of platforms in capital and power was not initially foreseen. Recognizing that platforms risk undoing precisely those rights, unions and grassroots initiatives have been investing more and more resources in organizing workers and broadening or supporting the labor movement – as we see with Amazon workers. Workers in the platform economy demonstrate, however, that when there is an absence of traditional structures to organize, they will organize themselves – whether this is through a discussion on a digital space or by setting up their own grassroots union or collective. It was, after all, the initiatives of workers that caught much of the attention of unions in the first place. In other cases, platform workers, like many others in our contemporary moment, associate joining an established union with a traditional structure that they may not identify with – additionally on racialized and gendered terms. Consequently, as unions navigate the terrain in attempting to strengthen power resources of workers, we see workers claiming their technologies and establishing their very own structures and even grassroot unions.

As previously mentioned, just as it is important not to project responsibility on to the everyday users of platforms, so it is equally important to recognize the efforts of workers, and their various associations, but not to unload all responsibility onto them. It is crucial that a wider movement to regulate the platform economy accompanies the labor struggle to both protect and support workers, as well as curb the growing powers of platforms. As this book has demonstrated, the platform economy has not developed in isolation from the wider technological and political–economic contexts. Indeed the latter, characterized by neoliberal policies and deregulation of the labor market, have not just allowed platforms to grow but have in many ways *facilitated* this growth. This has become even more so pressing within the context of COVID-19, as platforms have taken center stage in mediating a large portion of our social and labor relations, in many cases leading to an exponential growth of certain platforms and their capital. Reflecting much of what scholars have been highlighting over the last decade, ranging from contract status, wages and labor rights to algorithmic management and the lack of transparency (Aloisi and De Stefano, 2022), it seems that finally some initial efforts and possibilities to regulate platforms are appearing – so much of which has been also the result of labor organization and struggles.

In order to at least protect the bare minimum of working conditions, these have highlighted the necessity to reclassify gig workers as actual workers, guarantee a minimum wage for workers according to the national context in which they labor and protect their basic labor rights, such as the right to organize and form associations. Given the centrality of algorithmic management in platform work, there has also been a push for increased transparency, including the ability to challenge decisions and bring a human being back in to monitor the process (European Commission, 2021a, 2021b; Aloisi and De Stefano, 2022). It remains to be seen to what extent the gig economy can still retain its very fabric once and if regulation takes effect. While the growth of the platform economy was in part facilitated by operating largely outside of regulation to begin with, as we see with the gig economy, it has also benefited from the conditions of the labor market. These too must be more strongly regulated, such as by limiting the use of temporary contracts and generally outsourcing labor. Such regulatory frameworks 'from above' are crucial for the workers struggling on a daily basis for their agency 'from below'. These too are dialectically related. The former would lead to a strengthening of the legal basis to the latter's associational and institutional power, where workers could, if they so wish, organize without fear of termination, retaliation, loss of their residence status and essentially their livelihoods. This is crucial, as it would in turn mean that workers can further claim their workplace power in combination to their other powers. They can strike and bargain for higher wages and better working conditions, which would in turn lead to an improvement of their marketplace and overall structural power.

The lack of regulation has benefited not only the way in which platforms structure their labor relations but also directly the growing dimensions of its capital through subsidies and tax avoidance. Amazon has been accompanied by direct subsidies, explaining the public outrage at Amazon's initial plan to open HQ2 in New York City, where it would have received financial benefits. It has also been reported that Amazon was generally allocated at least US$ 4.7 billion in subsidies, of which US$ 4.18 billion have been recorded in the US, though less is known about those elsewhere (Thomas et al, 2022). It is only in recent years that we hear politicians advocating for regulating platforms: from breaking up those that have monopolized, centralized and concentrated power to obligatory minimum taxation that platforms can no longer dodge. One crucial effort has been the G7's deal, concluded in 2021, in which multinational corporations are to pay at least 15 percent in tax regardless of sales location. It is yet to be seen to what extent corporations will find ways to circumvent these and avoid being held accountable, but there have been increased cases of the European Commission investigating platforms over their anti-competitive behavior, embodied most recently in the Digital Markets Act. This is meant to directly counter platforms and foster competition by regulating the behavior of market-dominating platforms, where they require user consent to collect data from different services to show targeted ads (Satariano, 2022). Recognizing the growing economic power of platforms, it appears that regulators are finally pushing to counter their monopolization, which essentially squashes competition.

With its ever-increasing and ever-expanding range of powers and trend towards monopolization, it becomes crucial to accompany the regulation of capital with regulation of its labor relations to guarantee workers their basic rights and improve their working conditions. As these platforms are characterized by their transnational dimensions, regulation too must take place transnationally both in the Global North and the Global South. If changes in one part of the world are not accompanied by those elsewhere, capital may find ways to continue to dodge and circumvent regulation – both for its capital, by relocating, and for its workers, who may, depending on the organization of the platform, be confronted with an increasing race to the bottom. The latter is especially crucial in those contexts where labor rights are already undermined and the informal economy has long normalized these conditions. As these too operate in space and time, it remains to be seen how the COVID-19 pandemic has affected both capital–labor relations in general and the platform economy more specifically, which has presumably come to be among the 'winners' of the pandemic. The current political–economic and material conditions have thus far favored capital's interests, here of platforms, and the wealth they have accumulated, contributing to the further unequal distribution of wealth on a global scale and widening class inequalities.

Given these wide-ranging repercussions for the world of work and workers, both in terms of their alienating working conditions and their agency, we must take platforms seriously. We need to conceive these not only as products of neoliberalism but also as directly producing and reproducing its trends. It is a daunting image of the future, should class relations become dehumanized altogether and instead be veiled behind algorithmic management and the complete quantification and datafication of our existence. Our political–economic, social and technological discussions today need to aim at (re)humanizing the debate around workers of the Internet and to underline their agency at a time in which precarity is normalized and inequalities exacerbated. While capital in the platform economy alienates, fragments and impedes labor organization across platforms, workers claim time and time again their agency when regulation has failed to protect them from these very working conditions. The landscape of their labor activity and mobilization is becoming increasingly dynamic and vibrant, possibly fostering a labor movement of their own, built on solidarity in their respective platforms and across these. Just as capital evolves, so too must our analysis include the ways by which labor evolves, not in correlational and deterministic terms dictated by the former, but in dialectical and dynamic terms that shape these very class relations. Otherwise we may risk constructing a narrative of our current moment within the written record that is devoid of agency and resistance, and of any possibility for change.

# Notes

## Chapter 4

[1] https://www.webfoundation.org/about/vision/history-of-the-web/ [Accessed 22 February 2022].

[2] https://www.ebayinc.com/company/our-history/ [Accessed 24 February 2022].

[3] https://about.google/our-story/?hl=en [Accessed 28 February 2022].

[4] Own calculations for Meta based on https://www.statista.com/statistics/267031/facebooks-annual-revenue-by-segment/ [Accessed 28 February 2022]; https://www.statista.com/statistics/271258/facebooks-advertising-revenue-worldwide/ [Accessed 28 February 2022]; Google Ads calculations were based on https://www.statista.com/statistics/266206/googles-annual-global-revenue/ [Accessed 28 February 2022]; https://www.statista.com/statistics/266249/advertising-revenue-of-google/.

[5] https://news.airbnb.com/about-us/ [Accessed 1 March 2022]; https://www.uber.com/en-DE/newsroom/history/ [Accessed 1 March 2022].

## Chapter 5

[1] https://www.aboutamazon.com/about-us [Accessed 2 March 2022].

[2] https://www.mturk.com [Accessed 2 March 2022].

[3] https://www.mturk.com/help [Accessed 2 March 2022].

[4] https://www.mturk.com/help [Accessed 2 March 2022].

[5] https://aws.amazon.com/what-is-aws [Accessed 2 March 2022].

[6] https://aws.amazon.com/solutions/case-studies [Accessed 2 March 2022].

[7] https://www.aboutamazon.co.uk/innovation/amazon-prime [Accessed 2 March 2022].

[8] https://flex.amazon.com/why-flex [Accessed 2 March 2022].

[9] https://logistics.amazon.com/marketing/getting-started [Accesssed 21 September 2022].

[10] For continuously updated numbers, one resource is mwpvl.com/html/amazon_com.html [Accessed 2 March 2022].

[11] https://www.nasdaq.com/market-activity/stocks/amzn [Accessed 2 March 2022].

## Chapter 6

[1] https://www.amazon.jobs/en/landing_pages/diversity-and-inclusion [Accessed 3 March 2022].

[2] https://hiring.amazon.com/job-opportunities/fulfillment-center-jobs [Accessed 3 March 2022].

[3] https://www.aboutamazon.eu/working-at-amazon/amazon-fulfillment-network [Accessed 3 March 2022].

[4] https://hiring.amazon.com/why-amazon/work-life-balance [Accessed 3 March 2022].

[5] https://hiring.amazon.com/why-amazon/culture [Accessed 21 September 2022].

[6] https://hiring.amazon.com/why-amazon/work-life-balance [Accessed 3 March 2022].
[7] https://sites.google.com/site/thefaceofamazon/home/amazon-isn-t-worth-it [Accessed 3 March 2022].

## Chapter 7

[1] https://sites.google.com/site/thefaceofamazon/home/fulfillment-center-injury [Accessed 7 March 2022].
[2] https://hiring.amazon.com/hiring-process [Accessed 7 March 2022].
[3] https://www.amazon.jobs/en/landing_pages/diversity-and-inclusion [Accessed 3 March 2022].
[4] https://hiring.amazon.com/why-amazon/work-life-balance [Accessed 7 March 2022]; https://hiring.amazon.com/why-amazon/benefits [Accessed 7 March 2022].
[5] https://www.aboutamazon.eu/our-company/amazon-certified-as-a-2022-top-employer-in-italy-spain-france-and-poland [Accessed 7 March 2022].
[6] https://www.aboutamazon.eu/job-creation-and-investment/amazon-a-major-european-employer [Accessed 7 March 2022].
[7] https://www.aboutamazon.eu/press-release/amazon-pl-launches-in-poland [Accessed 7 March 2022].
[8] https://www.aboutamazon.eu/job-creation-and-investment/amazon-a-major-european-employer [Accessed 7 March 2022].
[9] www.awoodcenter.org [Accessed 7 March 2022].
[10] https://www.bundestag.de/parlament/aufgaben/rechtsgrundlagen/grundgesetz/gg_01-245122 [Accessed 7 March 2022]; https://handel.verdi.de/unternehmen/a-c/amazon [Accessed 7 March 2022].
[11] https://www.gov.uk/trade-union-recognition-employers [Accessed 7 March 2022].
[12] https://www.amazoniansunited.org/actions [Accessed 25 July 2022].
[13] https://fortune.com/fortune500/2021/search/?f500_%20employees=desc [Accessed 7 March 2022].
[14] https://sites.google.com/site/thefaceofamazon/home/unionization-process [Accessed 8 March 2022]; https://sites.google.com/site/thefaceofamazon/#openletter [Accessed 8 March 2022].
[15] https://makeamazonpay.com [Accessed 8 March 2022].
[16] https://amazonfctours.com [Accessed 8 March 2022]; now https://amazontours.com [Accessed 22 September 2022]; see also https://www.aboutamazon.com/news/company-news/response-to-senator-sanders [Accessed 8 March 2022].
[17] This was expressed by Abdirahman Muse during the "Symposium on the unchecked power of Amazon in today's economy and society".

## Chapter 8

[1] https://docs.aws.amazon.com/AWSMechTurk/latest/RequesterUI/amt-ui.pdf [Accessed 4 March 2022]; https://www.mturk.com/pricing [Accessed 4 March 2022].
[2] https://docs.aws.amazon.com/AWSMechTurk/latest/RequesterUI/amt-ui.pdf [Accessed 4 March 2022].
[3] https://www.mturk.com [Accessed 4 March 2022].
[4] https://www.mturk.com/help [Accessed 4 March 2022].
[5] https://docs.aws.amazon.com/AWSMechTurk/latest/RequesterUI/amt-ui.pdf [Accessed 4 March 2022].
[6] https://www.mturk.com/worker [Accessed 4 March 2022].
[7] https://www.mturk.com/help [Accessed 4 March 2022].

## Chapter 9

[1] https://www.mturk.com/help [Accessed 4 March 2022].

[2] https://docs.aws.amazon.com/AWSMechTurk/latest/RequesterUI/amt-ui.pdf [Accessed 4 March 2022].

[3] https://blog.mturk.com/how-to-be-a-great-mturk-requester-3a714d7d7436 [Accessed 11 February 2022].

[4] http://faircrowd.work [Accessed 11 March 2022].

[5] https://fair.work/about [Accessed 11 March 2022].

[6] http://platform.coop/who-we-are/pcc [Accessed 11 March 2022].

## Chapter 10

[1] As previously mentioned, one must keep in mind that not all workers within platforms are in the same position. Those for example working for Uber customer service are in a completely different (more traditional) employment relationship than Uber drivers. The emphasis in my discussion is on the latter, rather than the former.

[2] https://www.upwork.com/legal#privacy [Accessed 12 March 2022].

[3] For numbers see Statista, https://www.statista.com/statistics/311810/google-employee-ethnicity-us/; or https://www.statista.com/statistics/311810/google-employee-ethnicity-us/; for developments and efforts see for instance Google's Diversity Annual Report 2022 https://static.googleusercontent.com/media/about.google/en//belonging/diversity-annual-report/2022/static/pdfs/google_2022_diversity_annual_report.pdf?cachebust=1093852 [Accessed 30 July 2022].

[4] https://appen.com/solutions/platform-overview [Accessed 12 March 2022].

[5] https://help.uber.com/driving-and-delivering/article/driving-time?nodeId=a50a72e1-d315-4154-ac66-b17bd5bd050a [Accessed 26 September 2022].

[6] https://www.amazon.jobs/en/principles [Accessed 23 March 2022].

## Chapter 11

[1] https://techworkerscoalition.org [Accessed 12 March 2022].

[2] https://alphabetworkersunion.org/ [Accessed 23 March 2022].

# References

Abbate, J. (2000) *Inventing the Internet*, Cambridge/London: The MIT Press.

Alderman, L. (2020) "Amazon reaches deal with French Unions in coronavirus safety dispute", *The New York Times*, [online] 16 May, Available from: https://www.nytimes.com/2020/05/16/business/amazon-france-unions-coronavirus.html [Accessed 8 March 2022].

Alimahomed-Wilson, J. (2020) "The Amazonification of logistics: e-commerce, labor, and exploitation in the last mile", in J. Alimahomed-Wilson and E. Reese (eds) *The Cost of Free Shipping: Amazon in the Global Economy*, London: Pluto Press, pp 69–84.

Alimahomed-Wilson, J. and Reese, E. (eds) (2020) *The Cost of Free Shipping: Amazon in the Global Economy*, London: Pluto Press.

Alimahomed-Wilson, J., Allison, J. and Reese, E. (2020) "Introduction: Amazon capitalism" in J. Alimahomed-Wilson and E. Reese (eds) *The Cost of Free Shipping: Amazon in the Global Economy*, London: Pluto Press, pp 1–18.

Alimahomed-Wilson, J. and Reese, E. (2021) "Surveilling Amazon's warehouse workers: racism, retaliation, and worker resistance amid the pandemic", *Work in the Global Economy*, 1(1): 55–73.

Aloisi, A. (2021) "Demystifying flexibility, exposing the algorithmic boss: a note on the first Italian case classifying a (food-delivery) platform workers as an employee", *Comparative Labor Law & Policy Journal*, 35: 1–10.

Aloisi, A. and De Stefano, V. (2022) *Your Boss Is an Algorithm: Artificial Intelligence, Platform Work and Labour*, Oxford/New York/Dublin: Hart Publishing/Bloomsbury Publishing.

Aloisi, A. and Potocka-Sionek, N. (2022) "De-gigging the labour market? An analysis of the 'algorithmic management' provisions in the proposed Platform Work Directive", *Italian Labour Law E-Journal*, 15(1): 29–50.

Amazon Employees for Climate Justice (2020) "How Amazon's emissions are hurting communities of color", [online] 26 May, Available from: https://amazonemployees4climatejustice.medium.com/environmental-justice-and-amazons-carbon-footprint-9e10fab21138 [Accessed 24 October 2022].

Amazon Mechanical Turk (2019) "New feature for the MTurk marketplace", [online] 9 July, Available from: https://blog.mturk.com/new-feature-for-the-mturk-marketplace-aaa0bd520e5b [Accessed 22 September 2022].

Amazon Mechanical Turk (2020) "Participation agreement", *Amazon Mechanical Turk*, [online] updated 25 March 2020, Available from: https://www.mturk.com/participation-agreement [Accessed 4 March 2022].

Amazon Staff (2020) "How we're taking care of employees during COVID-19", *Amazon*, [online] 16 July, updated 3 February 2021, Available from: https://www.aboutamazon.com/news/company-news/how-were-taking-care-of-employees-during-covid-19 [Accessed 8 March 2022].

AMWORKERS (2019) "Final declaration of the transnational meeting of Amazon workers in Leipzig, September 27–29, 2019", *Amazon Workers International* [online] 24 October, Available from: https://amworkers.wordpress.com/2019/10/24/final-declaration-of-the-transnational-meeting-in-leipzig [Accessed 8 March 2022].

Andrews, E.L. and Calmes, J. (2008) "Fed cuts key rate to a record low", *The New York Times*, [online] 16 December, Available from: www.nytimes.com/2008/12/17/business/economy/17fed.html [Accessed 3 March 2022].

Apicella, S. (2016) *Von en Gründen, (nicht) zu streiken*. Studien 09/16. Berlin: Rosa Luxemburg Foundation.

Apicella, S. (2021) *Das Prinzip Amazon*, Hamburg: VSA Verlag.

Apicella, S. and Hildebrandt, H. (2019) "Divided we stand: reasons for and against strike participation in Amazon's German distribution centres", *Work Organisation, Labour & Globalisation*, 13(1): 172–89.

Arcy, J. (2016) "Emotion work: considering gender in digital labor", *Feminist Media Studies*, 16(2): 365–8.

Aytes, A. (2013) "Return of the crowds: mechanical turk and neoliberal states of exception", in T. Scholz (ed) *Digital Labor – Internet as Factory and Playground* (1st edn), New York/London: Routledge, pp 79–97.

Azzelini, D. and Kraft, M.G. (2018) "Introduction: a return to the shop-floor or how to confront neoliberal capitalism", in D. Azzelini and M.G. Kraft (eds) *The Class Strikes Back: Self-Organized Workers' Struggles in the Twenty-First Century*, Leiden/Boston: Brill, pp 1–18.

Barnes, S.-A., Green, A. and De Hoyos, M. (2015) "Crowdsourcing and work: individual factors and circumstances influencing employability", *New Technology, Work and Employment*, 30(1): 16–31.

Barrett, B. (2011) "Google's secret class system", *Gizmodo*, [online] 29 April, Available from: gizmodo.com/googles-secret-class-system-5797022 [Accessed 12 March 2022].

Barthel, G. (2019) "Against the logistics of Amazon: challenges to build effective power", *Strike the Giant! Transnational Organization against Amazon,* Transnational Social Strike Platform, pp 64–71, Available from: https://www.transnational-strike.info/2019/11/29/pdf-strike-the-giant-transnational-organization-against-amazon-tss-journal/ [Accessed 3 March 2022].

Bayat, A. (2013) *Life as Politics: How Ordinary People Change the Middle East,* Stanford: Stanford University Press.

Berg, J. (2016) *Income Security in the On-Demand economy: Findings and Policy Lessons from a Survey of Crowdworkers,* Conditions of Work and Employment Series No. 74, Geneva: International Labour Organization.

Berg, J. and De Stefano, V. (2017) "Regulating for a fairer world of work", in M. Graham and J. Shaw (eds) *Towards a Fairer Gig Economy,* Manchester: Meatspace Press, pp 32–4.

Berg, J., Furrer, M. Harmon, E., Arani, U. and Silberman, M.S. (2018) *Digital Labour Platforms and the Future of Work – Towards Decent Work in the Online World,* Geneva: International Labour Organization.

Berg, J. and Rani, U. (2021) "Working conditions, geography and gender in global crowdwork", in J. Haidar and M. Keune (eds) *Work and Labour Relations in Global Platform Capitalism,* ILERA Publication series, Cheltenham/Northampton: Edward Elgar Publishing, pp 93–110.

Bergfeld, M. (2019) "Delete your app", *Jacobin,* [online] 8 May, Available from: https://www.jacobinmag.com/2019/05/uber-lyft-rideshare-strike-misclassification [Accessed 11 March 2022].

Bergvall-Kåreborn, B., and Howcroft, D. (2014) "Amazon Mechanical Turk and the commodification of labour", *New Technology, Work and Employment,* 29(3): 213–23.

Berinsky, A.J., Huber, G.A. and Lenz, G.S. (2012) "Evaluating online labor markets for experimental research: Amazon.com's Mechanical Turk", *Political Analysis,* 20(3): 351–68.

Bhattacharya, T. (ed) (2017) *Social Reproduction Theory: Remapping Class, Recentering Oppression,* London: Pluto Press.

Bieler, A. (2018) "Agency and power resources approach: asserting the importance of the structuring conditions of the capitalist social relations of production", *Global Labour Journal,* 9(2): 243–8.

Bilić, P., Prug, T. and Žitko, M. (2021) *The Political Economy of Digital Monopolies: Contradictions and Alternatives to Data Commodification,* Bristol: Bristol University Press.

Biron, B. (2021) "Amazon workers in 20 countries will strike or protest on Black Friday for better working conditions", [online] 25 November, Available from: https://www.businessinsider.com/make-amazon-pay-campaign-staffers-will-strike-on-black-friday-2021-11 [Accessed 7 March 2022].

Bispinck, R. and Schulten, T. (2011) *Trade Union Responses to Precarious Employment in Germany*, WSI-Diskussionspapier Nr.178. Düsseldorf: Wirtschafts- und Sozialwissenschaftliches Institut in der Hans-Böckler-Stiftung.

Blest, P. (2020) "Leaked Amazon memo details plan to smear fired warehouse organizer: 'he's not smart or articulate'", *Vice News*, [online] 2 April, Available from: https://www.vice.com/en_us/article/5dm8bx/leaked-amazon-memo-details-plan-to-smear-fired-warehouse-organizer-hes-not-smart-or-articulate [Accessed 8 March 2022].

Block, J. and Sandner, P. (2009) "What is the effect of the financial crisis on venture capital financing? Empirical evidence from us internet start-ups", *Venture Capital*, 11(4): 295–309.

Bloomberg (2019) "Amazon doubles holiday hiring to 200,000 temporary workers", *Bloomberg Technology*, [online] 27 November, Available from: www.bloomberg.com/news/articles/2019-11-27/amazon-doubles-holiday-hiring-to-200-000-temporary-workers [Accessed 19 March 2022].

Boewe, J. and Schulten, J. (2019) *The Long Struggle of the Amazon Employees. Laboratory of Resistance – Laboratory of Resistance: Union Organising in E-Commerce Worldwide* (2nd edn), Brussels: Rosa Luxemburg Stiftung.

Boewe, J. and Schulten, J. (2020) "Amazon strikes in Europe: seven years of industrial action, challenges and strategies", in J. Alimahomed-Wilson and E. Reese (eds) *The Cost of Free Shipping: Amazon in the Global Economy*, London: Pluto Press, pp 209–24.

Bogen, M. (2019) "All the ways hiring algorithms can introduce bias", *Harvard Business Review*, [online] 6 May, Available from: hbr.org/2019/05/all-the-ways-hiring-algorithms-can-introduce-bias [Accessed 12 March 2022].

Bohrer, A.J. (2019) *Marxism and Intersectionality: Race, Gender, Class and Sexuality under Contemporary Capitalism*, Bielefeld: transcript Verlag.

Booth, D.E. (1978) "Collective action, Marx's class theory, and the union movement", *Journal of Economic Issues*, 12(1): 163–85.

Botsman, R. and Rogers, R. (2011) *What's Mine Is Yours: The Rise of Collaborative Consumption*, London: HarperCollins Publishers.

Boto, J.M.M. and Brameshuber, E. (eds) (2022) *Collective Bargaining and the Gig Economy: A Traditional Tool for New Business Models*, Oxford/New York/Dublin: Hart Publishing/Bloomsbury Publishing.

Brandom, R. (2013) "Union 2.0 how a browser plug-in is organizing Amazon's micro-laborers", *The Verge*, [online] 27 June, Available from: www.theverge.com/2013/6/27/4467296/turkopticon-a-labor-union-for-amazons-mechanical-turk [Accessed 11 March 2022].

Braverman, H. (1974) *Labor and Monopoly Capital: The Degradation of Work in the 20th Century*, New York: Monthly Review Press.

Brevini, B. (2021) "Conclusion", in B. Brevini, and L. Swiatek (eds) *Amazon: Understanding a Global Communication Giant*, New York/Abingdon: Routledge, pp 65–70.
Brevini, B. and Swiatek, L. (2021) *Amazon: Understanding a Global Communication Giant*, New York/Abingdon: Routledge.
Briken, K., Chillas, S., Krzywdzinski, M. and Marks, A. (eds) (2017) *The New Digital Workplace: How New Technologies Revolutionise Work*, Basingstoke: Critical Perspectives on Work and Employment.
Bucher, E. and Fieseler, C. (2017) "The flow of digital labor", *New Media & Society*, 19(11): 1868–86.
Buhrmester, M.D., Talaifar, S. and Gosling, S.D. (2018) "An evaluation of Amazon's Mechanical Turk, its rapid rise, and its effective use", *Perspectives on Psychological Science*, 13(2): 149–54.
Burawoy, M. (1979) *Manufacturing Consent: Changes in the Labor Process under Monopoly Capitalism*, Chicago: The University of Chicago Press.
Butler, S. (2018) "Amazon accused of treating UK warehouse staff like robots", *The Guardian*, [online] 31 May, Available from: https://www.theguardian.com/business/2018/may/31/amazon-accused-of-treating-uk-warehouse-staff-like-robots [Accessed 8 March 2022].
Butler, J., Gambetti, Z. and Sabsay, L. (eds) (2016) *Vulnerability in Resistance*, Durham: Duke University Press.
Campbell, A.F. (2019) "Google will extend some benefits to contract workers after internal protest", *Vox*, [online] 4 April, Available from: www.vox.com/2019/4/4/18293900/google-contractors-benefits-policy [Accessed 12 March 2022].
Casilli, A. (2017) "Digital labor studies go global: toward a digital decolonial turn", *International Journal of Communication*, 11: 3934–54.
Castells, M. (1996) *The Information Age: Economy, Society and Culture*, vol 1, *The Rise of the Network Society*, Oxford: Blackwell.
Cattero, B. and D'Onoforio, M. (2018) "Organizing and collective bargaining in the digitized 'tertiary factories' of Amazon: a comparison between Germany and Italy", in E. Alas, Y. Curzi, T. Fabbri, O. Rymkevich, I. Senatori and G. Solinas (eds) *Working in Digital and Smart Organizations: Legal, Economic and Organizational Perspectives on the Digitalization of Labour Relations*, Cham: Palgrave Macmillan, pp 141–64.
Cerf, V.G. (2004) "On the evolution of internet technologies", *Proceedings of the IEEE*, 92(9): 1360–70.
Chaudhry, A. (2020) "How to order takeout safely and ethically", *The Verge*, [online] 1 April, Available from: https://www.theverge.com/2020/3/17/21183919/food-take-out-delivery-order-safe-restaurants-coronavirus [Accessed 12 March 2022].
Chayko, M. (2018) *Superconnected: The Internet, Digital Media, and Techno-Social Life* (2nd edn), Thousand Oaks/London: SAGE Publications, Inc.

Christiaens, T. (2022) *Digital Working Lives: Worker Autonomy and the Digital Gig Economy*, London: Rowman & Littlefield.

Clark, K. (2019) "Uber's first day as a public company didn't go so well", *TechCrunch*, [online] 10 May, Available from: techcrunch.com/2019/05/10/ubers-first-day-as-a-public-company-didnt-go-so-well/ [Accessed 2 March 2022].

Cleaver, H. (1979) *Reading Capital Politically*, Austin: University of Texas Press.

Cockayne, D.G. (2016) "Sharing and neoliberal discourse: the economic function of sharing in the digital on-demand economy", *Geoforum*, 77: 73–82.

Collier, R.B., Dubal, V. and Carter, C. (2017) "Labor platforms and gig work: the failure to regulate". IRLE Working Paper No. 106-17, UC Hastings Research Paper No. 251.

Collinson, D. (1994) "Strategies of resistance: power, knowledge and subjectivity in the workplace", in J.M. Jermier, D. Knights and W.R. Nord (eds) *Resistance and Power in Organizations*, London: Routledge, pp 25–68.

Comor, E. (2014) "Revisiting Marx's value theory: a critical response to analyses of digital prosumption", *The Information Society*, 31(1): 13–19.

Cook, J. (2015) "Uber's internal charts show how its driver-rating system actually works", *Business Insider*, [online] 11 February, Available from: www.businessinsider.com/leaked-charts-show-how-ubers-driver-rating-system-works-2015-2?r=DE&IR=T [Accessed 12 March 2022].

Curry, B. (2022) "Amazon stock split: what you need to know", *Forbes Advisor*, [online] 6 June, Available from: https://www.forbes.com/advisor/investing/amazon-stock-split [Accessed 21 September 2022].

Dalla Costa, M. and James, S. (1975) *The Power of Women and the Subversion of the Community* (3rd edn), Bristol: Falling Wall Press Ltd.

Dastin, J. (2018) "Amazon scraps secret AI recruiting tool that showed bias against women", *Reuters*, [online] 10 October, Available from: www.reuters.com/article/us-amazon-com-jobs-automation-insight/amazon-scraps-secret-ai-recruiting-tool-that-showed-bias-against-women-idUSKCN1MK08G [Accessed 12 March 2022].

Dastin, J. (2019) "Exclusive: Amazon rolls out machines that pack orders and replace jobs", *Reuters*, [online] 13 May, Available from: www.reuters.com/article/us-amazon-com-automation-exclusive/exclusive-amazon-rolls-out-machines-that-pack-orders-and-replace-jobs-idUSKCN1SJ0X1 [Accessed 12 March 2022].

Day, M. and Gu, J. (2019) "The enormous numbers behind Amazon's market reach", *Bloomberg*, 27 March, Available from: www.bloomberg.com/graphics/2019-amazon-reach-across-markets/ [Accessed 2 March 2022].

Debter, L. (2020) "Bezos is $12.8 billion richer after Amazon delivers strong holiday sales", *Forbes*, [online] 31 January, Available from: www.forbes.com/sites/laurendebter/2020/01/30/amazon-jeff-bezos-13-billion-richer-holiday-quarter/ [Accessed 2 March 2022].

Delfanti, A. (2021a) "Machinic dispossession and augmented despotism: Digital work in an Amazon warehouse", *New Media & Society*, 23(1): 39–55.

Delfanti, A. (2021b) *The Warehouse: Workers and Robots at Amazon*, London: Pluto Press.

Delfanti, A., Radovac, L. and Walker, T. (2021) *The Amazon Panopticon: A Guide for Workers, Organizers and Policymakers*, UNI Global Union, Available from: https://uniglobalunion.org/report/the-amazon-panopticon.

Del Rey, J. (2022) "Leaked Amazon memo warns the company is running out of people to hire", *Vox*, [online] 17 June, Available from: https://www.vox.com/recode/23170900/leaked-amazon-memo-warehouses-hiring-shortage [Accessed 26 September 2022].

De Stefano, V. (2016) *The Rise of the "Just-in-Time Workforce": On-Demand Work, Crowdwork and Labour protection in the "Gig-Economy"*, Conditions of Work and Employment Series No.71, Geneva: International Labour Organization.

Dewhurst, M. (2017) "We are not entrepreneurs", in M. Graham and J. Shaw (eds) *Towards a Fairer Gig Economy*, Manchester: Meatspace Press, pp 20–23.

Difallah, D., Filatova, E. and Ipeirotis, P. (2018) "Demographics and dynamics of Mechanical Turk workers", in *Proceedings of WSDM 2018: The Eleventh ACM International Conference on Web Search and Data Mining*, Available from: https://www.ipeirotis.com/wp-content/uploads/2017/12/wsdmf074-difallahA.pdf.

Dinerstein, A.C. and Pitts, F.H. (2021) *A World beyond Work? Labour, Money and the Capitalist State Between Crisis and Utopia*, Bingley: Emerald Publishing Ltd.

Dinerstein, A., Vela, A.G., González, E. and Holloway, J. (eds) (2019) *Open Marxism 4: Against a Closing World*, London: Pluto Press.

Domhoff, G.W. (2013) "The rise and fall of labor unions in the U.S. – from the 1830s until 2012 (but mostly 1930s–1980s)", *Who Rules America?*, University of California Santa Cruz [online] Available from: https://whorulesamerica.ucsc.edu/power/history_of_labor_unions.html [Accessed 8 March 2022].

Dribbusch, H. (2015) "Where is the European general strike? Understanding the challenges of trans-European trade union action against austerity", *Transfer: European Review of Labour and Research*, 21(2): 171–85.

Dubal, V. (2022a) "Essentially dispossessed", *South Atlantic Quarterly*, 121(2): 285–96.

Dubal V. (2022b) "Economic security & the regulation of gig work in California: From AB5 to Proposition 22", *European Labour Law Journal*, 13(1): 51–65.

Duménil, G. and Lévy, D. (2011) *The Crisis of Neoliberalism*, Cambridge, MA: Harvard University Press.

Dunayevskaya, R. (1975) *Marxism and Freedom: From 1776 until Today* (4th edn), London: Pluto Press.

Dunn, B. (2004) *Global Restructuring and the Power of Labour*, London: Palgrave Macmillan.

Dzieza, J. (2020) "Robots aren't taking our jobs – they're becoming our bosses", *The Verge*, [online] 27 February, Available from: www.theverge.com/2020/2/27/21155254/automation-robots-unemployment-jobs-vs-human-google-amazon [Accessed 2 March 2022].

*The Economist* (2017) "The world's most valuable resource is no longer oil, but data", *The Economist*, [online] 6 May, Available from: www.economist.com/leaders/2017/05/06/the-worlds-most-valuable-resource-is-no-longer-oil-but-data [Accessed 4 March 2022].

*The Economist* (2018), "Technology may help to revive organised labour", *The Economist*, [online] 15 November, Available from: www.economist.com/briefing/2018/11/15/technology-may-help-to-revive-organised-labour [Accessed 4 March 2022].

Ellmer, M. (2015) "The digital division of labor: socially constructed design patterns of Amazon Mechanical Turk and the governing of human computation labor", *Momentum Quarterly – Zeitschrift für Sozialen Fortschritt*, 4(3): 174–86.

Englert, S, Woodcock, J, Cant, C. et al. (2020) "Digital workerism: technology, platforms, and the circulation of workers' struggles", *TripleC: Communication, Capitalism and Critique*, 18(1): 132–45.

Ettlinger, N. (2017) "Paradoxes, problems and potentialities of online work platforms", *Work Organisation, Labour & Globalisation*, 11(2): 21–38.

ETUC (2021) "Time to Europeanise Amazon – Statement by the ETUC Collective Bargaining and Wage Coordination Committee", [online] 27 May, Available from: https://www.etuc.org/en/document/time-europeanise-amazon-statement-etuc-collective-bargaining-and-wage-coordination [Accessed 9 March 2022].

Eurofound (2021) "Gorillas Workers Collective", *Eurofound*, 27 October, Available from: https://www.eurofound.europa.eu/nb/node/105423 [Accessed 25 October 2022].

Eurofound (2022) "Riders' Union Netherlands", *Eurofound*, 14 February, Available from: https://www.eurofound.europa.eu/data/platform-economy/initiatives/riders-union-netherlands [Accessed 25 October 2022].

European Commission (2021a) "Commission proposals to improve the working conditions of people working through digital labour platforms", *European Commission*, 9 December, Available from: https://ec.europa.eu/commission/presscorner/detail/en/ip_21_6605 [Accessed 2 March 2022].

European Commission (2021b) "Questions and answers: improving working conditions in platform work", *European Commission*, 9 December, Available from: https://ec.europa.eu/commission/presscorner/detail/en/qanda_21_6606 [Accessed 11 March 2022].

Evans, T. (2015) "Five explanations for the international financial crisis", in E. Hein, D. Detzer and N. Dodig (eds) *The Demise of Finance-Dominated Capitalism. Explaining the Financial and Economic Crisis*, Cheltenham: Edward Elgar Publishing, pp 219–39.

Fantasia, R. (1988) *Cultures of Solidarity: Consciousness, Action, and Contemporary American Workers*, Berkeley and Los Angeles: University of California Press.

Faus, J. and Carreño, B. (2021) "Gig-economy riders in Spain must become staff within 90 days under new rule", *Reuters*, [online] 11 May, Available from: https://www.reuters.com/business/sustainable-business/gig-economy-riders-spain-must-become-staff-within-90-days-under-new-rule-2021-05-11 [Accessed 11 March 2022].

The Federal Ministry of Labour and Social Affairs (2019) *Co-Determination 2019*. Available from: https://www.bmas.de/SharedDocs/Downloads/EN/PDF-Publikationen/a741e-co-determination.pdf?__blob=publicationFile&v=2 [Accessed 8 March 2022].

The Federal Reserve Board (2000) "Remarks by Chairman Alan Greenspan – the revolution in information technology", [online], Available from www.federalreserve.gov/boarddocs/speeches/2000/20000306.htm [Accessed 28 February 2022].

Federici, S. (2004) *Caliban and the Witch: Women, the Body and Primitive Accumulation* (1st edn), New York: Autonomedia.

Forbes Technology Council (2018) "13 reasons Google deserves its 'best company culture' award", *Forbes*, [online] 8 February, Available from: https://www.forbes.com/sites/forbestechcouncil/2018/02/08/13-reasons-google-deserves-its-best-company-culture-award/?sh=519157953482 [Accessed 26 September 2022].

Foucault, M. (1995) *Discipline and Punish: The Birth of the Prison* (2nd edn), trans. A. Sheridan, New York: Vintage Books.

*Frankfurt Paper on Platform-Based Work: Proposals for Platform Operators, Clients, Policy Makers, Workers, and Worker Organizations* (2016), Available from: http://crowdwork-igmetall.de/Frankfurt_Paper_on_Platform_Based_Work_EN.pdf.

Frenken, K. and Schor, J. (2017) "Putting the sharing economy into perspective", *Environmental Innovation and Societal Transitions*, 23: 3–10.

Fuchs, C. (2012) "Critique of the political economy of web 2.0 surveillance", in C. Fuchs, K. Boersma, A. Albrechtslund and M. Sandoval (eds) *Internet and Surveillance: The Challenges of Web 2. 0 and Social Media*, New York/Abingdon: Routledge, pp 31–70.

Fuchs, C. and Mosco, V. (eds) (2016) *Marx in the Age of Digital Capitalism*, Leiden/Boston: Brill.

Fuchs, C. (2019) *Marxism: Karl Marx's Fifteen Key Concepts for Cultural and Communication Studies* (1st edn), New York: Routledge.

Gallagher, R. (2019a) "Google accused of creating spy tool to squelch worker dissent", *Bloomberg*, [online] 24 October, Available from: www.bloomberg.com/news/articles/2019-10-23/google-accused-of-creating-spy-tool-to-squelch-worker-dissent [Accessed 11 March 2022].

Gallagher, R. (2019b) "Swiss Google employees defy managers, stage labor event", *Bloomberg*, [online] 24 October, Available from: [Accessed 11 March 2022].

Gandini, A. (2019) "Labour process theory and the gig economy", *Human Relations*, 72(6): 1039–56.

Gault, M. (2021) "Amazon introduces tiny 'ZenBooths' for stressed-out warehouse workers", *Motherboard Tech by Vice*, [online] 27 May, Available from: https://www.vice.com/en/article/wx5nmw/amazon-introduces-tiny-zenbooths-for-stressed-out-warehouse-workers [Accessed 19 March 2022].

Gearhart, D. (2017) "Giving Uber drivers a voice in the gig economy", in M. Graham and J. Shaw (eds) *Towards a Fairer Gig Economy*, Manchester: Meatspace Press, pp 13–14.

Gent, E. (2019) "The 'ghost work' powering tech magic", *BBC*, [online] 2 September, Available from: www.bbc.com/worklife/article/20190829-the-ghost-work-powering-tech-magic [Accessed 11 March 2022].

Gerber, C. (2022) "Gender and precarity in platform work: old inequalities in the new world of work", *New Technology, Work and Employment*, Early View, Available from: https://onlinelibrary.wiley.com/doi/10.1111/ntwe.12233?s=03 [Accessed 27 September 2022].

Gilbert, D. (2020) "Facebook is forcing its moderators to log every second of their days – even in the bathroom", *Vice news*, [online] 9 January, Available from: www.vice.com/en_ca/article/z3beea/facebook-moderators-lawsuit-ptsd-trauma-tracking-bathroom-breaks [Accessed 12 March 2022].

GMB Union (2018a) "Play Amazon warehouse whack-a-mole", *GMB Union*, [online] 18 December, Available from: https://www.gmb.org.uk/news/play-amazon-warehouse-whack-mole [Accessed 8 March 2022].

GMB Union (2018b) "This #BlackFriday Amazon workers worldwide have come together with one message for billionaire Jeff Bezos. We are not robots, treat us with dignity and respect. Please share their message #AmazonWeAreNotRobots.", *Twitter*, [online] 23 November, Available from: https://twitter.com/gmb_union/status/1065909252269793280?lang=en [Accessed 8 March 2022].

Gompers, P. and Lerner, J. (2001) "The venture capital revolution", *The Journal of Economic Perspectives*, 15(2): 145–68.

Gonzalez, A.L. (2019) "The 'microworkers' making your digital life possible", *BBC*, [online] 2 August, Available from: www.bbc.com/news/business-48881827 [Accessed 4 March 2022].

Goodkind, N. (2021) "Jeff Bezos thanks Amazon workers and customers after space flight: 'You paid for all of this'", *Fortune*, [online] 21 July, Available from: https://fortune.com/2021/07/20/jeff-bezos-thanks-amazon-workers-and-customers-after-space-flight-you-paid-for-all-of-this/ [Accessed 27 September 2022].

Goodnight, G.T. and Green, S. (2010) "Rhetoric, misk, and markets: the dot-com bubble", *Quarterly Journal of Speech*, 96(2): 115–40.

Goodwin, T. (2015) "The battle is for the customer interface", *TechCrunch*, [online] 3 March, Available from: https://techcrunch.com/2015/03/03/in-the-age-of-disintermediation-the-battle-is-all-for-the-customer-interface [Accessed 2 March 2022].

Graham, M., Hjorth, I. and Lehdonvirta, V. (2017) "Digital labour and development: impacts of global digital labour platforms and the gig economy on worker livelihoods", *Transfer: European Review of Labour and Research*, 23(2): 135–62.

Graham, M. and Shaw, J. (eds) (2017) *Towards a Fairer Gig Economy*, Manchester: Meatspace Press.

Graham, M. and Woodcock, J. (2020) *The Gig Economy: A Critical Introduction*, Cambridge/Medford: Polity Press.

Gramsci, A. (1971) *Selections from the Prison Notebooks*, trans. and ed. Q. Hoare and G.N. Smith, New York: International Publishers.

Gray, N., and Clare, N. (2022). "From autonomous to autonomist geographies", *Progress in Human Geography*, 46(5), https://doi.org/10.1177/03091325221114347 [Accessed 27 September 2022].

Gray, M.L. and Suri, S. (2019) *Ghost Work – How to Stop Silicon Valley from Building a New Global Underclass*, Boston/New York: Houghton Mifflin Harcourt.

Gregg, A. (2019) "CIA long relied exclusively on Amazon for its cloud computing. now it is seeking multiple providers for a massive new contract", *The Washington Post*, [online] 2 April, Available from: www.washingtonpost.com/business/2019/04/02/cia-long-relied-exclusively-amazon-its-cloud-computing-now-it-is-seeking-multiple-providers-massive-new-contract/ [Accessed 2 March 2022].

Gregg, M. (2011) *Work's Intimacy*, Cambridge/Malden: Polity.

Gurley, L.K. (2020) "Secret Amazon reports expose company spying of labor, environmental groups", *Motherboard Tech by Vice*, [online] 23 November, Available from: www.vice.com/en/article/5dp3yn/amazon-leaked-reports-expose-spying-warehouse-workers-labor-union-environmental-groups-social-movements [Accessed 8 March 2022].

Gurley, L.K. (2022a) "Google had secret project to 'convince' employees 'that unions suck'", *Motherboard Tech by Vice*, [online] 10 January, Available from: https://www.vice.com/en/article/v7d7j9/google-had-secret-project-to-convince-employees-that-unions-suck [Accessed 8 March 2022].

Gurley, L.K. (2022b) "Unionizing Amazon workers in Bessemer have no shot. Or do they?", *Motherboard Tech by Vice*, [online] 3 February, Available from: https://www.vice.com/en/article/z3nqe5/amazon-workers-could-have-a-better-chance-of-winning-a-union-this-time-around [Accessed 8 March 2022].

Gumbrell-McCormick, R. and Hyman, R. (2013) *Trade Unions in Western Europe*, Oxford: Oxford University Press.

Gupta, N., Martin, D., Hanrahan, B.V. and O'Neill, J. (2014) "Turk-life in India", *Group' 14*: Proceedings of the 18th International Conference on Supporting Group Work: 1–11.

Haidar, J, and Keune, M. (eds) (2021) *Work and Labour Relations in Global Platform Capitalism*, ILERA Publication series, Cheltenham/Northampton: Edward Elgar Publishing.

Haiven, M. (2011) "Finance as capital's imagination?: Reimagining value and culture in an age of fictitious capital and crisis", *Social Text* 29(3 (108)): 93–124.

Hall, M. (2017) "The ghost of the Mechanical Turk", *Jacobin*, [online] 16 December, Available from: http://www.jacobinmag.com/2017/12/middle-east-digital-labor-microwork-gaza-refugees-amazon [Accessed 4 March 2022].

Hamilton, I.A. (2018) "Amazon is raising its minimum wage to $15 following pressure from Bernie Sanders", *Business Insider*, [online] 2 October, Available from: https://www.businessinsider.com/amazon-raises-minimum-wage-to-15-dollars-2018-10?r=DE&IR=T [Accessed 8 March 2022].

Hamilton, I.A. (2021) "Amazon is changing how it measures a key productivity metric called 'Time off Task,' which workers have blamed for a culture of relentless monitoring and punishing staff who fall behind", *Business Insider*, [online] 2 June, Available from: https://www.businessinsider.com/amazon-changing-how-it-measures-time-off-task-metric-2021-6 [Accessed 3 March 2022].

Hansell, S. (2002) "TECHNOLOGY; a surprise from Amazon: Its First Profit", *The New York Times*, [online] 23 January, Available from: https://www.nytimes.com/2002/01/23/business/technology-a-surprise-from-amazon-its-first-profit.html, [Accessed 2 March 2022].

Hara, K., Abigail, A., Milland, K., Savage, S., Callison-Burch, C. and Bigham, J.P. (2018) "A data-driven analysis of workers' earnings on Amazon Mechanical Turk", *Proceedings of the 2018 Conference on Human Factors in Computing System*, Paper No.449.

Harmon, E. and Silberman, M.S. (2019) "Rating working conditions on digital labor platforms", *Computer Supported Cooperative Work (CSCW)*, 28: 911–60.

Harris, M. (2014) "Amazon's Mechanical Turk workers protest: 'I am a human being, not an algorithm'", *The Guardian*, [online] 3 December, Available from: https://www.theguardian.com/technology/2014/dec/03/amazon-mechanical-turk-workers-protest-jeff-bezos [Accessed 11 March 2022].

Harvey, D. (2005) *A Brief History of Neoliberalism*, Oxford: Oxford University Press.

Harvey, D. (2010a) *A Companion to Marx's Capital*, London: Verso.

Harvey, D. (2010b) "The enigma of capital and the crisis this time", *Reading Marx's Capital with David Harvey*, [online] 30 August, Available from: http://davidharvey.org/2010/08/the-enigma-of-capital-and-the-crisis-this-time/#fn-585-18 [Accessed 2 March 2022].

Heikkilä, M. (2020a) "Inside Amazon's global worker movement", *Politico*, [online] 19 October, Available from: https://www.politico.eu/article/amazon-workers-of-the-world-unite-jeff-bezos-protest/ [Accessed 8 March 2022].

Heikkilä, M. (2020b) "'This is crazy:' Rage boils over Amazon sites over coronavirus risks", *Politico*, [online] 20 March, Available from: https://www.politico.eu/article/coronavirus-amazon-employees-rage [Accessed 2 March 2022].

Helling, B. (2022) "Uber services: the company's ride options, products, and services", *Ridester*, [online] 16 July, Available from: https://www.ridester.com/uber-services/ [Accessed 27 September 2022].

Hill, S. (2018) "The distributed workforce: what will jobs of the future look like?", *Mitbestimmungsportal, Hans Böckler Stiftung*, [online] 18 July, Available from: https://www.mitbestimmung.de/html/the-distributed-workforce-what-will-jobs-8374.html [Accessed 2 March 2022].

Howcroft, D., and Bergvall-Kåreborn, B. (2019) "A typology of crowdwork platforms", *Work, Employment and Society*, *33*(1), 21–38.

Howe, J. (2006) "The rise of crowdsourcing", *Wired*, [online] 6 January, Available from: www.wired.com/2006/06/crowds/ [Accessed 2 March 2022].

Huws, U. (2014) *Labor in the Global Digital Economy: The Cybertariat Comes of Age*, New York: Monthly Review.

Hyman, R. (2005) "Trade unions and the politics of the european social model", *Economic and Industrial Democracy*, 26(1): 9–40.

IOL (2018) "Uber, Taxify drivers strike over 'slavery-like' conditions", *IOL*, [online] 13 November, Available from: https://www.iol.co.za/motoring/industry-news/uber-taxify-drivers-strike-over-slavery-like-conditions-18094851 [Accessed 12 March 2022].

International Labour Organization (2019) *Work for a Brighter Future – Global Commission on the Future of Work*, Geneva: International Labour Organization, Available from: https://www.ilo.org/wcmsp5/groups/public/---dgreports/---cabinet/documents/publication/wcms_662410.pdf.

Ipeirotis, P. (2018) "How many Mechanical Turk workers are there?", *A Computer Scientist in a Business School*, [online] 29 January, Available from: https://www.behind-the-enemy-lines.com/2018/01/how-many-mechanical-turk-workers-are.html [Accessed 10 March 2022].

Irani, L. (2013) "The cultural work of microwork", *New Media & Society*, 17(5): 720–39.

Irani, L. (2015) "Difference and dependence among digital workers: the case of Amazon Mechanical Turk", *South Atlantic Quarterly*, 114(1): 225–34.

Irani, L. and Silberman, M.S. (2013) "Turkopticon: interrupting worker invisibility in Amazon Mechanical Turk", *Proceedings of the CHI Conference on Human Factors in Computing System*, 611–20.

Jaeggi, R. (2014) *Alienation*, ed. F. Neuhouser, trans. F. Neuhouser and A.E. Smith, New York: Columbia University Press.

Jermier, J.M., Knights, D. and Nord, W.R. (eds) (1994) *Resistance and Power in Organizations*, London: Routledge.

Jolly, J. (2021) "Global G7 deal may let Amazon off hook on tax, say experts", *The Guardian*, [online] 6 June, Available from: https://www.theguardian.com/technology/2021/jun/06/global-g7-deal-may-let-amazon-off-hook-on-tax-say-experts [Accessed 2 March 2022].

Jones, S. (2018) "The Pinkertons still never sleep", *The New Republic*, [online] 23 March, Available from: newrepublic.com/article/147619/pinkertons-still-never-sleep [Accessed 8 March 2022].

Joyce, S., Stuart, M. and Forde, C. (2022) "Theorising labour unrest and trade unionism in the platform economy", *New Technology, Work and Employment*, online version, Available from: https://doi.org/10.1111/ntwe.12252 [Accessed 27 September 2022].

Kantor, J. and Streitfeld, D. (2015) "Inside Amazon: wrestling big ideas in a bruising workplace", *The New York Times*, [online] 15 August, Available from: www.nytimes.com/2015/08/16/technology/inside-amazon-wrestling-big-ideas-in-a-bruising-workplace.html [Accessed 8 March 2022].

Kassem, S. (2020) "Amazon in the time of coronavirus", *HesaMag* 22, ETUI, pp 14–17, Available from: https://etui.org/sites/default/files/2020-11/4-Sarrah_Kassem_Amazon%20in%20the%20time_of_coronavirus_2020.pdf.

Kassem, S. (2022) "Labour realities at Amazon and COVID-19: obstacles and collective possibilities for its warehouse workers and MTurk workers", *Global Political Economy*, 1(1): 59–79.

Kassem, S. (2023) "(Re)shaping Amazon Labour Struggles on both sides of the Atlantic: the power dynamics in Germany and the US amidst the pandemic", *Transfer: European Review of Labour and Research*, 28(4), Available from: https://doi.org/10.1177/10242589221149496 [Accessed 17 January 2023].

Kässi, O. and Lehdonvirta, V. (2018) "Online labour index: measuring the online gig economy for policy and research", *Technological Forecasting and Social Change*, 137: 241–8.

Katz, M. (2017) "Amazon's Turker crowd has had enough", *Wired*, [online] 23 August, Available from: www.wired.com/story/amazons-turker-crowd-has-had-enough [Accessed 11 March 2022].

Keefer, A. and Baiget, T. (2001) "How it all began: a brief history of the Internet", VINE, 31(3): 90–5.

Kelly, J. (1998) *Rethinking Industrial Relations: Mobilization, Collectivism and Long Waves*, London/New York: Routledge.

Kenney, M. (2003a) "The growth and development of the Internet in the United States", in B. Kogut (ed) *The Global Internet Economy*, Cambridge: MIT Press, pp 69–108.

Kenney, M. (2003b) "What goes up must come down: the political economy of the US Internet industry", in J.F. Christensen and P. Maskell (eds) *The Industrial Dynamics of the New Digital Economy*, Cheltenham/Northampton: Edward Elgar Publishing, pp 35–55.

Kenney, M. and Zysman, J. (2016) "The rise of the platform economy", *Issues in Science and Technology*, 32(3): 61–9.

Kessler, S. (2017) "Amazon is using peer pressure to keep German warehouse workers from calling in sick", *Quartz*, [online] 20 April, Available from: qz.com/962717/amazon-pays-german-warehouse-workers-bonuses-partly-based-on-when-their-coworkers-call-in-sick [Accessed 2 March 2022].

Keuschnigg, C. (2004) "Venture capital backed growth", *Journal of Economic Growth*, 9: 239–361.

Khaleeli, H. (2016) "The truth about working for Deliveroo, Uber and the on-demand economy", *The Guardian*, [online] 15 June, Available from: www.theguardian.com/money/2016/jun/15/he-truth-about-working-for-deliveroo-uber-and-the-on-demand-economy [Accessed 12 March 2022].

Kim, E. (2016) "There's a website just for upset Amazon employees to post reviews, and its organizers want a union", *Business Insider*, [online] 17 February, Available from: www.businessinsider.com/theres-an-anonymous-group-of-amazon-employees-to-complain-about-the-company-and-they-want-to-unionize-2016-2?r=DE&IR=T [Accessed 8 March 2022].

Knights, D. and Willmott, H. (eds) (1990) *Labour Process Theory*, London: Palgrave Macmillan.

Kocher, E. (2022) *Digital Work Platforms at the Interface of Labour Law: Regulating Market Organisers*, Oxford/New York/Dublin: Hart Publishing, Bloomsbury Publishing.

Kollewe, J. (2020) "Trade unions urge EU to investigate Amazon effort to spy on workers", *The Guardian*, [online] 30 September, Available from: www.theguardian.com/technology/2020/sep/30/trade-unions-urge-eu-to-investigate-amazon-effort-to-spy-on-workers [Accessed 8 March 2022].

Koloğlugil, S. (2015) "Digitizing Karl Marx: the new political economy of general intellect and immaterial labor", *Rethinking Marxism*, 27(1): 123–37.

Krähling, C. (2019) "Common strategy to gain power and think bigger", interview in *Strike the Giant! Transnational Organization against Amazon,* Transnational Social Strike Platform, pp 12–17. Available from https://www.transnational-strike.info/2019/11/29/pdf-strike-the-giant-transnational-organization-against-amazon-tss-journal/ [Accessed 3 March 2022].

Kruse, A. (2004) *Online bestellen – offline lesen: Das Buch als Verkaufserfolg im Internet*, Norderstedt: Books on Demand.

Krzywdzinski, M. (2014) "How the EU's Eastern Enlargement Changed the German Productive Model. The Case of the Automotive Industry", *Revue de la regulation*, 15 [online], Available from: http://journals.openedition.org/regulation/10663.

Kuek, S.C., Paradi-Guilford, C., Fayomi, T., Imaizumi, S. and Ipeirotis, P. (2015) *The Global Opportunity in Online Outsourcing*, Washington, D.C.: World Bank Group. Available from: http://documents.worldbank.org/curated/en/138371468000900555/pdf/ACS14228-ESW-white-cover-P149016-Box391478B-PUBLIC-World-Bank-Global-OO-Study-WB-Rpt-FinalS.pdf. [Accessed 27 September 2022].

LaVecchia, O. and Mitchell, S. (2016) *Amazon's Stranglehold: How the Company's Tightening Grip Is Stifling Competition, Eroding Jobs, and Threatening Communities*, Institute for Local Self-Reliance, Available from: https://ilsr.org/wp-content/uploads/2020/04/ILSR_AmazonReport_final.pdf [Accessed 27 September 2022].

Lecher, C. (2019) "How Amazon automatically tracks and fires warehouse workers for 'productivity'", *The Verge*, [online] 25 April, Available from: www.theverge.com/2019/4/25/18516004/amazon-warehouse-fulfillment-centers-productivity-firing-terminations [Accessed 2 March 2022].

Lee, M.K., Kusbit, D., Metsky, E. and Dabbish, L. (2015) "Working with machines: the impact of algorithmic and data-driven management on human workers", *Proceedings of the Association for Computing Machinery (ACM)*, Conference on Human Factors in Computing Systems (CHI), 1603–12.

Lee, T.L., Tapia, M., Pinto, S., Bustamente, A.R., Aranzaes, C.L. and Shimek, S. (2022) "Amazon's policing power: a snapshot from Bessemer", Available from: https://smlr.rutgers.edu/sites/default/files/Documents/News/Amazon_Policing_Power_Report.pdf [Accessed 27 September 2022].

Lehdonvirta, V. (2018) "Flexibility in the gig economy: managing time on three online piecework platforms", *New Technology, Work and Employment*, 33(1): 13–29.

Leiner, B.M., Cerf, V.G., Clark, D.D., Kahn, R.E., Kleinrock, L., Lynch, D.C., Postol, J., Roberts, L.G. and Wolff, S. (1997) *A Brief History of the Internet*, Internet Society, Available from: https://www.internetsociety.org/wp-content/uploads/2017/09/ISOC-History-of-the-Internet_1997.pdf [Accessed 27 September 2022].

Leisegang, D. (2014) *Amazon: Das Buch als Beute*, Stuttgart: Schmetterling-Verlag.

Liao, S. (2018) "Amazon warehouse workers skip bathroom breaks to keep their jobs, says report", *The Verge*, [online] 16 April, Available from: https://www.theverge.com/2018/4/16/17243026/amazon-warehouse-jobs-worker-conditions-bathroom-breaks [Accessed 12 March 2022].

Lieber, C. (2018) "Muslim Amazon workers say they don't have enough time to pray. Now they're fighting for their rights", *Vox*, [online] 17 December, Available from: https://www.vox.com/the-goods/2018/12/14/18141291/amazon-fulfillment-center-east-africa-workers-minneapolis [Accessed 8 March 2022].

Lilja, M. and Vinthagen, S. (2018) "Dispersed resistance: unpacking the spectrum and properties of glaring and everyday resistance", *Journal of Political Power*, 11(2): 211–29.

Logan, J. (2021) "Crushing unions, by any means necessary: how Amazon's blistering anti-union campaign won in Bessemer, Alabama", *New Labor Forum*, CUNY Academics Commons [online] November, Available from: https://newlaborforum.cuny.edu/2021/11/15/crushing-unions-by-any-means-necessary-how-amazons-blistering-anti-union-campaign-won-in-bessemer-alabama [Accessed 8 March 2022].

Lopatto, E. (2021) "Jeff Bezos appreciates your efforts to get Jeff Bezos to space", *The Verge*, [online] 20 July, Available from: https://www.theverge.com/2021/7/20/22585470/jeff-bezos-blue-origin-space-amazon-customers [Accessed 3 March 2022].

Lunden, I. (2017) "Amazon confirms acquisition of Souq, marking its move into the Middle East", *TechCrunch*, [online] 28 March, Available from: techcrunch.com/2017/03/28/amazon-confirms-acquisition-of-souq-marking-its-move-into-the-middle-east [Accessed 2 March 2022].

Lukács, G. (1920) *History and Class Consciousness*, Marxists Internet Archive, [online] Available from: https://www.marxists.org/archive/lukacs/works/history/lukacs3.htm [Accessed 2 March 2022].

Luxemburg, R. (1900) "Co-operatives, unions, democracy", in *Reform or Revolution*, Marxists Internet Archive, [online] Available from: https://www.marxists.org/archive/luxemburg/1900/reform-revolution/ch07.htm [Accessed 5 March 2022].

Mangalindan, J.P. (2011) "Timeline: where Facebook got its funding", *Fortune*, [online] 11 January, Available from: fortune.com/2011/01/11/timeline-where-facebook-got-its-funding/ [Accessed 2 March 2022].

Martin, C.J. (2016) "The sharing economy: a pathway to sustainability or a nightmarish form of neoliberal capitalism?", *Ecological Economics*, 121: 149–59.

Martin, D., Hanrahan, B.V., O'Neill, J., and Gupta, N. (2014) "Being a Turker", *Proceedings of the 17th ACM Conference on Computer Supported Cooperative Work & Social Computing* (CSCW '14), 224–35.

Marx, K. (1844) *Economic and Philosophic Manuscripts of 1844*, Marxists Internet Archive, [online] Available from: https://www.marxists.org/archive/marx/works/1844/manuscripts/labour.htm [Accessed 22 February 2022].

Marx, K. (1847) *The Poverty of Philosophy*, Marxists Internet Archive, [online] Available from: https://www.marxists.org/archive/marx/works/subject/hist-mat/pov-phil/ch02.htm [Accessed 22 February 2022].

Marx, K. (1852) *The Eighteenth Brumaire of Louis Bonaparte*, Marxists Internet Archive, [online] Available from: https://www.marxists.org/archive/marx/works/1852/18th-brumaire/ch01.htm [Accessed 22 February 2022].

Marx, K. (1859) *A Contribution to the Critique of Political Economy*, Marxists Internet Archive, [online] Available from: https://www.marxists.org/archive/marx/works/1859/critique-pol-economy/preface.htm [Accessed 22 February 2022].

Marx, K. (1977) *Capital: A Critique of Political Economy*, vol 1, trans. B. Fowkes, London: Vintage, in association with New Left Review.

Marx, K. (1978) *Capital: A Critique of Political Economy*, vol 2, trans. D. Fernbach, London: Penguin Books, in association with New Left Review.

Marx, K. (1981) *Capital: A Critique of Political Economy*, vol 3, trans. D. Fernbach, London: Penguin Books, in association with New Left Review.

Massimo, F. (2020) "A struggle for bodies and souls: amazon management and union strategies in France and Italy", in J. Alimahomed-Wilson and E. Reese (eds) *The Cost of Free Shipping: Amazon in the Global Economy*, London: Pluto Press, pp 129–44.

Meta (2007) "Facebook unveils Facebook Ads", *Meta*, 6 November, [online] Available from: newsroom.fb.com/news/2007/11/facebook-unveils-facebook-ads [Accessed 2 March 2022].

Metz, C. (2019) "A.I. is learning from humans. Many humans.", *The New York Times*, [online] 16 August, Available from: www.nytimes.com/2019/08/16/technology/ai-humans.html [Accessed 4 March 2022].

Metz. C. and Conger, K. (2020) "Uber, after years of trying, is handing off its self-driving car project", *The New York Times* [online] 7 December, Available from: https://www.nytimes.com/2020/12/07/technology/uber-self-driving-car-project.html [Accessed 26 September 2022].

Milland, K. (2019) "From bottom to top: how Amazon Mechanical Turk disrupts employment as a whole", *Brookfield Institute for Innovation + Entrepreneurship*, [online] 14 March, Available from: brookfieldinstitute.ca/commentary/from-bottom-to-top-how-amazon-mechanical-turk-disrupts-employment-as-a-whole [Accessed 4 March 2022].

Mohandesi, S. (2013) "Class consciousness or class composition?", *Science and Society*, 77(1): 72–97.

Moore, P.V. (2018) *The Quantified Self in Precarity: Work, Technology and What Counts*, Abingdon/New York: Routledge.

Moore, P.V. and Joyce, S. (2020) "Black box or hidden abode? The expansion and exposure of platform work managerialism", *Review of International Political Economy*, 27(4): 926–48.

Morozov, E. (2013) "The 'sharing economy' undermines workers' rights", *Financial Times*, [online] 14 October, Available from: https://www.ft.com/content/92c3021c-34c2-11e3-8148-00144feab7de [Accessed 2 March 2022].

Mosco, V. (2016) "Marx in the cloud", in C. Fuchs and V. Mosco (eds) *Marx in the Age of Digital Capitalism*, Leiden/Boston: Brill, pp 516–35.

Murillo, D., Buckland, H. and Val, E. (2017) "When the sharing economy becomes neoliberalism on steroids: unravelling the controversies", *Technological Forecasting and Social Change*, 125: 66–76.

Musser, J., O'Reilly, T. and the O'Reilly Radar Team (2007) *Web 2.0 Principles and Best Practices*, Sebastopol: O'Reilly Media, Inc.

Naughton, J. (2016) "The evolution of the Internet: from military experiment to general purpose technology", *Journal of Cyber Policy*, 1(1): 5–28.

Nedzhvetskaya, N. and Tan, J.S. (2019) "What we learned from over a decade of tech activism", *The Guardian*, [online] 23 December, Available from: www.theguardian.com/commentisfree/2019/dec/22/tech-worker-activism-2019-what-we-learned [Accessed 12 March 2022].

Negri, A. (2022) *Marx in Movement: Operaismo in Context*, trans. E. Emery, Cambridge/Medford: Polity Press.

Newton, C. (2019) "The trauma floor: the secret lives of Facebook moderators in America", *The Verge*, [online] 25 February, Available from: www.theverge.com/2019/2/25/18229714/cognizant-facebook-content-moderator-interviews-trauma-working-conditions-arizona [Accessed 12 March 2022].

New York Times (2022) "How two friends beat Amazon and built a union", podcast with Christian Smalls and Derrick Palmer, "The Daily", *New York Times*, [online] 11 April, Available from: https://www.nytimes.com/2022/04/11/podcasts/the-daily/new-york-amazon-union.html [Accessed 27 September 2022].

O'Brien, S.A. (2022) "Amazon is closing all of its physical bookstores", *CNN Business*, [online] 2 March, Available from: https://edition.cnn.com/2022/03/02/tech/amazon-closing-bookstores/index.html?utm_source=fbCNN&utm_medium=social&utm_content=2022-03-03T01%3A30%3A04&utm_term=link [Accessed 19 March 2022].

OECD (2009) "Venture capital in the economic crisis", *OECD Science, Technology and Industry Scoreboard*.

Ofek, E. and Richardson, M. (2003) "DotCom mania: the ise and fall of internet stock prices", *The Journal of Finance*, 53(8): 1113–37.

Ollman, B. (1971) *Alienation: Marx's Conception of Man in Capitalist Society*, Cambridge: Cambridge University Press.

Ollman, B. (1972) "Toward class consciousness next time: Marx and the working class", *Politics and Society*, 3(1): 1–24.

Ollman, B. (1987) "How to study class consciousness, and why we should", *Insurgent Sociologist*, 14(1): 57–96.

Ollman, B. (2003) *Dance of the Dialectic: Steps in Marx's Method*, Urbana and Chicago: University of Illinois Press.

Osborne, H. and Farrell, S. (2016) "Deliveroo workers strike again over new pay structure", *The Guardian*, [online] 15 August, Available from: www.theguardian.com/business/2016/aug/15/deliveroo-workers-strike-again-over-new-pay-structure [Accessed 12 March 2022].

Owczarek, D. and Chełstowska, A. (2018) *Amazon in Polen: Arbeitsbedingungen und Arbeitsbeziehungen*, Warsaw: Friedrich-Ebert-Stiftung, [online] Available from: https://library.fes.de/pdf-files/bueros/warschau/14103.pdf [Accessed 28 September 2022].

OZZ Inicjatywa Pracownicza (2019) "Warning signals for Amazon – struggles in Poland and beyond", in *Strike the Giant! Transnational Organization against Amazon,* Transnational Social Strike Platform, pp 18–25, Available from: https://www.transnational-strike.info/2019/11/29/pdf-strike-the-giant-transnational-organization-against-amazon-tss-journal [Accessed 3 March 2022].

Palmer, A. (2022) "Amazon hired an influential Democratic pollster to fight Staten Island union drive", *CNBC,* [online] 31 March, Available from: https://www.cnbc.com/2022/03/31/amazon-hired-pro-democrat-consultant-to-fight-staten-island-union-vote.html.

Paul, K. (2020) "Hundreds of Amazon warehouse workers to call in sick in coronavirus protest", *The Guardian,* [online] 21 April, Available from: https://www.theguardian.com/technology/2020/apr/20/amazon-warehouse-workers-sickout-coronavirus [Accessed 7 March 2022].

Pepitone, J. (2012) "Amazon buys army of robots", *CNNMoney,* [online] 20 March, Available from: money.cnn.com/2012/03/20/technology/amazon-kiva-robots/index.htm [Accessed 2 March 2022].

Perticone, J. (2019) "Bernie Sanders and Elizabeth Warren want to break up Amazon, but their campaigns spend more money there than anyone else", *Business Insider,* [online] 17 July, Available from: www.businessinsider.com/bernie-sanders-elizabeth-warren-spent-most-amazon-2020-campaign-2019-7?r=DE&IR=T [Accessed 2 March 2022].

Pfeiffer, S. (2013) "Web, value and labour", *Work Organisation, Labour & Globalisation,* 7(1): 12–30.

Pitts, F.H. (2017) *Critiquing Capitalism Today: New Ways to Read Marx,* Cham: Palgrave Macmillan.

Progressive International (2021) "Time to make Amazon pay", Progressive International, [online] 18 November, Available from: https://progressive.international/movement/article/2021-11-18-time-to-make-amazon-pay/en [Accessed 9 March 2022].

PwC (2015) *Sharing or Paring? Growth of the Sharing Economy,* PwC, Available from: https://www.pwc.com/hu/en/kiadvanyok/assets/pdf/sharing-economy-en.pdf [Accessed 28 September 2022].

Rajaraman, S. (2017) "The on-demand economy is a bubble-and it's about to burst", *Quartz,* [online] 28 April, Available from: qz.com/967474/the-on-demand-economy-is-a-bubble-and-its-about-to-burst [Accessed 2 March 2022].

Ravenelle, J. (2020) *Hustle and Gig: Struggling and Surviving in the Sharing Economy,* Oakland: University of California Press.

Reese, E. (2020) "Gender, race, and Amazon warehouse labor in the United States" in J. Alimahomed-Wilson and E. Reese (eds) *The Cost of Free Shipping: Amazon in the Global Economy,* London: Pluto Press, pp 102–15.

Reese, H. and Heath, N. (2016) "Inside Amazon's Clickworker platform: how half a million people are being paid pennies to train AI", *TechRepublic* [online] 16 December, Available from: www.techrepublic.com/article/inside-amazons-clickworker-platform-how-half-a-million-people-are-training-ai-for-pennies-per-task [Accessed 4 March 2022].

Richardson, L. (2015) "Performing the sharing economy", *Geoforum*, 67: 121–9.

Robinson, B. (2014) "With a different Marx: value and the contradictions of web 2.0 capitalism", *The Information Society*, 31(1): 44–51.

Rose, S. (1997) "Class Formation and the Quintessential Worker" in J.R. Hall (ed) *Reworking Class*, Ithaca: Cornell University Press, pp 133–66.

Rosenberg, E. (2019) "Amazon had New York City in the bag. Then left-wing activists got fired up", *The Washington Post*, [online] 15 February, Available from: https://www.washingtonpost.com/nation/2019/02/14/how-amazons-big-plans-new-york-city-were-thwarted-by-citys-resurgent-left-wing [Accessed 8 March 2022].

Ross, J, Irani, L., Silberman, M.S., Zaldivar, A. and Tomlinson, B. (2010) "Who are the crowdworkers? Shifting demographics in Mechanical Turk", *CHI '10 Extended Abstracts on Human Factors in Computing Systems*, 2863–72.

Różycki, M. and Kerr, I. (2019) "Amazon is set to disrupt Germany's last mile", *Parcel and Postal Technology International*, [online] 23 September, Available from: www.parcelandpostaltechnologyinternational.com/analysis/amazon-is-set-to-disrupt-germanys-last-mile.html [Accessed 7 March 2022].

RWDSU (2021) "Amazon illegally interfered in union vote – RWDSU to file objections and related ULP charges to hold Amazon accountable for their actions", *RWDSU*, [online] 9 April, Available from: https://www.rwdsu.info/amazon_illegally_interfered_in_union_vote_rwdsu_to_file_objections_and_related_ulp_charges_to_hold_amazon_accountable_for_their_actions [Accessed 7 March 2022].

Sainato, M. (2019) "'We are not robots': Amazon warehouse employees push to unionize", *The Guardian*, [online] 1 January, Available from: www.theguardian.com/technology/2019/jan/01/amazon-fulfillment-center-warehouse-employees-union-new-york-minnesota [Accessed 2 March 2022].

Sainato, M. and Paul, K. (2019) "Uber and Lyft strikes: US drivers stop taking rides in protest over pay", *The Guardian*, [online] 8 May, Available from: www.theguardian.com/technology/2019/may/08/uber-lyft-strikes-us-new-york-la-latest-news-updates [Accessed 12 March 2022].

Salehi, N., Irani, L., Bernstein, M., Alkhatib, A., Ogbe, E., Milland, K., Clickhappier (2015) "We are Dynamo: overcoming stalling and friction in collective action for crowd workers", *Proceedings of the ACM CHI'15 Conference on Human Factors in Computing Systems*, 1621–30.

Samuel, A. (2018) "Amazon's Mechanical Turk has reinvented research", *JSTOR Daily*, [online] 15 May, Available from: https://daily.jstor.org/amazons-mechanical-turk-has-reinvented-research [Accessed 4 March 2022].

Satariano, A. (2021) "In a first, Uber agrees to classify british drivers as 'workers'", *The New York Times*, [online] 16 March, Available from: https://www.nytimes.com/2021/03/16/technology/uber-uk-drivers-worker-status.html [Accessed 4 March 2022].

Satariano, A. (2022) "E.U. takes aim at big tech's power with landmark digital act", *The New York Times*, [online] 16 March, Available from: https://www.nytimes.com/2022/03/24/technology/eu-regulation-apple-meta-google.html [Accessed 25 March 2022].

Satterwhite, J.H. (2009) *Varieties of Marxist Humanism: Philosophical Revision in Postwar Eastern Europe*, Pittsburgh and London: University of Pittsburgh Press.

Savage, S. and Jarrahi, M. H. (2020) "Solidarity and A.I. for transitioning to crowd work during COVID-19", *Association for the Advancement of Artificial Intelligence*, Available from: https://www.microsoft.com/en-us/research/uploads/prod/2020/07/NFW-Savage-Jarrahi.pdf [Accessed 28 September 2022].

Sayers, S. (2011) *Marx and Alienation: Essays on Hegelian Themes*, Basingstoke/New York: Palgrave Macmillan.

Schafer, V. and Serres, A. (2017) "Introduction", *Histories of the Internet and the Web*, Infoclio, [online] Available from: https://livingbooksabouthistory.ch/uploads/media/pdf/en/histories-of-the-internet-and-the-web.pdf [Accessed 28 September 2022].

Schaverien, A. (2018) "Five reasons why amazon is moving into bricks-and-mortar retail", *Forbes* [online] 29 December, Available from: https://www.forbes.com/sites/annaschaverien/2018/12/29/amazon-online-offline-store-retail/?sh=6bbd395a5128 [Accessed 21 September 2022].

Scheiber, N. (2020) "Uber and Lyft drivers face hurdles to stimulus bill benefits", *The New York Times*, [online] 8 April, Available from: https://www.nytimes.com/2020/04/08/business/economy/coronavirus-gig-unemployment.html [Accessed 12 March 2022].

Scheiber, N. (2022) "Labor board official says Amazon effort to overturn Staten Island warehouse election should be rejected", *New York Times*, [online] 1 September, Available from: https://www.nytimes.com/2022/09/01/technology/nlrb-amazon-union-staten-island.html [Accessed 21 September 2022].

Schiffer, Z. (2020) "Google fires prominent AI ethicist Timnit Gebru", *The Verge*, [online] 3 December, Available from: https://www.theverge.com/2020/12/3/22150355/google-fires-timnit-gebru-facial-recognition-ai-ethicist [Accessed 24 March 2022].

Schiller, D. (2000) *Digital Capitalism: Networking the Global Market System*, Cambridge: MIT Press.

Schmalz, S. and Dörre, K. (2014) "Der Machtressourcenansatz: Ein Instrument zur Analyse gewerkschaftlichen Handlungsvermögens", *Industrielle Beziehungen*, 21(3): 217–37.

Schmalz, S., Ludwig, C. and Webster, E. (2018) "The power resources approach: developments and challenges", *Global Labour Journal*, 9(2): 113–34.

Schmidt, F.A. (2017) *Digital Labour Markets in the Platform Economy – Mapping the Political Challenges of Crowd Work and Gig Work*, Friedrich-Ebert-Stiftung [online], Available from: https://library.fes.de/pdf-files/wiso/13164.pdf [Accessed 28 September 2022].

Scholz, T. (2015) "Think outside the boss: cooperative alternatives to the sharing economy", *Public Seminar*, [online] 5 April, Available from: https://publicseminar.org/2015/04/think-outside-the-boss [Accessed 4 March 2022].

Scholz, T. (2016) *Platform Cooperativism: Challenging the Corporate Sharing Economy*, New York: Rosa Luxemburg Stiftung, [online] Available from: https://rosalux.nyc/wp-content/uploads/2020/11/RLS-NYC_platformcoop.pdf [Accessed 28 September 2022].

Schor, J. (2020) *After the Gig: How the Sharing Economy Got Hijacked and How to Win It Back*, Oakland: University of California Press.

Schwär, H. (2018) "Jeff Bezos responded to reports of poor working conditions at Amazon – here's what he said", *Business Insider*, [online] 26 April, Available from: https://www.businessinsider.com/jeff-bezos-responded-to-reports-on-amazon-warehouse-working-conditions-2018-4 [Accessed 22 September 2022].

Schwartz, O. (2019) "Untold History of AI: How Amazon's Mechanical Turkers Got Squeezed Inside the Machine", *IEEE Spectrum*, [online] 22 April, Available from: https://spectrum.ieee.org/untold-history-of-ai-mechanical-turk-revisited-tktkt [Accessed 2 March 2022].

Scott, J.C. (1985) *Weapons of the Weak: Everyday Forms of Peasant Resistance*, New Haven/London: Yale University Press.

Shehata, S. (2010) *Shop Floor Culture and Politics in Egypt*, New York: SUNY Press.

Silberman, M.S. (2017) "Fifteen criteria for a fairer gig economy" in M. Graham and J. Shaw (eds) *Towards a Fairer Gig Economy*, Manchester: Meatspace Press, pp 16–19.

Silver, B.J. (2003) *Forces of Labor: Workers' Movements and Globalization since 1870*, Cambridge: Cambridge University Press.

Simon, M. (2020) "Where gig economy workers and freelancers can look for some relief today", *Forbes*, [online] 23 March, Available from: https://www.forbes.com/sites/morgansimon/2020/03/23/where-gig-economy-workers-and-freelancers-can-look-for-some-relief-today/#2c03b41850cc [Accessed 12 March 2022].

Simonite, T. (2020) "Newly unemployed, and labeling photos for pennies", *Wired*, [online] 23 April, Available from: www.wired.com/story/newly-unemployed-labeling-photos-pennies [Accessed 10 March 2022].

Sloan, J.W. (1999) *The Reagan Effect: Economics and Presidential Leadership*, Lawrence: University Press of Kansas.

Smith, A. (1776) *The Wealth of Nations,* Book V, *On the Expenses of the Sovereign or Commonwealth*, Marxists Internet Archive, [online] Available from: https://www.marxists.org/reference/archive/smith-adam/works/wealth-of-nations/book05/ch01c-2.htm [Accessed 16 March 2022].

Solon, O. (2018) "Amazon patents wristband that tracks warehouse workers' movements", *The Guardian*, [online] 1 February, Available from: www.theguardian.com/technology/2018/jan/31/amazon-warehouse-wristband-tracking [Accessed 3 March 2022].

Spector, R. (2002) *Amazon.com: Get Big Fast*, New York: HarperBusiness.

Srnicek, N. (2017) *Platform Capitalism*, Cambridge: Polity Press.

Statista (2021a) *Amazon*, Available from: https://www.statista.com/study/10137/amazoncom-statista-dossier [Accessed 28 September 2022].

Statista (2021b) "Number of Internet users worldwide 2005–2021" [online] Available from: https://www.statista.com/statistics/273018/number-of-internet-users-worldwide/ [Accessed 2 March 2022].

Statista (2022) "Number of Amazon.com employees from 2007 to 2021", [online] Available from: https://www.statista.com/statistics/234488/number-of-amazon-employees/ [Accessed 21 September 2022].

Stephany, F., Dunn, M., Sawyer, S. and Lehdonvirta, V. (2020) "Distancing bonus or downscaling loss? The changing livelihood of us online workers in times of COVID-19", *Special Issue: The Geography of the COVID-19 Pandemic*, 11(3): 561–73.

Stone, B.S. (2013) *The Everything Store: Jeff Bezos and the Age of Amazon*, New York: Little, Brown and Company.

Struna, J. and Reese, E. (2020) "Automation and surveillance-driven warehouse in inland Southern California", in J. Alimahomed-Wilson and E. Reese (eds) *The Cost of Free Shipping: Amazon in the Global Economy*, London: Pluto Press, pp 85–101.

Sundararajan, A. (2016) *The Sharing Economy: The End of Employment and the Rise of Crowd-Based Capitalism*, Cambridge: The MIT Press.

Syrovatka, F. (2022) "Europäischer Mindestlohn: Ein Schritt in die richtige Richtung", *Jacobin* [online], Available from: https://jacobin.de/artikel/europaischer-mindestlohn-ein-schritt-in-die-richtige-richtung-richtlinie-tarifbindung-lohnentwicklung/.

Taylor, F.W. (1911) "The principles of scientific management", in *The Principles of Scientific Management*, Marxists Internet Archive, [online] 16 June, Available from: https://www.marxists.org/reference/subject/economics/taylor/principles/ch02.htm [Accessed 2 March 2022].

Thomas, K.P., Tarczynska, K., Martinez, A., Wen, C. and LeRoy, G. (2022) *Amazon.com's Hidden Worldwide Subsidies*, Good Jobs First and UNI Global Union, Available from: https://uniglobalunion.org/wp-content/uploads/amazon_subsidies_final.pdf [Accessed 5 March 2022].

Thorbecke, C. (2022) "Amazon to buy One Medical for $3.9 billion as it expands healthcare footprint", *CNN Business*, [online] 22 July, Available from: https://edition.cnn.com/2022/07/21/tech/amazon-one-medical/index.html [Accessed 27 July 2022].

Tilly, C. (1978) *From Mobilization to Revolution*, New York: McGraw-Hill.

Tooze, A. (2018) *Crashed: How a Decade of Financial Crises Changed the World*, New York: Viking, Penguin Random House.

Tran, M. (2002) "WorldCom accounting scandal", *The Guardian*, [online] 9 August, Available from: www.theguardian.com/business/2002/aug/09/corporatefraud.worldcom2 [Accessed 2 March 2022].

Transnational Social Strike Platform (2019) *Strike the Giant! Transnational Organization against Amazon*, Available from: https://www.transnational-strike.info/2019/11/29/pdf-strike-the-giant-transnational-organization-against-amazon-tss-journal/.

Tronti, M. (2019) *Workers and Capital*, London: Verso.

Turner, L. (2005) "From transformation to revitalization: a new research agenda for a contested global economy", *Work and Occupations*, 32(4): 383–99.

Tynan, D (2018a) "Amazon's 'ambassador' workers assure Twitter: we can go to the toilet any time", *The Guardian*, [online] 24 August, Available from: https://www.theguardian.com/technology/2018/aug/23/amazon-fc-ambassadors-twitter-working-conditions?CMP=Share_iOSApp_Other [Accessed 8 March 2022].

Tynan, D. (2018b) "The glory that was Yahoo", *Fast Company*, [online] 20 March, Available from: www.fastcompany.com/40544277/the-glory-that-was-yahoo [Accessed 2 March 2022].

Uber Blog (2018) "Introducing a new feature: driving hours limit", *Uber*, [online] 23 April, https://www.uber.com/en-ZA/blog/driving-hours-limit/ [Accessed 12 March 2022].

UNI Global Union (2020) *Amazon & the COVID-19 Crisis – Essentially Irresponsible*, Available from: https://uniglobalunion.org/report/essentially-irresponsible-amazon-and-covid-19.

UNI Global Union Europa (2021a) "Make Amazon pay: from the streets to the European Parliament", *UNI Europa*, [online] 1 June, Available from: https://www.uni-europa.org/news/make-amazon-pay-from-the-streets-to-the-european-parliament [Accessed 9 March 2022].

UNI Global Union Europa (2021b) "UNI blasts Amazon for refusing to testify before EU Parliament", *UNI Europa*, [online] 27 May, Available from: https://www.uni-europa.org/news/uni-blasts-amazon-for-refusing-to-testify-before-eu-parliament [Accessed 9 March 2022].

UNI Global Union Europa (2022) "Amazon has a European Works Council, despite management", *UNI Europa*, [online] 12 May, Available from: https://www.uni-europa.org/news/amazon-has-a-european-works-council-despite-management/ [Accessed 29 July 2022].

UNI and ITUC (2019) *Symposium on the Unchecked Power of Amazon in Today's Economy and Society*, Brussels: UNI Global Union and the International Trade Union Confederation, [online] Available from: https://www.ituc-csi.org/symposium-on-the-unchecked-power [Accessed 2 March 2022].

Valenduc, G. and Vendramin, P. (2016) *Working in the Digital Economy: Sorting the Old from the New*, Working Paper 2016.03, Brussels: ETUI.

Vandaele, K. (2018) *Will Trade Unions Survive in the Platform Economy? Emerging Patterns of Platform Workers' Collective Voice and Representation in Europe*, Working Paper 2018.05, Brussels: ETUI.

Vandaele, K. (2021) "Collective resistance and organizational creativity amongst Europe's platform workers: a new power in the labour movement?", in J. Haidar and M. Keune (eds) *Work and Labour Relations in Global Platform Capitalism*, ILERA Publication series, Cheltenham/Northampton: Edward Elgar Publishing, pp 206–35.

Van Doorn, N. (2017) "Platform labor: on the gendered and racialized exploitation of low-income service work in the 'on-demand'economy", *Information, Communication & Society*, 20(6): 898–914.

Van Doorn, N., Ferrari, F., and Graham, (2022) "Migration and migrant labour in the gig economy: an intervention", *Work, Employment and Society*, online version, Available from: https://doi.org/10.1177/09500170221096581 [Accessed 28 September 2022].

Van Doorn, N. and Vijay, D. (2021) "Gig work as migrant work: the platformization of migration infrastructure", *Environment and Planning A: Economy and Space*, online version, Available from: https://doi.org/10.1177/0308518X21106504 [Accessed 28 September 2022].

ver.di (2014) "ver.di erstmals im Aufsichtsrat von Amazon", *ver.di*, [online] 28 August, Available from: https://www.verdi.de/presse/pressemitteilungen/++co++bb938af4-2eb8-11e4-b592-52540059119e [Accessed 22 September 2022].

ver.di (2021) "Gorillas haben Betriebsrat gewählt", ver.di, [online] 28 November, Available from: https://www.verdi.de/themen/recht-datenschutz/++co++5accc95e-47a8-11ec-a96c-001a4a160129 [Accessed 25 October 2022].

ver.di (2022) "Erster Amazon Streik in Niedersachsen", ver.di, [online] 14 September, Available from: https://nds-bremen.verdi.de/presse/pressemitteilungen/++co++0fb32076-33f2-11ed-85e5-001a4a160129 [Accessed 22 October 2022].

The Verge (2018) "Google's 20th anniversary: how an internet search engine reshaped the world", *The Verge*, [online] 27 September, Available from: www.theverge.com/2018/9/5/17823490/google-20th-birthday-anniversary-history-milestones [Accessed 2 March 2022].

Vgontzas, N. (2020) "A new industrial working class? Challenges in disrupting Amazon's fulfillment process in Germany", in J. Alimahomed-Wilson and E. Reese (eds) *The Cost of Free Shipping: Amazon in the Global Economy*, London: Pluto Press, pp 116–28.

Weaver, M., Hern, A., Bekiempis, V., Hepler, L. and Fermoso, J. (2018) "Google walkout: global protests after sexual misconduct allegations", *The Guardian*, [online] 1 November, Available from: www.theguardian.com/technology/2018/nov/01/google-walkout-global-protests-employees-sexual-harassment-scandals [Accessed 12 March 2022].

Webster, J. (2016) "Microworkers of the gig economy: separate and precarious", *New Labor Forum*, 25(3): 56–64.

Webster, J. and Randle, K. (2016) "Positioning virtual workers within space, time and social dynamics", in J. Webster and K. Randle (eds) *Virtual Workers and the Global Labour Market*, London: Palgrave Macmillan, pp 3–34.

Weise, K. (2021) "Amazon illegally fired activist workers, labor board finds", *The New York Times*, [online] 15 June, Available from: https://www.nytimes.com/2021/04/05/technology/amazon-nlrb-activist-workers.html [Accessed 23 March 2022].

Wendling, A.E. (2011) *Karl Marx on Technology and Alienation*, Basingstoke/New York: Palgrave Macmillan.

Wilhelm, A. (2017) "A look back in IPO: Amazon's 1997 move", *TechCrunch*, [online] 28 June, Available from: techcrunch.com/2017/06/28/a-look-back-at-amazons-1997-ipo [Accessed 2 March 2022].

Williams, D.M. (2020) "Power accrues to the powerful: amazon's market share, customer surveillance, and internet dominance", in J. Alimahomed-Wilson and E. Reese (eds) *The Cost of Free Shipping: Amazon in the Global Economy*, London: Pluto Press, pp 35–49.

Wong, J.C (2019) "Google staff condemn treatment of temp workers in 'historic' show of solidarity", *The Guardian*, [online] 2 April, Available from: www.theguardian.com/technology/2019/apr/02/google-workers-sign-letter-temp-contractors-protest [Accessed 12 March 2022].

Wood, A.J. (2020) *Despotism on Demand: How Power Operates in the Flexible Workplace*, Ithaca: ILR Press.

Woodcock, J. (2021) "Towards a digital workerism: workers' inquiry, methods, and technologies", *Nanoethics*, 15: 87–98.

Woodcock, J., and Graham, M. (2019) "How can we better regulate digital platform capitalism to protect workers?", *LabourList*, [online] 22 February, Available from: https://labourlist.org/2019/02/how-can-we-better-regulate-digital-platform-capitalism-to-protect-workers [Accessed 5 March 2022].

Woodcock, J., and Johnson, M.R. (2019). "The affective labor and performance of live streaming on Twitch.tv", *Television & New Media*, 20(8): 813–23.

Wright, E.O. (2000) "Working-class power, capitalist-class interests, and class compromise", *American Journal of Sociology*, 105(4): 957–1002.

Wright, S (2008) "Mapping pathways within Italian autonomist Marxism: a preliminary survey", *Historical Materialism*, 16(4): 111–40.

Wright, S. (2017) *Storming Heaven: Class Composition and Struggle in Italian Autonomist Marxism*, London: Pluto Press.

Yang, L. (2017) "13 Incredible perks of working at Google, according to employees", *Insider*, [online] 11 July, Available from: www.insider.com/coolest-perks-of-working-at-google-in-2017-2017-7#perhaps-one-of-googles-most-well-known-perks-employees-can-eat-every-meal-at-work-for-free-and-save-a-ton-of-money-1 [Accessed 12 March 2022].

Zittrain, J. (2009) "The Internet creates a new kind of sweatshop", *Newsweek*, [online] 7 December, Available from: www.newsweek.com/internet-creates-new-kind-sweatshop-75751 [Accessed 11 March 2022].

Zuboff, S. (2019) *The Age of Surveillance Capitalism: The Fight for the Future at the New Frontier of Power*, New York: Public Affairs.

# Index

References to figures appear in *italic* type;
those in **bold** type refer to tables.

Printed and bound by CPI Group (UK) Ltd, Croydon, CR0 4YY

19/11/2023

08190732-0001